The Freedom
of Information
Officer's Handbook

The Freedom
of Information
Officer's Handbook

Paul Gibbons

© Paul Gibbons 2019

Published by Facet Publishing
7 Ridgmount Street, London WC1E 7AE
www.facetpublishing.co.uk

Facet Publishing is wholly owned by CILIP: the Library and Information Association.

Paul Gibbons has asserted his right under the Copyright, Designs and Patents Act 1988 to be identified as author of this work.

British Library Cataloguing in Publication Data
A catalogue record for this book is available from the British Library.

ISBN 978-1-78330-353-3 (paperback)
ISBN 978-1-78330-354-0 (hardback)
ISBN 978-1-78330-355-7 (e-book)

First published 2019

Text printed on FSC accredited material.

Typeset from editors' files in 11/14pt Elegant Garamond and Myriad Pro by Flagholme Publishing Services.
Printed and made in Great Britain by CPI Group (UK) Ltd, Croydon, CR0 4YY.

Contents

Acknowledgements

Writing a book about freedom of information (FOI) at a time when everyone else is talking about data protection requires a certain mindset. Several people have encouraged my obsession with the right to access information over the years, for which I would like to thank them: Frances Grey, who involved me in FOI preparations in the House of Lords and made me want her job; Annabel Davies, who appointed me as an FOI officer, pointed me in the right direction, and supported me during the occasional difficult moments that inspired the section in this book on 'uncooperative colleagues'; and Ibrahim Hasan, who in 2012 invited me to develop a training course called 'Practical FOI', which ultimately led both to Part 3 of this book and a significant change in my career direction. By asking me to supply an article for every issue of PDP's Freedom of Information Journal, Rezzan Huseyin helped convince me that I had anywhere near enough to say about FOI to fill a book.

Nonetheless, it is unlikely that the idea of writing this book would even have been entertained had it not been for regular enquiries from Nicholas Lovell and Ben Worthy as to when it was coming out. Those questions kept the idea ticking away at the back of my mind even when I was convinced that it wasn't going to happen. Ben, Maurice Frankel and Elizabeth Lomas provided invaluable feedback on drafts of some of the chapters. My good friend Alison Drew agreed to act as guinea pig and read the whole thing for the first time. I would also like to thank my commissioning editor at Facet Publishing, Damian Mitchell, who as well as giving me the opportunity to do this in the first place provided comments on draft chapters which were of much more use to me than I may have indicated at the time. I take pride in claiming ownership of any faults that remain since they help demonstrate the central thesis of this book, that FOI officers are human.

This book owes much to the many colleagues and users of FOI I have engaged with over the years, from the lawyers and the Public Liaison Unit at the Greater London Authority, to the journalists and campaigners who have contacted me as a result of my FOIMan blog and Twitter feed. It is aimed at FOI officers, and many of them have inspired its content, through discussion of difficult requests at meetings, and questions raised on training courses. Then there are the many officials who answered my FOI requests, whose responses helped ground the last few chapters in the real world.

The most thanks of all go to my extraordinary wife, Sally, who provided support beyond that which I might have expected or deserved. Aside from her patience and encouragement, as my unpaid research assistant she spent several weekends inputting over 750 responses to questions asked under FOI into a spreadsheet. I am also grateful to my parents, Len and Sue, for their constant support over many years. This book is dedicated to them and Sally, without whom in their respective ways 'FOIMan' and this book would never have existed. My final thanks go to my nephews Leo and Toby, and my niece Josie (who displayed impeccable timing by arriving on the very morning that I completed the manuscript), for providing much needed perspective and great joy throughout the many months that I spent writing this book.

Abbreviations

ATI	access to information
CDPA	the Copyright, Designs and Patents Act 1988
CFOI	the Campaign for Freedom of Information
DPA	the Data Protection Act (1984, 1998 or 2018)
DPO	data protection officer
EIR	the Environmental Information Regulations 2004
EI(S)R	the Environmental Information (Scotland) Regulations 2004
FOI	freedom of information (as a concept)
FOIA	the UK's Freedom of Information Act 2000
FOI(S)A	the Freedom of Information (Scotland) Act 2002
FTT	the First-Tier Tribunal (Information Rights)
GDPR	the General Data Protection Regulation (EU) 2016/679
ICO	the Information Commissioner's Office
PRA	the Public Records Act 1958
PRA(NI)	the Public Records Act (Northern Ireland) 1923
PRONI	the Public Record Office of Northern Ireland
RoPSI	the Re-use of Public Sector Information Regulations 2015
RTI	right to information
TNA	the National Archives
UT	Upper Tribunal

.

Introduction

In testing whether a Freedom of Information regime is meeting its objectives, it is
no good making a judgement on the basis of the statute alone. The most elegant
and liberal legislation would be valueless unless supported by an administration
that creates records systematically, retrieves them efficiently, and then provides them
promptly. And so Freedom of Information administrators are critical to the success
of this Act.   Lord Falconer (2004)[1]

Welcome to the *Freedom of Information Officer's Handbook*. As the name
suggests, this book is intended as an indispensable guide for those with
responsibility for managing their organisations' compliance with freedom of
information (FOI) laws.

The Freedom of Information Act 2000 (FOIA) has been in force in the United
Kingdom (UK) since 1 January 2005. Like similar laws elsewhere in the world,
it introduced a right of access to information held by specified public authorities
(for the most part such laws only apply to the public sector). Many have taken
advantage of this right, and there is hardly a news report that goes by these days
without the inclusion of the phrase 'the information, released under freedom of
information'. Because of FOIA, the public found out about MPs' expenses claims,
what the Prince of Wales wrote to government ministers about, and less high-
profile public interest stories such as the dangers of trampolines.[2]

The UK was far from the first to adopt such legislation. There are now over
100 similar laws around the world, also commonly referred to as access to
information or right to information laws. Even within the UK there is more than
one FOI law, since Scotland has its own FOI Act.

Those affected in all these countries will have learnt that the right to access
information is a simple concept in theory, but less so in practice. Within the pages

of this book are copious examples of the legal, political and logistical challenges faced by organisations subject to FOI laws. There are people within those bodies whose job it is to manage them.

Lord Falconer was the UK minister responsible for implementing the FOIA in the lead up to 2005. Experience over the last 13 years has shown his assertion in the quotation at the start of this introduction to be correct: the officials with responsibility for managing FOIA obligations within public authorities have been absolutely critical to its success.

FOI officers

Since this is a handbook for FOI officers, we should explain who they are. The difficulty with doing so is that there are very few people whose job title is 'FOI officer'. Most of those with responsibilities for managing the FOI process within their organisation are called information governance officers, or information officers or similar. In many cases FOI is only a part of their responsibilities, so they may be the records manager, the data protection officer, the legal services officer or even the customer services officer. They come from different backgrounds, sometimes with experience in information management disciplines, but just as often not. As we will see in later chapters, they may carry out different activities, depending on how FOI administration is organised in their authority. They have in common a responsibility for leading on FOI within their organisation. They establish the procedures for others to follow, they advise their colleagues, they log and monitor compliance. They are the contact for FOI in their authority.

What they also have in common is that they have a very challenging job. Acting as the 'gatekeeper', they are stuck in the middle between applicants who may underestimate the difficulties involved in considering their request, and colleagues with other priorities who may have strong convictions that information should not be disclosed. Often the interpretation of the legal requirements of FOI laws are the least of their troubles. There are the logistics of receipt, distribution, collation and response to consider. There are the difficulties of persuading people often more senior than themselves to do something they don't want to. They have to understand what their colleagues are telling them and apply the law accordingly. These are complex tasks requiring tact, skill and knowledge.

The aims of this book

These challenges are rarely acknowledged, and therefore support in meeting them is scarce. Many FOI officers may have found themselves placed in the role with little relevant experience to rely on. Even seasoned information professionals, such as archivists and librarians, used to the complexities of data management, are less comfortable with the legal underpinning of FOI administration. FOI stirs up strong convictions among colleagues and those in charge, requiring excellent people skills from those in the firing line. Nobody coming to the job of FOI officer for the first time finds it easy, and everyone in this position needs help with carrying out the role from time to time.

The first aim of this book is therefore to be a handy work of reference for anyone involved in fulfilling FOI obligations within a public authority. In these pages, the UK FOIA is explained, analysed and compared with other FOI laws around the world. Exemptions from the right to know are explained and related obligations in other laws recounted.

The second aim of this book is to provide a practical guide in how to manage FOI, which has not often been addressed. How should authorities best organise themselves to ensure that they can meet the obligations of FOI laws? What systems should they use to monitor and report on their performance? How do they protect their own rights?

Connected to these first two aims, and implicit in the title of this book, is a third aim. This book seeks to define what an FOI officer is today, and what they should be. In the UK the concept of FOI is still relatively new. People fulfilling the role of FOI officer can come from a range of backgrounds, with differing levels of interest, and varying views on the value of FOI. The way they work needs to be better understood. Looking to the future, FOI officers need to start thinking of themselves as being part of a profession with its own ethics and aims beyond those of the organisations that employ them.

Professional FOI officers need to be appropriately supported, and there are suggestions in this book as to how employers should do this. Getting FOI right depends on recruiting the right people, developing them and empowering them.

One caveat on the scope of this book. As it is aimed at practitioners – those doing the job – and is written by someone who used to do the job, it focuses on the day-to-day work of FOI officers and their colleagues. There are deliberately no detailed discussions of case law related to tribunal procedure in these pages. At the point at which an authority needs to know about such matters, it has usually appointed legal representatives, who can be approached for advice as necessary. Indeed, most authorities rarely need such advice. This book focuses on the matters that crop up for FOI officers and their colleagues during the normal handling of FOI requests and in seeking to comply with FOI obligations.

While this book is primarily aimed at FOI officers and those involved in handling FOI requests, what follows will still be of use to others. Those who manage FOI officers can gain better insight into their roles and understand the support that they need. Other public employees who have to respond to requests or supply information will find much to help them here. Records managers and archivists who are not directly involved in processing FOI requests will find explanations of how FOI affects their work. Finally, journalists and others who make regular FOI requests may find that this book helps them to make better requests, or at least to understand why they might not always get the answer that they would like.

Around the world

It is hoped that this book is of interest to an international audience, although much of it focuses on the legislation in place in the UK and the experiences of UK officials.

There are good reasons for this. With over 100 laws in place, with significant variations between them, it would be impossible to cover the way that every law works. Such a book would be a very different beast from the one that I set out to write.

Furthermore, every book is influenced by the experiences and prejudices of their author, and this one is no different. I live in the UK, have worked as a FOI officer in the UK, and have followed the decisions and case law of the UK's regulator and courts. The book focuses on the UK because that is where my experience lies.

Nonetheless, I think there is much here for FOI officers and others wherever they may be based. First, case studies looking at FOI laws in other jurisdictions can be useful in identifying solutions to common problems. Even if I haven't spelt out how a particular situation would be relevant to someone working in a different jurisdiction, readers can take what they need from examples provided here. Second, while the first two-thirds of this book are necessarily focused on UK legislation and its application, the last third considers the practical implementation of FOI. Much of this is not UK specific, and should be thought provoking to anyone, wherever they may be carrying out this work. Third, researching this book has reinforced my fascination with how FOI laws work around the globe, and I'm sure there are many practitioners, academics and others who are interested in what happens in the UK.

In many of the chapters there are boxed out sections on FOI 'around the world' where I have provided examples of how other jurisdictions have addressed aspects of the FOIA. What kinds of organisation do other laws cover? What constitutes a valid request in India or the Isle of Man? How do other countries manage the process of answering FOI requests? Just as some FOI officers abroad may be inspired by examples of UK practice, there is much for the UK to learn from what happens elsewhere, particularly as many FOI laws outside the UK have been in place for a lot longer.

A note on the British islands

Readers outside the UK may be puzzled by the references to other FOI laws around the British islands. Indeed many people living in the UK get confused by the interaction between nations in this small, but complex, part of the world. Briefly, the UK is made up of England, Wales, Northern Ireland and Scotland. All the UK is subject to the FOIA. However, Scotland has its own FOI Act, the Freedom of Information (Scotland) Act 2002 (FOI(S)A), which applies only to 'devolved institutions' – those bodies that are under control of the Scottish Government. This includes Scottish government departments, local councils, the police, health service and universities among other authorities. It does not include cross-border bodies – UK government agencies operating across the UK that happen to have offices in Scotland. The Welsh and Northern Ireland administrations have varying levels of autonomy, but are subject to the FOIA, as are other public authorities that they are responsible for.

In addition, there are several other nations on the UK's doorstep. The Republic of Ireland (covering all the island of Ireland except for Northern Ireland) is a sovereign state with its own laws. It has had an FOI law since 1997, replaced by a new law in 2014.

The Channel Islands and the Isle of Man are crown dependencies in the English Channel and the Irish Sea respectively. Crown dependencies have the same monarch as the UK, but are independent nations. However, the UK is responsible for their foreign policy and their defence, and they often follow the UK's approach to laws. The States of Jersey in the Channel Islands adopted its own FOI Law in 2011 (Acts are called 'Laws' there), while the Isle of Man adopted a FOI Act in 2015.

The structure of this book

This book is split into three parts. The first part looks at FOI legislation itself: its history, content and application, focusing particularly on the FOIA. Importantly, the exemptions are examined, looking at when and how to apply them correctly. Other sources of assistance are identified and assessed, from codes of practice to decisions of the Information Commissioner, tribunals and courts, to blogs and social media.

In Part 2, the wider context in which FOI laws operate is examined. The Environmental Information Regulations 2004 (EIR) set out rules for the disclosure of information on environmental matters. A new European data protection law – the General Data Protection Regulation (GDPR) (EU) 2016/679 – affects how requests involving personal information should be handled. Recently introduced rules on re-use require an understanding of how FOI laws interact with copyright. Other legal requirements dictate what information must be published proactively, affecting the content of publication schemes, and FOI actively changes the way that archivists select, preserve and provide access to records. The FOIA requires government to issue guidance on managing records, recognising that the way that records are managed affects their availability under FOI laws.

Finally, Part 3 explores the practical implications of FOI. The role of FOI officers is analysed, looking at what they do, who should be given the role, their responsibilities and how they should be supported. Ways to embed FOI within public authorities, and to change attitudes, are considered. The journey of an FOI request from receipt to response is traced, identifying what needs to be in place to support compliance. The importance of good communication is stressed: how to provide advice, what is best practice when responding to requests and how to deal with complaints.

As well as the 'around the world' features there is a series of boxed out articles called 'The gist'. Sometimes the sheer volume of guidance and case law can be daunting for even the most experienced FOI officer, many of whom have had no legal training. 'The gist' sections aim to distil the essence of the most significant case law and other lessons from the last 13 years into simple messages that everyone can understand.

Research

This book is the result of 15 years of involvement in FOI. I was recruited as the Greater London Authority's (GLA's) FOI and records manager in 2003 to lead its preparations for the FOIA. My experiences there for six years, and since then in an NHS hospital trust and a higher education college, significantly inform this book. Some readers will be aware that in 2010 I started writing a blog called FOIMan about my experiences as an FOI officer, and some of the content in this book has its origins in blog posts written there. Since 2014 I have been working as a freelance trainer and consultant, and research for my training courses has also found its way into these pages.

Perhaps most importantly, over the many years that I have worked as an FOI officer and trainer I have encountered hundreds of hard-working practitioners. Discussions with them have helped develop and consolidate my thinking on many of the issues explored here.

Chapter 4 looks at the range of guidance, case law, websites, social media, professional organisations and other resources that FOI officers have at their disposal, and I have used all of these in the preparation of this book. In addition, I have benefitted hugely from the academic research that has been conducted over the last decade or so into FOI, most notably by University College London's Constitution Unit and its alumni.

Inspired by their fascinating work, I attempted some original research of my own when preparing this book. Part 3 in particular benefits from the responses received to an FOI request I sent to several local authorities in autumn 2017. You can read more about this research in Appendix 1, including about the questions asked and methodology used.

Terminology

As noted, FOI laws are called different things around the globe. For the purposes of this book, the acronym 'FOI' is used to refer to the concept of FOI in general, and 'FOI laws' for all the various laws covering FOI around the world whether they are called 'access to information', 'right to information' or any of the many and various other terms used.

Finally

Every chapter in this book ends with a box summarising the key conclusions reached in that chapter. This introduction is no exception.

> **Summing up**
> - The UK's FOIA has proved a success by most measures, due in no small part to the hard work of FOI officers and other public employees who have helped make it work in practice.
> - FOI officers are the people who lead on FOI in their authority, establishing procedures, providing advice and monitoring compliance.
> - FOI officers may be lawyers, data protection officers, records managers, archivists or customer service officers – they come from a range of backgrounds.

- FOI officers have a complex and demanding job, often requiring the postholder to act as a gatekeeper.
- The book aims to identify the challenges facing FOI officers, provide tools and solutions to help meet these challenges, define the role of the FOI officer, and be an essential resource for anyone wanting to understand how FOI really works in practice.
- It focuses on FOI in the UK, but draws on practice in other jurisdictions; it is hoped that it will be useful to FOI officers everywhere.
- It is structured in three parts: understanding the FOIA; FOI in context; and the practical management of FOI.
- It explores what it means to be an FOI officer and provides the tools to do the job

Part 1

Understanding FOI

Chapter 1

A brief history of freedom of information

Introduction

The UK's Freedom of Information Act 2000 (FOIA) did not become law on a sudden whim of the government of the time. When it received royal assent on 30 November 2000 it was the culmination of a long campaign for a right to information law in the UK. It was also a relatively late instance of such a law being introduced in the western world.

Internationally, FOI laws in various forms are becoming commonplace. From Albania to Zimbabwe, access to information is increasingly seen as a fundamental right. Very often, the right to information is high on the agenda of those seeking the overthrow of tyranny. As well as providing a check on power, FOI laws are an important symbol of the freedom and democracy that many nations aspire to.

For many years, there was resistance to the introduction of such a right in the UK. It was argued that it was incompatible with the way that the country was governed, and that it was unnecessary. It was only after years of campaigning by groups such as the Campaign for Freedom of Information, the media, individuals and politicians that FOIA became a reality.

Even then, many people working for public bodies could not understand why the government had chosen to inflict such an administrative burden on them. Why us? Why now? Those questions persist in some parts of the public sector.

FOI officers carry out their role in this context. Understanding where FOI comes from, why it is seen as so important by campaigners and politicians, and how it came to be helps them to better understand their role and argue the case for transparency more effectively.

We didn't start the FOIA

When was the first FOI law passed? Few know, and if pushed will guess at the origins of FOI lying anywhere from the time of classical Greece (500-300 BC) to the late 20th century (in fact, there are suggestions that the principle of FOI may have its roots in ancient China).[1] The ancient world undoubtedly could provide examples of what might be loosely termed transparency, mostly to suit the political tactics of politicians. However, there was nothing that we would recognise as a right of access like that enshrined in the FOIA.

The answer is nonetheless surprising. It was as long ago as 1766 that the Swedes adopted a Freedom of the Printing Press Act, which allowed citizens to have access to information held by government ministries.[2] It didn't survive long on the statute book, but there it was – the first attempt to give the public a statutory right to government information.

FOI in the 20th century

Fast forward 200 years and FOI laws are becoming established as a feature of (primarily) democratic states. Sweden was again among those leading the charge, with its modern-day Freedom of the Press Act in 1949.[3]

More importantly perhaps for the spread of the concept, in 1966 President Lyndon B. Johnson declined to block the passage of a US FOI Bill.[4] If one of the superpowers could adopt an FOI law without it compromising its people's safety or good government at the height of the Cold War, then gradually the arguments against these laws would become harder to make, at least by governments claiming to champion democracy.

Since 1966 many countries have introduced FOI laws and there are now over 100 countries with some form of FOI legislation. They include obvious candidates like the UK's European neighbours, but also more unexpected examples such as China. Right to information laws are often seen as a way for opposition to contrast itself with governing parties with a reputation for secrecy or corruption.[5] This perhaps explains why FOI laws are a growing phenomenon across the developing world, as when those oppositions achieve power, they often feel obliged to follow through on the promises they made outside government.

Some of these laws are more progressive than those found in older democracies. For example, in Mexico's Transparency and Access to Government Information Act 2002, a failure to respond to a request within the statutory deadline constitutes a positive response, and information has to be disclosed within a further ten working days. Not surprisingly, perhaps, Mexico's government tends to respond promptly to requests – on average within 11 working days. The Act explicitly prevents the government from withholding information about human rights violations and crimes against humanity.[6]

In India, the Right to Information Act passed in 2005 is seen as an important tool for tackling corruption. Unfortunately those under scrutiny have occasionally resorted to extreme methods and applicants have been murdered for their interest, the so-called 'right to information martyrs'. Reforms have sought to safeguard applicants from violence. The Act is a good example of a 21st-century FOI law, containing requirements to keep and index records, proactively publish information, and appoint 'public information officers' – FOI officers in all but name. Most significantly, the Right to Information Act applies to a broad range of bodies from federal government departments down to local government offices and publicly financed organisations. India is also innovating, with applicants able to track the progress of their request using their mobile phones.[7]

FOI is now an international phenomenon. The UK is not the first to tread this path, and neither is its law the most demanding. Figure 1.1 illustrates the global spread of FOI legislation in 2017. Throughout the following chapters, the 'around the world' features highlight examples of FOI laws and how they compare with those in the UK.

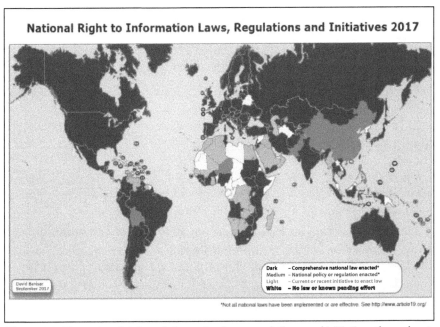

Figure 1.1 The national right to information laws, regulations and initiatives throughout the world in 2017 (reproduced with kind permission of David Banisar)[8]

The UK's path towards FOIA

While FOI legislation spread around the world, there was resistance in the UK. A common argument was that a statutory right to information was incompatible with a Westminster parliamentary system.[9] This was somewhat undermined in the 1980s as Canada, Australia and New Zealand, all with parliamentary systems closely modelled on the UK's, all introduced FOI laws.

Across the world, as well as at home, the UK had a reputation for secrecy.[10] Not only was there no right for people to access government information, but civil servants could be prosecuted and even imprisoned for disclosing it under the Official Secrets Act 1911 (which was updated in 1989). Despite attempts to reform this situation in the 1970s, and several Labour manifestos promising an FOI law, by the time the Labour government fell in 1979, nothing had changed.[11] The new Conservative prime minister, Margaret Thatcher, was an FOI-sceptic.[12] However, in the 1980s, the newly established Campaign for Freedom of Information (CFOI) successfully pushed FOI up the agenda, slowly but tenaciously building up a powerful coalition of support inside and outside Parliament. The canny tactics of Des Wilson and Maurice Frankel, the Campaign's directors, succeeded in ensuring that the next time Labour were in a position to implement their manifesto, their options for retreat would be limited.[13]

In the 1990s, John Major sought to use openness to draw a distinction between his government and that of his predecessor.[14] The Code of Practice on Access to Government Information was introduced, which while without a statutory basis and often described as 'one of government's best kept secrets'[15] continued to erode the idea that FOI couldn't work in the UK.

From the 'right to know' to the FOIA

It was in no way inevitable that the FOIA would become law after Labour's victory in the 1997 election. There were question marks over the commitment of the new government.[16]

The introduction of an FOI Act was one of a suite of new constitutional changes planned by Labour.[17] It was initially seen as a potential quick win and very swiftly a white paper was produced promising an ambitious FOI Bill.[18] There was a backlash within government, and the result was a Bill which disappointed campaigners,[19] but they fought on and with parliamentary allies it was strengthened.[20]

The FOIA's passage through Parliament was not smooth, and this is reflected in its final form. The fossilised remains of earlier drafts poke through the sediment, occasionally requiring awkward manoeuvres to avoid embarrassing stumbles. Compromises designed to appease MPs favouring more, or less, openness have sometimes resulted in language that is not easy for courts to interpret, let alone for the average public sector worker trying their best to understand their obligations. Chapter 2 examines what emerged from all the argument and compromise.

The Act eventually received royal assent on 30 November 2000. The requirement to adopt publication schemes was brought into force gradually between 2002 and 2004, before the rest of the legislation – including the right to make FOI requests – came into force on 1 January 2005.

What's the point of the FOIA?

The aims of the FOIA were identified by the Labour government as being:

- to improve the openness and transparency of public bodies
- to increase the accountability of public body decision making and spending
- to improve decision making
- to allow the public to engage in decision making
- to increase trust in public authorities.[21]

In 2012, the post-legislative scrutiny conducted by the House of Commons' Justice Select Committee found that except for the last of these points – which it considered to have been unrealistic – these aims had been met. Indeed it concluded that 'the Freedom of Information Act has been a significant enhancement of our democracy'.[22]

Changes to the FOIA

Famously, political leaders tend to go off FOI once in government. Tony Blair described himself as a 'nincompoop' for introducing the FOIA,[23] while David Cameron complained about 'this endless discovery process that furs up the whole of Government'.[24] This leads to sporadic attempts to neuter the Act. Academic Dr Ben Worthy estimates that there is an attempt to amend the FOIA every 18 months to 2 years.[25]

The only successful attempt to do this came at the end of Gordon Brown's premiership in 2010 (brought into force by the coalition government in 2011). This resulted in the qualified exemption from the FOIA covering

communications with the royal household being changed so that communications with the monarch and her two closest heirs are now absolutely
protected.[26] Such a change was later resisted in Scotland.[27]

Another change to the FOIA, this time enhancing people's rights, came
because of the Protection of Freedoms Act 2012, which introduced new
requirements in relation to datasets.[28] These changes are explored in Chapter 9.

The GDPR has led to some minor changes to the FOIA and the handling of
requests that include personal information, the relevant amendments being made
by the Data Protection Act 2018 (DPA 2018).

Other laws providing access to information

The FOIA is not the only law providing access to information in the UK.
Governments less keen on their own transparency have nonetheless embraced
the concept of local government openness for decades. Despite her objection to
FOI at a national level, Mrs Thatcher was very keen on local level transparency,
speaking in support of a Private Members Bill opening up local authority
meetings to the media in her maiden speech in 1960.[29] During her premiership,
the Local Government (Access to Information) Act 1985 required councils to
make papers available to attendees, inserting a schedule containing exemptions
from the duty into the Local Government Act 1972.[30] Councils are also required
to provide access to their accounts and supporting documentation once a year
under audit rules.[31] More recent local government reforms have resulted in more
transparency for executive mayors and cabinets,[32] requirements to provide
information about their decisions on request,[33] and a right for citizens to film or
blog about council meetings.[34] A transparency code with legal force in England
requires certain categories of information to be published proactively.[35] Some of
these laws are explored in Chapter 8.

Similarly there is a long history of legislation addressing environmental
concerns. In the 1970s, while FOI proposals were floundering, the Control of
Pollution Act introduced registers of water pollution incidents that would be open
for inspection by the public. It even required water authorities to provide copies
of entries on the registers on request.[36] The Environment and Safety Information
Act 1988 opened up enforcement notices that were issued following breaches of
environmental laws.[37] A European directive on environmental information in
1990 resulted in the Environmental Information Regulations 1992.[38] The Aarhus
Convention of 1998 eventually led to a revision of the directive and ultimately the
current EIR, which are discussed in Chapter 5.

A series of laws in the last decades of the 20th century provided rights to individuals to access information about themselves or their children. These included the Access to Health Records Act 1990, which allowed individuals rights to access their medical records, and the Access to Personal Files Act 1987, which allowed them to see their social care and housing records.[39] While at the time these laws were significant steps forward, they have mostly been superseded by data protection laws. Starting with the Data Protection Act 1984, continuing with the Data Protection Act 1998, and now with the GDPR and DPA 2018, individuals have gradually had more right to access information that organisations – public sector and beyond – hold about them. Data protection laws have a significant relationship with the FOIA and this is explored in Chapter 6 and at various points throughout this book.

The next frontier in openness is the move towards open data, and there have been several developments in this regard. Open data laws consider not just access to information, but what applicants are then allowed to do with the data obtained. In the absence of reforms in this area, the Copyright, Designs and Patents Act 1988 (CDPA) has long been the relevant legislation, and those who republished or re-used released information risked being subject to legal action. The Protection of Freedoms Act 2012 amended the FOIA to require public authorities to allow re-use of electronic datasets on request where 'reasonably practicable'.[40] More significantly, the Re-use of Public Sector Information (RoPSI) Regulations 2005 permitted and encouraged public authorities to license the re-use of specified information. In 2015, a new iteration of the regulations went further, requiring them to do so, and limiting the exceptions to this rule.[41]

In 2011, the UK joined the Open Government Partnership, an international group aimed at promoting transparency, fighting corruption and empowering citizens.[42] Each member country publishes a national action plan committing it to specific actions designed to promote these aims. The UK's most recent action plan covering 2016–2018 includes commitments to establish a register of company beneficial ownership information, following growing pressure in recent years for increased transparency around corporate activities. Other commitments in the UK Open Government National Action Plan include more disclosure of information about sales of oil, gas and minerals, new standards for open government contracting, and more proactive publication of details about government grants.[43]

Different parts of the UK and the British islands have adopted their own FOI laws over the last 20 years. Scotland passed the FOI(S)A in 2002, coming into force with the UK's FOIA in January 2005. In the Channel Islands, Jersey adopted its Freedom of Information Law in 2011,[44] and another crown dependency, the Isle of Man, joined the FOI club in 2015.[45] Summaries of the differences between these laws and the UK's legislation can be found in the 'around the world' features in later chapters.

The future of FOI in the UK

In 2016, the Supreme Court curtailed the ability of government to veto disclosures under the FOIA. A Guardian journalist won a ten-year fight to obtain Prince Charles's letters to ministers. An earlier tribunal had ruled they should be released, but Attorney General Dominic Grieve had used the Act's veto to prevent this. The Supreme Court ruled that the veto was unlawful, and in doing so circumscribed its use so that it was almost unusable.[46]

The prime minister responded furiously,[47] and soon afterwards the Independent Commission on Freedom of Information was established.[48] The general perception was that the Commission's aim was to justify substantial reforms to the FOIA. Despite this, the Commission's conclusions were generally supportive of the FOIA,[49] influenced no doubt by a high-profile media campaign with even tabloid newspapers publishing editorials criticising any proposal to weaken the FOIA.[50] In the event, the government appeared to rule out any changes.[51]

One recommendation that the government accepted was that the s.45 code of practice should be revised.[52] The code, which the government is required to publish under s.45 of the FOIA, had not been updated since 2004. Following a consultation in late 2017, a revised s.45 code was published in July 2018, providing guidance on how the government believes public authorities should comply with FOIA's provisions.

The Commission considered whether to extend FOIA to private companies that provide public services, though it stopped short of recommending this.[53] In recent years this move has been proposed several times, included in recent Labour Party manifestos,[54] and supported by the current Information Commissioner.[55] The House of Commons Public Accounts Select Committee, looking at public sector contracts, has commented that it is 'vital that Parliament and the public are able to follow the taxpayers' pound to ensure value for money'.[56] The CFOI regularly persuades MPs successful in the ballot for Private Members Bills to put forward a Bill to achieve this.[57] Some moves have already been made to extend FOI to private contractors in Scotland,[58] and it is perhaps only a matter of time before one of these attempts succeeds in the UK.

Summing up

- FOI has a long history going back at least to 1766.
- Over 100 countries have now adopted FOI legislation.
- Before the FOIA, the UK had a reputation for secrecy, as represented by the Official Secrets Acts 1911, under which civil servants could face prosecution for disclosing even non-sensitive information.
- The FOIA is the result of a long campaign by the CFOI and others, starting in the 1970s.
- Other laws were introduced along the way giving access to information on local government administration, the environment and private individuals among other matters.
- The FOIA received royal assent on 30 November 2000, coming fully into force on 1 January 2005, the same day as the EIR.
- The aims of the FOIA are:
  - to improve the openness and transparency of public bodies
  - to increase the accountability of public body decision making and spending
  - to improve decision making
  - to allow the public to engage in decision making
  - to increase trust in public authorities.
- There have been several attempts to reform the FOIA since 2005, most of which have failed because of media and political resistance.
- The next frontier in openness is open data – what people can do with data once they get it.
- A revised code of practice, providing guidance on how to fulfil FOIA's obligations, was published in July 2018.
- In future the FOIA in the UK may be extended to cover private companies that provide public sector services.

Chapter 2

Understanding the Act

Introduction

In the UK and everywhere else FOI derives from legislation. If FOI officers want to know what they have to do, and be able to provide advice to colleagues and applicants, they need to understand that legislation. Although there are other places to go for help, some of which are described in Chapter 4, all the codes, guidance, books, decisions of regulators and courts are based on the statute itself.

It is surprising how often a seemingly intransigent problem that an FOI officer has to deal with can be resolved simply by going back to a battered, dog-eared copy of the FOIA, and re-reading what the UK Parliament has set down. Myths build up over what the FOIA does and doesn't require, and going back to the original legislation often helps to establish fact over rumour. Questions as to whether a request is valid, whether information is held, whether it is possible to withhold information – all unlocked at times by simply going back to the source. To be an FOI officer, and to be good at it, it is necessary to read the legislation itself.

Those not used to working with statute may be nervous about reading legislation in its raw state, but the FOIA can be (though isn't always) straightforward to understand. If anything, legislation in other jurisdictions tends to be even clearer.

This chapter looks at the process of creating laws in the UK, how they are structured, and how to access them, before going on to examine the main features of the FOIA. The way that those features are approached in other countries' FOI laws are highlighted. It is important to recognise that FOI doesn't have to be the way that it is, and that the choices made by legislators have been made for a reason.

Legislation in the UK

The FOIA is an Act of Parliament agreed by the House of Commons, the House of Lords and the monarch, who gave royal assent to the Act on 30 November 2000. Legislation that is still going through the process of reaching agreement by those institutions is referred to as a Bill. Acts are referred to as 'primary legislation'.

In the UK, there is also 'secondary legislation'. This consists of regulations or orders made by government ministers. They are given the power to issue secondary legislation by Acts of Parliament – in this way Parliament has ultimate control over the powers of government. Even when the power to make secondary legislation exists, ministers still have to make it available to Parliament and it may, on occasion, be challenged by MPs or peers.

Primary legislation is usually divided into parts and sections. Parts are the equivalent of chapters in a book. Sections, or clauses (as they are referred to in a Bill), contain the detailed provisions. They are often divided into subsections or sub-clauses. For example, section 40, subsection 2 – s. 40(2) – of the FOIA is an important provision of the exemption covering personal information. Many pieces of primary legislation also contain schedules – effectively appendices – containing more detailed or extensive information that might clutter the main body of the law. There are also 'explanatory notes' issued alongside legislation, which can help those reading the Act understand the intention of a particular section.

Secondary legislation tends to be much shorter than primary legislation. It is broken down into regulations. So we might refer to regulation 2 (reg. 2) of the EIR for example.

There are common features to legislation. For instance, each Act has a long title and a short title: 'An Act to make provision for the disclosure of information held by public authorities or by persons providing services for them and to amend the Data Protection Act 1998 and the Public Records Act 1958; and for connected purposes' is thankfully usually referred to as the 'Freedom of Information Act 2000'.[1]

Legislation usually also contains sections explaining how to interpret certain terms, and listing ways that it affects other laws, perhaps through amendments or repeal of those laws.

All UK legislation can be found on the website legislation.gov.uk, which staff at The National Archives (TNA) handily update when amendments are made. This is the best place to view or download a copy of the FOIA, or for that matter the EIR. Legislation of the Scottish Parliament and other UK administrations can also be found on this website.

Duties under the FOIA

Turning to the FOIA itself, part I of the Act sets out the scope of the right to access information under the legislation. It cuts straight to the chase at s. 1(1), stating:

> Any person making a request for information to a public authority is entitled –
>
> (a) to be informed in writing by the public authority whether it holds information of the description specified in the request, and
> (b) if that is the case, to have that information communicated to him.

So right from the start, it is clear that public authorities have to respond to requests in writing, and that they have a duty to say both whether they hold the requested information, and if they do to communicate that information to the applicant.

This isn't the only duty under the Act though. Section 19 states that public authorities are also required to 'adopt and maintain' a publication scheme, publish information in line with this scheme, and review it 'from time to time'.

Which organisations have to comply with the FOIA?

All public authorities must comply with the FOIA. The Act defines what a public authority is at s. 3(1). First, it refers to schedule 1 of the Act, which lists most bodies subject to the FOIA. This list can be amended by the secretary of state with responsibility for FOI policy (s.4), which at the time of writing is the Chancellor of the Duchy of Lancaster, the lead minister in the Cabinet Office. It includes government departments, local authorities, universities, schools, NHS trusts, GPs and pharmacists, along with some less familiar bodies such as the Committee on Chemicals and Materials of Construction for Use in Public Water Supply and Swimming Pools. A small number of bodies are only subject to the FOIA in part. These include the BBC, Channel 4 (neither of which are covered in respect of journalism or the arts) and the Bank of England (its private banking activities remain private).

If the secretary of state considers that organisations 'exercise functions of a public nature', or are providing a public service under contract, they can be made subject to the Act by order (s. 5). The secretary of state must consult them first. The Universities and Colleges Admissions Service, the Financial Ombudsman Service and Network Rail are among the organisations that have become subject to the FOIA in this way.

Finally, if a company is 'publicly owned' it is subject to the FOIA under s. 6. For this to be the case, the company must be wholly owned by the Crown or one or more public bodies listed in schedule 1.

Around the world: which organisations are covered?

Scotland's FOI(S)A applies to a similar range of bodies to the UK Act. It has now been extended by statutory instrument to cover 'arms-length' bodies set up by local authorities to deliver certain public services, contractors who run privately managed prisons, providers of secure accommodation for children, grant-aided schools and independent special schools.

In the States of Jersey, the government is a single legal entity, so the list of bodies covered by its FOI Law is rather short. Along with the government, the police, bodies established by the States administration, and parishes (local government) appear on the list.

India's Right to Information Act covers federal government institutions, but also bodies controlled and financed by the various states. Most observers praise the broad scope of the Act.[2]

Talking of broad scope, South Africa's Promotion of Access to Information Act 2000 is unusual. Most FOI laws apply only to public sector bodies. Private sector organisations are covered in South Africa – not just if they provide public services, as is sometimes the case in other countries – but in their own right.

Many countries, especially those with federal-type constitutions, adopt laws which only apply to the federal government or central government institutions. These include Canada, Mexico, New Zealand and the USA. They have usually adopted separate legislation providing access to information held at state or local level, such as the Local Government Official Information and Meetings Act 1987, which provides access to local government information in New Zealand.

Communicating with the applicant

Public authorities are obliged to provide advice and assistance to applicants and potential applicants under s. 16 of the FOIA. Where a public body conforms with the s. 45 code of practice's guidance on the provision of advice and assistance, it is taken to have complied with this duty.

Public authorities must issue a 'refusal notice' to applicants if they are refusing a request for any reason (s. 17). This should set out the reason for refusal including which provision is being applied and why, along with instructions on how to appeal the decision and the contact details for the Information Commissioner.

Valid requests

A valid 'request for information' is defined at s. 8 of the FOIA and must:

- be in writing (the form is not stated, so it is accepted that requests submitted by e-mail or other electronic means are valid, as are letters)
- state the name of the applicant; the ICO suggests there should be at least an initial and surname for an individual, but a company name can also be valid
- provide an address for correspondence (an e-mail address is sufficient if the information can be sent digitally)
- describe the information requested
- be legible (the s. 45 code of practice suggests that requests submitted in languages other than English or Welsh are not valid on this basis)[3]
- be in permanent form.

In theory at least, unless a request meets these requirements, it need not be processed. However, the ICO reminds public authorities of the aim of the FOIA to improve openness and accountability, and that there is nothing to stop them from responding even if a request does not meet all these requirements (unless it is the lack of an address for communication that is at issue). The ICO also stresses the duty to advise and assist (set out at s. 16), and suggests that if, for example, an applicant has not provided their name, the authority should advise them to do so rather than just ignoring the request. If it is suspected that a pseudonym has been used, this arguably makes the request invalid, but an authority needs to be sure of its ground before refusing such a request. The ICO looks dimly on authorities that insist on the provision of proof of identity before handling a request.[4] Ultimately, the UK ICO suggests it will not consider complaints unless an applicant has provided their real name. If the regulator will not enforce where a request is invalid, many authorities not unreasonably take the view that they do not need to comply with requests in these circumstances.

Around the world: valid requests
Many countries (e.g. Canada, New Zealand, the USA) define a valid request as one that is in writing, describes the information required and provides contact details for correspondence. The requirements of the law may dictate other criteria though.

In Malta, applicants must provide proof of identity and/or residence, since their FOI law only provides residents of the island with rights of access. The Isle of Man similarly only permits residents to make requests, and Manx residents must submit requests using a specified form, otherwise their request will not be valid.

In Australia, applicants must specify that they are making a request under the Australian FOI Act.

How long can public authorities take to answer requests?

The time allowed for public authorities to answer requests is specified in the FOIA at s. 10. In most circumstances requests should be answered 'promptly and in any event not later than the twentieth working day following the date of receipt'. Those 'working days' do not include weekends or bank holidays 'in any part of the United Kingdom'.[5] This can be handy for FOI officers in England, Wales and Northern Ireland when Scotland is celebrating St Andrew's Day or recovering from Hogmanay.

Exceptions to the 20 working day deadline include:

- The clock can be stopped while waiting for a fee to be paid (s. 10(2)).
- Where applying a qualified exemption and more time is required to consider the public interest a refusal notice still has to be issued within the normal deadline, but a final decision can be delayed 'until such time as is reasonable in the circumstances' (s. 10(3)).
- If an authority has told an applicant that their request is not clear enough, they do not need to start the clock until a clarified request has been submitted (s. 1(3)).
- Schools (including academies)[6] are permitted a potentially longer period of 20 school days or 60 working days, whichever is sooner[7].
- Permission can be sought from the Information Commissioner to extend the deadline to a maximum of 60 working days if the information is stored overseas or is with armed forces on active service.[8]
- If the information is in a public record that has been transferred to TNA, the Public Record Office of Northern Ireland (PRONI) or an approved place of deposit (e.g. a local authority record office), then the deadline can be extended to 30 working days.[9]

One common dispute is over exactly when the 20 working days begins, especially if a request is received on a non-working day. Arguably, this is one of those situations where returning to the text of the Act can be helpful. Section 10 refers to the date of receipt as being 'the day on which the public authority receives the request for information'. Notably, unlike elsewhere in s. 10, it doesn't refer to 'the working day'. So if a request is received on a Saturday, that is still the date of receipt. The following Monday will normally be the first working day. Similarly, if a request is received at 11.59 p.m. on Tuesday, Tuesday is the day on which the request is received, and day 1 will be Wednesday. This is the approach taken by the Information Commissioner in their guidance.[10] Confusingly, however, the s. 45 code of practice published in July 2018 ignores the Information Commissioner's position and the wording of the Act itself, stating that:

> The date on which a request is received is the day on which it arrives or, if this is not a working day, the first working day following its arrival.[11]

Whichever view the FOI officer may subscribe to in relation to the date of receipt, they should note that s. 10 states that requests should be answered 'promptly'. For the most part, the Commissioner and the tribunals have been sympathetic to public authorities when interpreting the word 'promptly'. They should answer them 'without delay', but it is recognised that authorities have to process requests and do not have unlimited resources. They have to conduct their core business as well as answer FOI requests,[12] so answering requests within 20 working days of receipt may be regarded 'as prompt within the meaning and intendment of the legislation'.[13] That said, FOI officers must be able to explain any delay to responses – the Information Commissioner stresses that 20 working days should be seen as a 'long stop', and that responses just before or on the 20th day may need to be justified.[14]

Around the world: time limits

It is common for authorities to have to answer requests within 20 working days – this is the normal period in which requests have to be answered in Ireland, the Isle of Man, Scotland, the States of Jersey, and many other places beside. Other countries have adopted different time limits.

The European Union's institutions must answer requests within 15 working days.

In Australia, requests must be acknowledged within 14 days of receipt (acknowledgements are good practice in the UK, but not required under the FOIA), and a decision must be communicated within 30 days. Failing to respond within this period is a 'deemed refusal' and can trigger a complaint to the authority or Information Commissioner.

Canada also has a 30-day limit for answering requests, which can be extended to allow for consultation or if there is a lot of information to go through.

Mexico requires requests to be answered in 20 working days but, as noted in Chapter 1, has an unusual provision stating that if a request is not answered within that period, the information must be released automatically within 10 working days.

US government guidance states that agencies 'typically process requests in the order of receipt'. The existence of a backlog, or a particularly complex request, can delay responses significantly (see www.foia.gov/how-to.html).

What is 'information'?

'Information' is defined at s. 84 as 'information recorded in any form'. This is rather a circular definition, but it does at least indicate that the form of information will not make a difference to whether it is covered by the legislation. It also establishes that non-recorded information – such as knowledge in employees' heads – will not be covered. If for example someone makes a request asking for the authority's view on a recently announced government policy, in many cases it is true to say that this is not held, since while a view may have been taken, it might not be written down anywhere. However, FOI officers should be careful not to take too rigid a stance on this. It is not true to say that opinions are not covered by the FOIA – if an opinion has been written down or otherwise recorded, it is subject to the FOIA in the same way as any recorded fact.

The ICO's guidance on identifying FOI requests highlights some other situations where FOI officers might debate whether 'information' is being described. These are all valid requests for information:

- a request for 'all the e-mails in [named person]'s e-mail account'
- a request for all documents containing a specific keyword
- questionnaires.

In summary, the ICO considers 'any description that allows the requested information to be distinguished from other information held by the authority as valid'.[15] Remember, though, that even when a request is valid, it is not always necessary for the information to be provided. For example, some requests falling under the categories listed above may well be estimated to exceed the cost limit, so could be refused using s. 12.

FOI laws around the world vary in that some provide a right of access to 'documents', and some, like the UK's Act, to 'information'. It is sometimes suggested that the use of the word 'information' in the FOIA means that applicants are not entitled to receive copies of specific documents. However, it is often most practical to provide information in the form of a copy of the document, rather than extracting the text and pasting it into a different one. In any case, the form of the document itself may constitute information. In one case, the Independent Parliamentary Standards Authority was ordered to disclose copies of receipts submitted by MPs in support of their expenses claims. The tribunal observed:

a signature on an invoice may indicate fraud if it was identical to the claimant's signature or that of a member of his team; a shoddily presented invoice may call into question the legitimacy of the company said to have issued it, or a letterhead or logo may have changed or be different to the one usually associated with a particular company – again bringing the legitimacy of the invoice into question.[16]

Is information held?

The Act defines when information is considered to be held at s. 3(2). This is the case firstly if 'it is held by the authority'. So far so (apparently) straightforward. As one judge put it, 'hold' 'is an ordinary English word and is not used in some technical sense in the Act'.[17]

However, the FOIA then qualifies the definition, excluding information held 'on behalf of another person'. The Act is allowing for the fact that there may be circumstances where information happens to be on the premises of a public authority, but has nothing to do with its operations. For example, an employee's personal diary does not become subject to FOIA merely because that person brings it to work. Similarly, councillors using their council's IT facilities to correspond with their constituents about concerns that they have raised do not need to worry about whether such correspondence is accessible under the Act (as long as they don't copy in council officers).

Section 3(2) continues: 'or…it is held by another person on behalf of the authority'. Here the legislation is making it clear that its effects cannot be avoided by merely moving the business of the authority to a different location. The employee referred to above will not remove information from the FOIA's coverage by taking it home or sending it off-site. Similarly, where a company is contracted by a public authority to provide public services, information relating to the provision of those services is subject to the FOIA (though this is not always straightforward to establish).

Table 2.1 on the next page summarises a sample of decisions made by the Information Commissioner and tribunals in disputes over whether information was held.

Creating new information

Some FOI laws explicitly state that authorities are not obliged to create new information to answer a request (for example, the Isle of Man's FOI Act includes such a provision). This is instead implicit in the FOIA. It can be

Table 2.1 *When information is held or not held under the FOIA*

Held	Not held
E-mail held in a personal e-mail account relating to a public authority's business *ICO decision FS50422276*	E-mail held in a corporate e-mail account sent by an employee in a personal capacity (non-business related) *Montague v IC & Liverpool John Moores University*, EA/2012/0109, 13 December 2012
Number of e-mails sent by an employee in a personal capacity *Lotz v IC & DWP*, EA/2016/0150, January 2017, para. 29	Information in an online database that an authority has access to, but does not host *Glen Marlow v the Information Commissioner*, EA/2005/0031, 15 August 2006
Information that has been deleted, but still exists on a backup tape or similar *Catherine Whitehead v the Information Commissioner*, EA/2013/0262, 29 April 2014, para. 16	Information that the authority has the right to inspect, but does not otherwise have control over *Alan Dransfield v the Information Commissioner and Devon County Council*, EA/2010/0152, 30 March 2011
Information created by a company to fulfill contractual obligations to provide a public service *Visser v Information Commissioner and London Borough of Southwark*, EA/2012/0125, 11 January 2013	Information created for its own purposes by a company, where it is under no contractual obligation to provide it to the public authority *ICO decisions FS50463474 and FS50478617*

difficult to understand the difference between collating information from various resources that are held and creating something new.

The ICO says that if an authority holds the 'building blocks' that can be used to collate the answer, then the information is normally considered to be held. So, an applicant might ask for a list of information, and the authority does not hold that list in the form asked for. If the list can be constructed using information taken from various existing resources, the requested information is held. It is possible that the process of pulling that information together may exceed the cost limit, so even if information is 'held', the authority may not have to provide it. This was the situation in *Mr M L Johnson v Information Commissioner and Ministry of Justice* (EA 2006/0085, 13 July 2007), a case used by the ICO to illustrate this issue.[18]

Table 2.2 opposite provides two examples of common mistakes related to whether information must be created or not to answer a FOI request.

Table 2.2 *Two examples of common mistakes related to whether information must be created or not to answer a FOIA request*

Description of request	X Wrong	✓ Right
Please provide the number of complaints received by the authority in 2018. (The authority normally reports complaint numbers by financial year, but monthly totals are recorded).	The figure for the financial year 2017-18 is provided. The FOI officer claims that the figure for the calendar year is not held.	The monthly totals of complaints received are added up to calculate a figure for the calendar year of 2018 and this is provided.
Please tell me how many linear metres of desk space are provided for student study. (The authority has never had any reason to record this information).	The FOI officer asks colleagues to measure every desk so that the request can be answered.	The request is refused by the FOI officer because the information is not recorded anywhere.

The format of information

Applicants can express a preference as to the form that they would like their information to be provided in. Section 11(1) provides that where this happens, the public authority 'shall so far as reasonably practicable' comply with their preference. Deciding whether it is 'reasonably practicable' to comply with their preference involves considerations such as the cost of doing so (s. 11(2)). Decisions not to provide the information in the specified format to the applicant must be explained (s. 11(3)).

The Court of Appeal has ruled that 'form' is equivalent to 'format', so applicants can specify that they would like to receive information in the form of an Excel spreadsheet, for example.[19] The Act offers the options of provision in a 'form acceptable to the applicant', provision of 'a reasonable opportunity to inspect a record containing the information', or the provision of 'a digest or summary of the information'. Again, the provision of a summary of information is not normally seen as an example of new information being created.

The Protection of Freedoms Act 2012 amended s. 11 to the effect that where applicants specify that they would like to receive a dataset in an electronic form capable of re-use, the authority has to meet this as far as reasonably practicable, and as long as they own the copyright in the information.[20] These changes are explored in Chapter 9.

Fees and cost limits

Public authorities can issue a 'fees notice' to the applicant (s. 9). The applicant must then pay within three months if they want the information. However, there are limited circumstances where fees can be charged, specifically where:

- 'disbursements' apply – reasonable charges may be made for photocopying, printing, postage and other such costs[21]
- the cost of answering the request exceeds the 'appropriate limit' (see below).[22]

It is also possible to charge for information listed in the authority's publication scheme (s. 19), and in certain circumstances for permission to re-use supplied information.[23] In practice, public authorities don't charge very often, as it is rarely seen as worthwhile charging for disbursements and, as we will see, requests that exceed the cost limit present an inviting alternative.

Regulations establish the 'appropriate limit'.[24] Section 12 of the Act states that authorities do not have to provide information where they estimate that to do so exceeds that limit. The limit is £600 for central government departments and the armed forces, and £450 for all other public authorities.[25] The regulations state that only the following activities can be considered in calculating the cost:

- establishing whether the information is held
- locating the information
- retrieving the information
- extracting the information.[26]

Consideration, redaction or reading time, or time spent consulting with third parties, cannot be taken into account. In addition, staff time must be calculated at £25 an hour, no matter who works on the request.[27] This is the basis of the commonly cited 18- and 24-hour time limits for FOI requests. There is no time limit specified within the FOIA or the fees regulations, but one can be calculated through simple mathematics: £600/£25 = 24 hours; and £450/£25 = 18 hours.

The regulations also permit public authorities to aggregate the cost of multiple requests as long as they are made within 60 working days, by the same person or people working in concert, and on a broadly similar topic.[28]

The gist: the tribunals on the appropriate limit

- Estimates must be 'sensible, realistic and supported by cogent evidence' (*Randall v IC*, EA/2007/0004).
- An example of this would be timing how long it took to extract relevant information from a single screen of a database, and multiplying the time by the number of screens that need to be looked at. Using the £25 an hour formula, the cost of looking through all the screens can be estimated (*Urmenyi v Information Commissioner & London Borough of Sutton*, EA/2006/0093).
- However, estimates do not have to be precise or involve 'scientific rigour'; and it is not necessary to say precisely how much more than the appropriate limit it would cost to answer a request, only to demonstrate that the appropriate limit will be exceeded (*Kirkham v Information Commissioner* [2018] UKUT 126 (AAC), paras. 23–26).
- If the reason that a request can't be answered within the appropriate limit is because the authority keeps its records in a particular way, or its records management practices are poor, this does not prevent them from refusing the request using s. 12 (*Francis v Information Commissioner & South Essex Partnership NHS Trust*, EA/2007/0091).
- Authorities may not be permitted to rely on s. 12 if they have failed to provide advice and assistance (*Brown v Information Commissioner*, EA/2006/0088).
- Authorities don't have to search up to the limit (even if the applicant asks them to) (*Kirkham v Information Commissioner* [2018] UKUT 126 (AAC), para. 14)
- Authorities can stop searching if they realise that they have already spent up to the cost limit (*Quinn v IC & Home Office*, EA/2006/0010).

Around the world: fees and cost limits

In Scotland, a different and complex approach to fees and cost limits applies. Authorities can consider the cost of locating, retrieving and providing information, but not the cost of establishing whether it is held. Time spent deciding whether exemptions apply can't be taken into account, but time spent on the physical activity of redaction can. Staff time is calculated on the basis of the actual salary paid to the staff working on the request up to £15 an hour (the Scottish Commissioner comments that they may check job descriptions to ascertain whether a lower paid member of staff should have carried out the work!). The cost of postage and packing can be added to the total estimated. Once a total estimate has been calculated:

- if it is less than £100, the request will be handled free of charge
- if it is more than £100, the authority can charge 10% of the estimated cost up to an estimated cost of £600
- if it is more than £600, the authority can refuse to comply with the request.[29]

In Malta, a charge of up to €40 can be made for the supply of a document.

In Australia, the first five hours of work on a request are free, but beyond this there is an hourly rate for specific activities. For example, searching is charged at A$15 an hour and decision making at A$20 an hour. Applicants can ask for fees to be waived.

South Africa permits an application fee. The level depends on whether the recipient is a public body (35 rand) or a private company (50 rand). Further charges can be made for locating and copying information.[30]

In Canada, the incoming Trudeau government simplified charges under the federal Access to Information Act in 2016 so that there is a single C$5 application fee.

Vexatious and repeated requests

Where a request is vexatious, a public authority can refuse it under s. 14(1) of the FOIA. The word 'vexatious' is not defined in the Act.

Where an applicant makes a request that is 'identical' or 'substantially similar' to a previous request that they have made, it can be refused (s. 14(2)). The Information Commissioner, perhaps surprisingly, interprets this to mean that repeated requests can only be refused where information was provided, and not where the applicant refuses to accept a valid refusal of their original request.[31]

The gist: what does 'vexatious' mean?
One of the problems with s. 14 is that the term 'vexatious' is not defined. It took until 2013 to gain some clarity on this issue, when the Upper Tribunal considered the case *Information Commissioner v Devon CC and Dransfield* [2012] UKUT 440 (AAC). In particular, the judge in this case identified four themes that can help in deciding whether a request is vexatious or not.

The burden – is this 'manifestly unjustified'?
The number of requests made by an applicant can be taken into account, the amount of work that would be involved, and anything that demonstrates that the latest request imposes an unjustified burden on the authority.

In *DfE v IC and McInerney* (EA/2013/0270, 2 July 2014), the First-Tier Tribunal (FTT) concluded that a request to the Department for Education (DfE) for copies of free school applications, and the DfE's responses to them, was vexatious after the DfE demonstrated that it would take 54 hours to locate and retrieve the information, and 11 civil servants would take three months to read through and redact it, costing an estimated £171,875. This was despite the case that there was 'no question here of anything in the tone of the request tending towards vexatiousness' and the tribunal being impressed by the applicant's 'genuine motives'.

What is the motive of the applicant?
In *Dr Gary Duke v ICO and the University of Salford* (EA/2011/0060, 26 July 2011), the applicant and a number of other individuals had made a significant number of requests following Dr Duke's dismissal from the university. The university persuaded the FTT that these requests were intended to disrupt its operations.

Does the request have a value or serious purpose?
In *Ainslie v Information Commissioner and Dorset CC* [2012] UKUT 441, the applicant was

able to demonstrate a serious purpose behind his request – namely holding the council to account over remedial works designed to prevent flooding.

Does the request harass staff or distress them?
In *Sanders v IC* (EA/2016/0221, 13 June 2017), the FTT accepted that the pattern and type of requests (e.g. asking for the FOI officer's job description, contact details of line manager, salary and job history) were likely to cause distress.

The codes of practice

Sections 45 and 46 require the relevant secretaries of state to issue codes of practice 'providing guidance to . . . authorities as to the practice which it would . . . be desirable for them to follow'. The former provides such guidance in relation to compliance with Part I of the Act (how to comply with the provisions thus far discussed in this chapter). The latter covers records management and the transfer of public records to TNA and other public records institutions in the UK. The codes of practice are discussed further in Chapter 4.

Exemptions

Part II of the FOIA sets out the exemptions that can be used to justify refusal of requests; these are explored in detail in Chapter 3.

The Information Commissioner

The Act (s. 18) renamed the then Data Protection Commissioner as the Information Commissioner and made that person the regulator for FOI. Their role is defined at ss. 47–9 of the Act as being to promote good practice and observance of the FOIA. The enforcement powers of the Information Commissioner are set out in Part IV of the FOIA. Chapter 14 examines the duties and powers of the Information Commissioner, and the procedures for appealing their decisions under the Act.

Other provisions

Famously, under s. 53 of the FOIA cabinet ministers are able to veto disclosure of information if they disagree with the Information Commissioner's decision. This ability extends to the Attorney General, the First Minister of Wales and the First and Deputy First Minister (in consultation) in Northern Ireland. Other public bodies have no veto. Even the government's ability to veto disclosures has been effectively limited by a Supreme Court ruling,[32] as mentioned in Chapter 1. One of the concerns of critics of this provision has been that the government has in the past used the veto to block disclosures following rulings of the FTT, effectively overruling a court. The government has now committed only to use the veto after the Commissioner has made a decision and before it reaches any tribunal or court.[33]

The FOIA has to interact with other legislation already on the statute book. The Public Records Act 1958 (PRA) and Public Records Act (Northern Ireland) 1923 (PRA(NI)) govern the selection and preservation of government records. Part VI of the FOIA sets out how the FOIA works with them, and places limits on how long certain exemptions can apply to information (s. 63). The FOIA's relationship to data protection laws and to the EIR is set out in parts VII and VIII of the Act. The way that these laws interact with the FOIA is discussed in more detail in Part 2 of this book (chapters 5–9).

Where other laws prevent disclosure, the Act makes provision at s. 75 for the relevant secretary of state to repeal or amend those laws by secondary legislation. Finally, there is protection in law for public bodies that disclose third-party information that contains 'defamatory matter' in response to a request, as long as they can show that the disclosure was not made with malice (s. 79).

Summing up

The FOI Act should be the first port of call for FOI officers seeking to resolve questions over its interpretation.

- It sets out the duties of public authorities and defines which organisations fall into this category.
- It provides definitions of key terms used in FOIA administration.
- It sets out when a request is valid.
- It explains the circumstances in which requests can be refused (where requests exceed a cost limit, when requests are vexatious and when exemptions apply), and how this should be done.
- It lists the responsibilities of the Information Commissioner and other bodies.
- The relationship between the FOIA and other legislation is also outlined.

Chapter 3

The exemptions in the FOIA

Introduction

The FOIA is intended to promote the disclosure of information. Ironically, though, any attempt to explain its working inevitably tends to focus on the various methods for refusing to do so. This is true whatever the author's agenda or interest.

This is not because the FOIA is really designed to obstruct access to information, whatever the most cynical commentators may say. It is because releasing information under the FOIA is relatively straightforward. If all the requested information is being disclosed, no more legal justification is required than the duty spelt out at s. 1.

If an authority wishes to depart from this duty, it is more difficult. Any attempt to refuse a request under the FOIA must be justified. This is true of the reasons for refusal already discussed in Chapter 2. If refusing on cost grounds, the reasoning must be outlined. It must be possible to explain – if not to the applicant, certainly to the Information Commissioner – why a request is considered vexatious. It is also true when other reasons must be found to refuse a request. These other reasons are called exemptions and can be found in Part II of the Act.

Some of these exemptions are very complex to apply. Added to the complexity of the drafting, nearly 15 years of case law has occasionally clarified, but more often complicated, our understanding of these provisions.

FOI officers must be able to advise their colleagues and where necessary apply these exemptions. Doing so successfully may be the key test of the practitioner's proficiency for many colleagues.

The FOIA is not alone in identifying the circumstances in which requests may be refused. Other FOI laws contain exemptions – broadly similar in coverage to those in the UK's Act.

Exemptions – some terminology

Before looking at the individual exemptions, it is important to be familiar with some of the terminology.

Section 2 of the Act establishes the concept of 'absolute' and 'qualified' exemptions. Any exemption that is 'qualified' is subject to a public interest test; even if the information falls within the exemption, it might still be disclosed if the public interest in disclosing it outweighs the public interest in withholding it. Most exemptions are qualified. A more detailed explanation of the public interest test is provided later in this chapter.

The exemptions listed at s. 2(3) as being 'absolute' are not subject to a public interest test. If the information falls within the scope of the exemption it can be withheld irrespective of any public interest considerations. Very often these exemptions are there to prevent the FOIA from conflicting with other legal requirements. For example, the exemption at s. 40 protects personal information, preventing the FOIA from contradicting the GDPR or the DPA 2018. The most obvious example is s. 44, which allows information to be withheld where its disclosure would contradict a separate legal requirement set out in statute or a court order.

The terms 'class' and 'prejudice' are also often employed in descriptions of exemptions and the way that they should be applied. Many of the exemptions (particularly, but not exclusively, the qualified exemptions) contain the following wording: 'Information is exempt information if its disclosure under this Act would, or would be likely to, prejudice...' Some use slightly different words such as 'endanger' or 'inhibit'. In these cases, the exemption only applies if disclosure is to some extent likely to prejudice – or harm – the particular interest that the exemption is focused on. Note also the phrasing 'would or would be likely to' in these exemptions. Whenever refusing a request on these grounds, the likelihood of the harm must be indicated – that might be whether the harm 'would' happen, or merely whether it 'would be likely' to happen.

If an exemption does not use the word 'prejudice' or similar, it is a 'class' exemption. This means that it is not necessary to demonstrate that any prejudice would be caused by disclosure, only that the requested information falls within the description set out in the relevant section of the Act. Effectively, with these exemptions Parliament has already decided that disclosing this particular kind

The gist: conducting the prejudice test

Hogan v Oxford City Council and IC, EA/2005/0026 and 0030, 17 October 2006

This very early case concerned a request from Mr Hogan for information about vehicles owned by the council. The council refused some of the information, citing s. 31(1)(a) of the FOIA (the exemption covering prejudice to the prevention or detection of crime). It is important because it established the following process for considering the application of prejudice-based exemptions:

1   Identify the applicable interest to be protected – which exemption is likely to be relevant?
2   Explain the nature of the prejudice that it is envisaged would result from disclosure. It should be possible to show a causal link between the disclosure of the information and the envisaged harm that would be caused. The prejudice should be 'real, actual or of substance'.
3   Consider the likelihood of the prejudice being caused. In choosing to say that disclosure 'would prejudice', the authority is claiming that the prejudice is 'more probable than not' (the Information Commissioner takes this to mean that there is a greater than 50% chance of prejudice).[1] If the alternative of 'would be likely to prejudice' is selected, the authority is still saying that there is a 'real and significant risk' of the prejudice being caused, though it falls short of being 'more probable than not' (i.e. the likelihood is less than 50%).

This test is regularly referenced by the Information Commissioner and tribunals when considering whether prejudice-based exemptions have been applied correctly.

of information would be harmful. Examples include information provided by specified national security bodies (s. 23) and documentation relating to an authority's investigation of a criminal offence (s. 30).

Around the world: prejudice

Both the Isle of Man and the States of Jersey take the terminology used in the UK Act for several of their exemptions, so that authorities have to demonstrate that disclosure 'would or would be likely to prejudice' particular interests.

The FOI(S)A's equivalent of 'prejudice' is 'prejudice substantially'. This suggests there is a higher threshold for withholding information than under the UK Act. The Scottish Commissioner observes that any harm caused by disclosure 'must be of real and demonstrable significance, rather than simply marginal'.[2]

The Irish Freedom of Information Act 2014 (which replaced the earlier 1997 Act) uses a mixture of terms. The security, defence and international relations exemption applies if 'access to it could reasonably be expected to affect adversely' those interests. Elsewhere, information can be withheld if disclosure 'could prejudice the competitive position' of a person.[3]

Prejudice, or harm, tests are common in FOI laws. They can be found in Mexico's law (though, as in the Irish Act, a range of terms are used), as well as the FOI laws of India, Jamaica, Japan, New Zealand, South Africa, Uganda and many others. Most of the exemptions in the USA's FOI Act are class-based.[4]

In rare circumstances, it may be necessary neither to confirm nor deny whether information is held. Remember that the first section of the Act gives public authorities two duties:

- to indicate whether requested information is held
- to communicate the information if so.

Most of the time it is sufficient to use an exemption to suspend only the second of these duties. It is rarely harmful to admit that information is held, even if it cannot be released. Occasionally, though, it is necessary to apply a particular exemption to both duties. This is what is meant by neither confirming nor denying whether information is held. All of the exemptions except for s. 21 (information reasonably accessible to the applicant) can be applied in this way where necessary. It is helpful for authorities to identify circumstances where they would not want to confirm whether information is held so that a consistent approach can be taken. The box below sets out an example of a situation where this might be necessary.

Request: I would like to see any information held on disciplinary action taken against Paul Gibbons.
If the public authority refuses to provide the information, citing s. 40(2), but complies with the duty to confirm whether information is held, it would be unfair to me. The authority would effectively be confirming that disciplinary action was taken against me. By neither confirming nor denying whether any information is held, the authority is able to ensure that such private information remains confidential. This only works if the authority always answers such requests in this way, even when there is no information held (no disciplinary action has ever taken place). Note that a refusal notice would still need to be sent to the applicant, and an exemption cited with an explanation of why it is necessary neither to confirm nor deny the request. Section 40(5B)(a)(i) would be the relevant exemption in this scenario.

The public interest test

Qualified exemptions are all subject to a public interest test. The public interest is not something in which the public will be interested, as some might expect. It is something that *benefits* the public as a whole. It might be better named the public benefit test!

This might seem an odd concept, but consider the ways that disclosure of information, or indeed withholding information, can be of benefit. The very fact that the FOIA exists is an acknowledgment that the public can benefit from more openness. The fact that decisions about public spending are likely to be disclosed may encourage officials and politicians to be more careful about how they reach them. Releasing information about that spending might make it possible for others to suggest ways to bring down the cost to the public. Similarly, openness about the way things are done and the performance of public authorities can make it easier for others to come up with alternative and more effective measures. If there are risks to people's health, or to their rights, it is not hard to see that they should know about this so that they can take appropriate action to protect themselves.

Sometimes, though, it is clear that the public will benefit most if information is withheld. Remember to consider the public as a whole. If disclosure of the information is likely to drive up the cost or reduce the effectiveness of a particular service, this does not benefit the public. If people's safety would be compromised by disclosure, or there would be an enhanced risk of them becoming the victims of crime, this is not in the public interest.

When carrying out a public interest test, it is a matter of identifying all the ways that the public will benefit from information being disclosed and from it being withheld, and judging which of these arguments are strongest. Some people talk about 'weighing the public interest'. This can be misleading as it suggests an emphasis on quantity – the more arguments in favour of withholding information the better. In reality, the focus should always be on how serious the arguments are. There might be half-a-dozen arguments in favour of disclosure, but if release of the information would be likely to put somebody's life at risk, that one argument may be sufficient.

The gist: the public interest in squatting
Voyias v London Borough of Camden, EA/2011/0007, 22 January 2013
Mr Voyias asked for a list of empty properties in Camden. The council refused this, applying s. 31(1)(a) on the basis that disclosure would prejudice the prevention of crime by facilitating squatting and other offences.

Section 31 is a qualified exemption. The FTT considered these public interest arguments in favour of disclosure:

- Disclosure would pressure the council into taking more action to bring housing stock back into use.
- Disclosure would ensure that the council's management of housing stock was accountable (the FTT considered that the benefits claimed by these first two arguments could equally be met by simply publishing statistics on empty properties).

- Disclosure would facilitate squatting (which the applicant considered desirable, though the council and the FTT were unsurprisingly less impressed by).

The FTT considered these arguments in favour of applying the exemption (and therefore withholding the information):

- Disclosure would be likely to prejudice crime prevention (by facilitating it).
- As a result there would be a rise in the cost of security, and if vandalism occurs, repairs.
- If squatters occupy properties, it will cost public money to evict them.
- The potential crime facilitated by the disclosure would impact on the local community, the police and other public officials (increasing public spending and risk to individuals' safety).

On this basis, the FTT agreed with the council that the public interest favoured withholding the information. Doing so would benefit the public more than disclosing the information.

It is essential to keep a record of the arguments considered in case of challenge. Section 17 of the FOIA does not require that they are set out in full in the refusal notice, though it does require that an explanation is provided as to why the public interest favours withholding the information. It is suggested that the easiest way to do this is to list the arguments considered in full in the response – thus providing a formal record in one place, and helping the applicant to better understand why information is being withheld.

Section 10 of the FOIA provides that the usual time limit for responding to requests may be extended to consider the public interest. In these circumstances, an initial refusal notice must be issued within the usual period, setting out which exemption(s) apply and why, and explaining that more time is required. The s. 45 code of practice recommends that the public interest extension be no longer than a further 20 working days.[5]

Around the world: public interest tests

The FOI(S)A follows the UK's approach to public interest for the most part, as do the States of Jersey and Isle of Man FOI Acts, though these Acts separate out the qualified exemptions into different parts of the legislation, making it clearer to see which exemptions are subject to a public interest test.

Many countries do not require the public interest to be assessed when applying exemptions. These include Bulgaria's Access to Public Information Act, Mexico's Transparency and Access to Government Information Act, and perhaps more surprisingly, the USA's FOI Act.[6] This effectively means that if a public authority is able to demonstrate that an exemption applies, it is difficult for an applicant to challenge the decision.

India and New Zealand incorporate strong public interest tests in their exemptions.

The Part II exemptions

Section 21: reasonably accessible

Applies to: information that is already reasonably accessible to the applicant.

Considerations:
- Is the information held? If not, the exemption cannot be applied (but the request can be refused on the basis that the information is not held).
- Is the information accessible to the applicant through other means? This can include publication on a website, in a book, or being open to public inspection in the public authority's offices or in a record office. It can still be considered accessible if the information has to be paid for. Putting information in an authority's publication scheme makes it accessible.
- Is it *reasonably* accessible *to the applicant*? Bear in mind obligations under the Equality Act 2010, as well as practical considerations. Information that is made available to the public in a council's record office in Cornwall may not be reasonably accessible to an applicant living in Aberdeen. It may present difficulties for someone with restricted mobility even if they live in the same town. If the requested information consists of a number on page 232 of a 350-page report, which would cost £150 to purchase, it is unlikely to be considered reasonably accessible to the applicant.
- What assistance can be provided? The duty to advise and assist often comes into play with this exemption. Always explain how the information can be accessed. This might be by providing a URL (web address) or explaining where and when information is available for inspection. If the information is within a large publication, state on which page it can be found.
- It is common practice where information is freely available (especially if on a website) not to formally refuse the request by citing the exemption in the response (a technical infringement of s. 17). As long as the applicant is able to access the information freely and easily, this is perfectly acceptable and unlikely to attract a complaint (indeed, citing the exemption in these circumstances can seem coldly formal and confusing to applicants).

Public interest test: this is an absolute exemption, so no public interest test is required.

Section 22: future publication

Applies to: information that the authority (or someone else) already intends to publish at a future date.

Considerations:
- Is there a settled intention to publish? The exemption does not apply if the authority was not already intending to publish the information before the request was received. Publication can be in a book or report, on a website, delivery of a speech, or making documents available to the public in a record office.
- Is refusal reasonable in all the circumstances? The period that the applicant would have to wait for publication is a key factor.[7] Another indication of reasonableness would be documented consideration of whether earlier disclosure is possible.
- Is all the information going to be published? For example, if the first draft contained the requested information in a table, but it has subsequently been decided that the table and its contents will be omitted from the published report, that information will no longer be protected by s. 22. Similarly, if there is uncertainty over whether information will be included in a publication, the exemption will not apply.[8]

These public interest test arguments are commonly relevant:

- Accelerating publication would require public resources to be diverted from other activities that benefit the public more.[9]
- Partial and piecemeal disclosures of information could result in confusion and inaccuracy.[10]
- Commercial exploitation of the information might be prejudiced.[11]

Around the world: future publication exemption in Scotland, the Isle of Man and the States of Jersey
The FOI(S)A has a similar exemption for information intended for future publication at s. 27. However, it only applies where there is an intention to publish the information within 12 weeks of the request being received. The States of Jersey's FOI Law follows the same approach at s. 36.

The Isle of Man's FOI Act future publication exemption (s. 41) operates in the same way as the UK's s. 22 exemption.

Section 22A: unpublished research data

Applies to: research data where there is an intention to publish a report of the research.

Considerations:
- Was the information obtained in the course of, or derived from, a research programme?
- Would disclosure of the information prejudice (or would it be likely to prejudice) the research itself, participants in the research, or the interests of the authority holding the information, or which carried out the research?
- Is there an intention to publish a report on the information? Even if a report has already been published, the exemption can still be applied as long as there is an intention to publish further reports in the future.

These public interest test arguments are commonly relevant:

- Researchers should be able to complete research before a research programme is subjected to external scrutiny.
- Established peer review process should not be undermined.
- Premature publication of research could lead to an incomplete and confusing picture emerging.[12]
- In favour of disclosure, it might be that contentious conclusions have been published and the disclosure of the raw data would allow these conclusions to be evaluated by a wider audience.

Sections 23–5: national security

Apply to: information supplied by or about a security body listed at s. 23(3) of the FOIA; other information to the extent that it requires protection for the purposes of safeguarding national security.

Considerations:
- Is the information about or supplied by a body listed at s. 23(3)? It is protected if it is about or supplied by MI5, MI6, GCHQ, the National Crime Agency and a number of other bodies.
- If it is not, is withholding the information considered 'reasonably necessary' to protect national security?[13]

- Members of the Cabinet, the Attorney General, the Advocate General for Scotland and the Attorney General for Northern Ireland are able to issue a certificate under s. 25 certifying that s. 23 or s. 24 applies.

These public interest test arguments are commonly relevant:

- For most purposes s. 23 is absolute, so no public interest test applies as long as information is retained by the authority.
- If the information is historical (see Chapter 7) and has been transferred to TNA, a public interest test applies to s. 23.
- The exemption at s. 24 is qualified, so a public interest test applies in every case where it is used.
- There is always a strong public interest in safeguarding national security, so if a good argument can be made as to why it is reasonably necessary to withhold the information (i.e. that s. 24 applies) it should be straightforward to argue that withholding the information is in the public interest.

Section 26: prejudice to defence

Applies to: information which if disclosed would, or would be likely to, prejudice the defence of the British Islands or colonies, or the capability, effectiveness or security of the armed forces (of the UK or its allies).

Considerations:
- Would disclosure assist an enemy? It is necessary to explain this to the extent possible without causing the prejudice.

These public interest test arguments are commonly relevant:

- There 'would need to be very weighty countervailing considerations' to justify disclosure of information that would place the security of the armed forces at risk.[14] Again, if the argument for prejudice can be made out, the public interest will almost certainly follow.
- Arguments in favour of disclosure include furthering public understanding, where there has been failure to control spending, and revealing health and safety issues.[15]

The gist: neither confirming nor denying the existence of 'directed energy weapons'
Donnie Mackenzie v IC, EA/2013/0251, 8 July 2014
Mr Mackenzie asked for a list of 'directed energy weapons' which the Ministry of Defence (MoD) had access to – in effect he wanted to know whether the UK had in use, or was developing, a ray gun or similar. The MoD responded by neither confirming nor denying whether such information existed, citing s. 26(3). This was upheld by both the Commissioner and the FTT, who agreed with the MoD that a hostile power would be assisted by the knowledge that such weapons did or did not exist. They noted that 'there was [an] exceptionally strong public interest in maintaining the safety and security of British forces'.

Section 27: prejudice to international relations

Applies to: information disclosure of which would, or would be likely to, prejudice relations between the UK and any other state, international organisation or court, the interests of the UK abroad, or the promotion or protection of the UK's interests abroad. Section 27(2) also provides a class exemption protecting confidential information obtained from another state, international organisation or court.

Considerations:

- Would disclosure be likely to have a negative impact on international relations? Even a relatively trivial matter might have this effect, though it depends on the government concerned.[16]
- Was the information provided in confidence? There is no need to demonstrate that a breach of the confidence would be actionable (unlike s. 41).
- When seeking the views of other nations, avoid asking leading questions (e.g. 'There is this awful tribunal in London that is threatening to release these documents, don't you think this will be a very bad idea?').[17]

These public interest test arguments are commonly relevant:

- There is an inherent public interest in avoiding loss of international confidence.[18]
- Arguments in favour of disclosure include that the matters are no longer current, and that the information would help the public understand issues better and inform their input.[19]

Section 28: relations within the UK

Applies to: information the disclosure of which would or would be likely to prejudice relations between the administrations of the UK.

Considerations:
- Is the information likely to prejudice relations between any of the following: the UK Government, the Scottish Administration, the Northern Ireland Assembly Executive Committee or the Welsh Assembly Government?

These public interest test arguments are commonly relevant:

- the importance of maintaining good relations between administrations
- the importance of administrations being able to discuss policy freely and frankly without inhibition[20]
- in favour of disclosure, the value of the public being able to understand why decisions have been made.[21]

Section 29: prejudice to the economy

Applies to: information the disclosure of which would or would be likely to prejudice the economic interests of the UK or any part of the UK, or the financial interests of any UK administration.

Considerations:
- Will disclosure negatively affect the economy of a region or part of the UK?
- Will disclosure negatively affect the financial interests of a UK administration?
- Will disclosure upset the normal operation of market forces, or damage relations between government and business?[22]
- Will disclosure have an impact on market confidence or investment in the UK economy?[23]

These public interest test arguments are commonly relevant:

- Disclosure would or would be likely to increase financial instability.
- Announcements, such as the budget, on the economy or public finances would be pre-empted.
- Confidence in financial markets would be undermined.

- Disclosure may damage relationships of trust with those who have provided information in confidence.[24]
- Disclosure might help the public understand the relationship between government and business.[25]
- Disclosure may enhance public understanding and stimulate debate, and promote greater public confidence in the management of the economy.[26]

Section 30: investigations and proceedings

Applies to: information which has been held at any time for the purposes of a criminal (or military service) investigation or prosecution which the authority had the power to conduct. Information obtained from confidential sources in the process of such an investigation or prosecution or in the process of certain civil investigations or proceedings set out at s. 31(2).

Considerations:
- Is the information held because the authority has a duty or power to investigate or prosecute a crime? If not, s. 30 will not apply; s. 31 is the most likely alternative.
- Sections 30 and 31 cannot be used together – one or the other will apply.

These public interest test arguments are commonly relevant:

- Reasons for withholding information include: not wishing to deter people from assisting criminal investigations; the vital interest in maintaining confidentiality so that there can be a full and frank exchange of views between police and the Crown Prosecution Service (CPS); the CPS being able to communicate 'frankly and fearlessly'.[27]
- Other factors might include: '(a) the stage a particular investigation or prosecution has reached, (b) whether and to what extent the information is already in the public domain, (c) the significance or sensitivity of the information requested and (d) whether there is any evidence that an investigation or prosecution has not been carried out properly which may be disclosed by the information'.[28]

Section 31: prejudice to law enforcement

Applies to: information the disclosure of which would, or would be likely to, prejudice the prevention, investigation or enforcement of a range of criminal or civil matters.

Considerations:
- Will disclosure prejudice any of: the prevention and detection of crime, the apprehension and prosecution of offenders, the administration of justice, assessment and collection of tax, operation of immigration controls, or the maintenance of security in prisons and other places of custody?
- Will disclosure prejudice civil proceedings, fatal accidents inquiries, or a range of regulatory or standards activities listed at s. 31(2)?

These public interest test arguments are commonly relevant:

- If a prejudice can be identified, there is an inherent public interest in preventing it.
- There is likely to be a cost to any mitigating actions that might be required as a result of the increased chance of prejudice.
- Prejudice to the interests identified at s. 31(1) is likely to have an impact on public officials and/or the public.
- In favour of disclosure, it may assist the public in holding the authority to account.[29] As with s. 30, it may expose the fact that an investigation or prosecution has been mishandled.[30]

Section 32: court records

Applies to: information held 'only by virtue' of being contained in documents created or held for the purposes of court, inquiry or arbitration proceedings. Examples include 'indices of court bundles, admissions, court orders and judgements and the like',[31] tape recordings and transcripts of proceedings, and statistics drawn from court records.[32]

Considerations:
- Was the information initially held for another purpose, but only later included in a court document? If so, the exemption will not apply.
- Is the information held in support of court proceedings that have commenced? The exemption applies.
- Was the document filed or placed in the custody of the court? The exemption applies.
- Was it served on or by a public authority? The exemption applies.
- Was it created by the court or a member of court administrative staff? The exemption applies.

Public interest test: this is an absolute exemption, so no public interest test is necessary.

Section 33: prejudice to audit functions

Applies to: information held by bodies that conduct audits of other public authorities which if disclosed would, or would be likely to, prejudice the exercise of their functions. Bodies covered include the National Audit Office, the Northern Ireland Audit Office, Ofsted, the Care Quality Commission and other similar organisations.[33] Information could include draft reports, audit methodologies, correspondence between auditors and bodies subject to audit, and information provided to auditors by whistle-blowers or other informants.[34]

Considerations:
- Is this a public authority that conducts audits of other public authorities' accounts or effectiveness?
- Would disclosure prejudice or be likely to prejudice their work?

These public interest test arguments are commonly relevant:

- Disclosure of information may interfere with the ability of auditors to carry out their work – notably if it made other authorities and their employees less likely to co-operate in future.
- The integrity of the audit may be damaged.
- In favour of disclosure, it may help the public to understand decisions made by public bodies, and promote accountability in relation to public spending and decision making (particularly if the information exposes a problem that has not been addressed).[35]

Section 34: parliamentary privilege

Applies to: information the disclosure of which would infringe the privileges of either House of Parliament. Examples include records of parliamentary proceedings, work undertaken as a result of proceedings (e.g. correspondence between the clerk of a select committee and a government department in relation to a current inquiry), and briefings prepared to inform debates or committee proceedings.

Considerations:
- Is this information relating to proceedings of either House of Parliament?

- Would disclosure infringe their privileges? It may be advisable to consult the relevant House to establish this if necessary.
- Has the Speaker of the House of Commons or Clerk of the Parliaments issued a certificate certifying that disclosure would infringe parliamentary privilege? If so, this is conclusive and the exemption applies.

Public interest test: this is an absolute exemption, so no public interest test is necessary.

Section 35: formulation of government policy

Applies to: information held by a government department, Northern Ireland's administration, or by the Welsh Assembly Government relating to formulation or development of government policy, ministerial communications, the provision of advice by any of the law officers or any request for the provision of their advice, or the operation of any ministerial private office.

Considerations:
- Is the authority a government department or the Welsh Assembly Government? If not, this exemption cannot apply and s. 36 should be considered.
- Does the information relate to the formulation or development of government policy? The Information Commissioner defines formulation as the process ending with royal assent for legislation or the announcement of a particular government policy. Development means the review, improvement or adjustment of policy. Interpret these terms broadly as they are meant to provide a safe space for government policy making.[36]
- Does the information include statistics used in the formulation or development of policy? If so, it will lose the protection of the exemption once the process of formulation or development is complete (but other information may still be protected even after the policy is announced).
- Does the information include other factual information used (or intended to be used) in the formulation or development of policy? Section 35(4) sets out a specific public interest argument in favour of disclosure of factual information supporting policy decisions – as a result, the Commissioner argues that such information normally should be disclosed.[37]
- Does the information relate to ministerial communications? These include cabinet papers as well as other communications (including meeting papers, correspondence and ministerial submissions). Correspondence about

ministerial communications is protected – not just the communications themselves.

- Is the information advice provided by the Attorney General, the Solicitor General, the Advocate General for Scotland, the Lord Advocate, the Solicitor General for Scotland or the Attorney General for Northern Ireland? Advice in this context is wider than the legal advice protected by s. 42.
- Does the information relate to the operation of a ministerial private office? The Commissioner suggests this should be interpreted narrowly as otherwise it would be possible to withhold almost anything that originated in or passed through the office.[38]

These public interest test arguments are commonly relevant:

- There remains a need for a private space while a decision is reached.
- The relationship between civil servants and ministers would be exposed to an unhelpful degree of scrutiny, preventing them from carrying out their jobs effectively.
- Ministers might be less likely to seek and rely on formal advice.
- Ministers' individual views might be disclosed, undermining cabinet collective responsibility.
- The length of time that has passed since formulation or development was completed.
- The level of public concern with a policy, or improving understanding of the process by which a decision was reached, would be arguments in favour of disclosure.
- Whether information is already in the public domain.

The gist: refusing requests for policy formulation information
DfES v Information Commissioner and the Evening Standard, EA/2006/0006, 19 February 2007
   A journalist from the Evening Standard asked the Department for Education & Skills (DfES) for copies of minutes of senior management meetings held between June 2002 and June 2003 on setting school budgets. Some of the requested information was withheld on the basis of s. 35(1)(a), that the information related to the formulation and development of government policy. The FTT ruled that the minutes should be disclosed but in the process established some principles for use in similar cases:

- Take a case-by-case approach.
- No information is automatically exempt on account of its status, its classification or the seniority of those whose actions are recorded.

- The aim of the exemption is to protect civil servants from unfair criticism, not ministers once they have reached a decision.
- The timing of a request is 'of paramount importance'. Disclosure of discussions of policy options while a policy is still being formulated is unlikely to be in the public interest:

  > Ministers and officials are entitled to time and space, in some instances to considerable time and space, to hammer out policy by exploring safe and radical options alike, without the threat of lurid headlines depicting that which has been merely broached as agreed policy.

- 'Formulation' ends with a parliamentary statement announcing the policy, though the circumstances will dictate the public interest in maintaining the exemption after that point.
- It was suggested by DfES that disclosure of information would have a 'chilling effect' – i.e. it would discourage civil servants from writing full and frank advice. In response to these suggestions, the FTT commented that 'we are entitled to expect of them the courage and independence that has been the hallmark of our civil servants since the Northcote–Trevelyan reforms' (in a separate case, a differently constituted tribunal panel made a similar point about BBC governors, saying that they were unlikely to be 'shrinking violets').[39]
- Expect politicians to display 'a substantial measure of political sophistication and, of course, fair-mindedness' – in other words, it is not reasonable to argue that information should not be disclosed in case a politician associated a civil servant with a specific policy.
- Similarly, the worst should not be assumed of the public – the answer to ill-informed criticism is to educate the public.

Section 36: prejudice to the effective conduct of public affairs

Applies to: information held which if disclosed would, or would be likely to, prejudice the convention of collective responsibility of ministers or the work of the Northern Ireland or Welsh Assembly ruling bodies (s. 36(2)(a)); or inhibit the free and frank provision of advice or exchange of views for the purposes of deliberation (s. 36(2)(b)); or prejudice the effective conduct of public affairs (s. 36(2)(c)).

Considerations:
- The protection for the convention of collective responsibility and similar protection for the Welsh and Northern Ireland administrations will only be relevant for central government departments or their equivalents in Northern Ireland and Wales.

- Government departments (including Northern Ireland departments) and the Welsh Assembly can only use s. 36 for information not covered by the exemption at s. 35 – the exemptions cannot be used together to protect the same information.[40]
- The protection for 'free and frank provision of advice' and 'free and frank exchange of views' at s. 36(2)(b) is designed – like s. 35 – to provide a safe space for deliberation within public bodies.
- The remaining area protected by s. 36, at (2)(c), might best be described as a 'safety net'. It is designed to be used in circumstances where no other exemption in the FOIA applies, but the authority takes the view that a prejudice that was not envisaged by the drafters of the FOIA would, or would be likely to, result from disclosure.[41]
- Information can only be withheld if it is the 'reasonable opinion' of the 'qualified person' that disclosure would, or would be likely to, cause the prejudice or inhibition that is envisaged. The requirement to obtain this opinion does not apply to statistical information.[42]
- Who is the qualified person? Section 36(5) lists several different types of organisation and who their qualified person will be. In other cases, it is up to the relevant cabinet minister to nominate the qualified person – which can be the organisation as a whole (effectively its board)[43] or one or more of its officers or employees. It can be very difficult establishing who the qualified person is as no list of qualified persons is actively maintained by government. A list prepared by the Ministry of Justice can be found on the UK web archive but this has not been updated since 2009.[44] Some examples are provided in Table 3.1. If no qualified person has been nominated (or it is not possible to establish whether this has happened), FOI officers are advised to contact the Cabinet Office for advice.
- Has the opinion of the qualified person been obtained? It will clearly be necessary to keep a record demonstrating that this has happened. The Information Commissioner provides a template form for obtaining the qualified person's opinion, which may be adapted for use by public authorities.
- Until recently, the view was taken that the opinion had to be reasonably arrived at – if the procedure followed to obtain the opinion was flawed, the opinion would not be valid. If, for example, the authority could not demonstrate that the qualified person had read all the information, this might lead to the decision being overturned. However, the accepted position is now that 'reasonable' means that the substance of the decision should be reasonable, not the way it was reached.[45]

- The qualified person is not expected to consider the public interest – their decision is about whether prejudice (or inhibition) would, or would be likely to, be caused (irrespective of the public interest).[46]
- Is the opinion rational? The 'substance of the opinion must be objectively reasonable'. It may be that other opinions would also be reasonable, but the important point is that the opinion given by the qualified person is reasonable.[47]

These public interest test arguments are commonly relevant:

- Section 36 is an absolute exemption when used by the House of Commons or House of Lords. In all other cases it is a qualified exemption and a public interest test should be conducted.
- The public interest arguments in relation to s. 36(2)(c) depend on what prejudice is being claimed, which in this case could be anything not covered by another exemption.
- The fact that the qualified person has given an opinion should itself be considered as part of the public interest test.[48]
- Where it is being claimed that disclosure would, or would be likely to, inhibit the free and frank provision of advice or exchange of views, the public interest arguments cover similar ground to those set out under s. 35 above.

Table 3.1 *Examples of who the qualified person can be under the FOIA*

Type of public authority	Qualified person	Basis
A government department headed by a minister of the Crown	A minister of the Crown	FOIA s. 36(5)(a)
A Northern Ireland department	A NI minister in charge of department	FOIA s. 36(5)(b)
Government departments not led by a minister	The commissioners or other person in charge of the department	FOIA s. 36(5)(c)
The House of Commons	The Speaker	FOIA s. 36(5)(d)
The House of Lords	The Clerk of the Parliaments	FOIA s. 36(5)(e)
The Northern Ireland Assembly	The Presiding Officer	FOIA s. 36(5)(f)
The Welsh Assembly Government	Welsh ministers or Counsel General to the Welsh Assembly Government	FOIA s. 36(5)(g)

Table 3.1 *Continued*

Type of public authority	Qualified person	Basis
The National Assembly for Wales	The Presiding Officer	FOIA s. 36(5)(ga)
Welsh public authorities	The public authority, or any officer or employee authorised by Welsh Ministers or the Presiding Officer of the Assembly	FOIA s. 36(5)(gb)/(gc)
The National Audit Office or the Comptroller and Auditor General	The Comptroller and Auditor General	FOIA s. 36(5)(i)
A Northern Ireland public authority	The public authority, or any officer or employee authorised by the First Minister and Deputy First Minister acting jointly	FOIA s. 36(5)(l)
The Greater London Authority	The Mayor of London	FOIA s. 36(5)(m)
A principal local authority in England	The monitoring officer and chief executive	Authorised by minister[49]
A parish or town council	The clerk to the council and the chairman of the council	Authorised by minister
A Welsh local authority	Either the public authority or any officer or employee of the authority authorised by the Assembly First Secretary	Authorised by minister
A Northern Ireland local authority	The chief executive	Authorised by minister
A maintained school	The chair of the governing body	Authorised by minister
University or other higher education body that receives financial support	The vice chancellor or chief executive (depending on title used)	Authorised by minister
A police force	The chief officer of police	Authorised by minister
British Museum	The director	Authorised by minister
The BBC	The BBC	Authorised by minister
The Financial Services Authority	All individual board members	Authorised by minister
The information commissioner	The information commissioner	Authorised by minister

Around the world: policy information exemptions

The FOI(S)A effectively reproduces the policy formulation exemption from s. 35 of the FOIA. There is also a much shorter version of the s. 36 exemption covering cabinet collective responsibility, inhibition of free and frank discussion, and the effective conduct of public affairs. The Isle of Man Act appropriates the Scottish versions of these exemptions. In the States of Jersey, there is a short and simple qualified exemption at s. 35 of their FOI law covering information relating to the formulation or development of any proposed policy by any public authority. There is no necessity to consult a qualified person in any of these laws.

The US has an exemption for 'inter-agency or intra-agency memorandums or letters'. New Zealand's Official Information Act provides for the maintenance of 'the constitutional conventions . . . which protect . . . collective and individual ministerial responsibility; the political neutrality of officials; [and] the confidentiality of advice tendered by Ministers of the Crown and officials'.[50] There is also an 'effective conduct of public affairs' exemption protecting the 'free and frank expression of opinions'.[51] In practice, it has become general practice in New Zealand to disclose policy advice as soon as a decision has been reached.[52] Both Acts apply only to central or federal government, so these exemptions are not designed to cover the work of local government or other public bodies outside the central administration.

Section 37: communications with the royal household and honours conferred by the Crown

Applies to: information relating to communications with the sovereign or her two closest heirs, the royal family, the royal household, or the conferring by the Crown of any honour or dignity.

Considerations:

- Does the information relate to a communication with the monarch or the two individuals next in line to the throne? 'Relate to' means that this will cover not just the communications themselves, but also any references to, or descriptions of, communications with them. If so, an absolute exemption has applied to this information since 2011.
- Does the information relate to a communication with another member of the royal family or the wider royal household (which we might describe as the 'administration' of the royal family, led by the monarch's private secretary)? If so, the information is exempt, but a public interest test must be conducted.
- Does the information relate to the conferring of an honour by the Crown? Again, if so, the information is exempt, but a public interest test must be conducted.

In relation to communications with the wider royal family, the royal household, or relating to honours, a public interest test must be conducted. These public interest test arguments are commonly relevant:

- Disclosure would allow the public to better understand the constitutional role of the royal family.
- Disclosure would reveal whether members of the royal family have sought to influence policy making.
- Disclosure of information might compromise the ability of members of the royal family to carry out their role.
- Disclosure of information would compromise the neutrality of the royal family.
- Disclosure would compromise security.
- There is a public interest in there being a safe space in which members of the Royal Family and Household can discuss matters with public bodies.[53]

The gist: correspondence sent on someone's behalf
Evans v Information Commissioner [2012], UKUT 313 (AAC), 18 September 2012, paras. 244–249
One of the many issues discussed during the long appeal process related to Rob Evans's attempts to obtain correspondence between Prince Charles and government ministers was the status of correspondence signed by an official, or between officials representing Prince Charles's or a minister's views.

It was common ground before the Upper Tribunal that letters signed by an official on behalf of (i.e. pp) the heir to the throne or a minister would count as correspondence from the prince or the minister. The judge decided that a broader definition applied: 'a letter from a private secretary to a private secretary which said, "The minister is aware of Prince Charles's interest in this topic, and I enclose a note on which the minister would welcome his views." In our view a communication of that kind would in substance be a letter from the minister to Prince Charles.'

In effect, a letter or e-mail summarising the views of a senior or elected official will count as being correspondence from them, even if it is written and signed by another person employed to act on their behalf.

Section 38: endanger health and safety

Applies to: information which if disclosed would, or would be likely to, endanger the physical or mental health, or the safety of any individual.

Considerations:
- Consider 'endanger' in the same way as 'prejudice'. The three-step test

identified for prejudice (see 'The gist: conducting the prejudice test' earlier in this chapter) needs to be applied when considering this exemption.[54]

● Would an individual's mental or physical health be endangered? It should be possible to show a causal link between the disclosure and the envisaged harm that the authority is seeking to avoid.[55]

● Endangerment of mental health means more than merely causing stress or worry.[56]

These public interest test arguments are commonly relevant:

● As with most exemptions, it can be argued that transparency and accountability of spending and decision making is in the public interest. The extent to which this is true varies depending on the specific circumstances of the request.

● The likelihood and degree of endangerment are significant factors. If an increased risk to life and limb has been identified, 'significant and conclusive weight' should be given to these arguments.[57]

Section 39: environmental information

Applies to: information falling under the definition of environmental information set out at reg. 2 of the EIR.

Considerations:
● Does the information fall under the definition of environmental information set out at reg. 2 of the EIR? If so, handle the request under the EIR, as the information is exempt from disclosure under the FOIA.

These public interest test arguments are commonly relevant:

Oddly, s. 39 is a qualified exemption. As discussed in Chapter 5, it is not necessary to carry out a public interest test in practice, since it is generally assumed that the public interest will favour handling requests under the EIR rather than the FOIA where the information falls under the relevant definition.

Section 40: personal information

Applies to: information falling under the definition of personal data in the GDPR or DPA 2018.

This exemption is discussed at length in Chapter 6.

Section 41: information provided in confidence

Applies to: information obtained from another person or organisation the disclosure of which would constitute an actionable breach of confidence.

Considerations:
- Was the information obtained from another person? If the public authority played any part in creating the information, it will not be possible to rely on this exemption.
- Was the information provided in circumstances that would give rise to an obligation of confidence? Was it obvious that the information should be treated as confidential, e.g. because it was clearly labelled as being such?
- Does the information have the 'nature of confidence' about it? This is unlikely to be the case if the information is trivial, widely known, or could be easily guessed.
- What harm would disclosure do to the person who provided the information?

These public interest test arguments are commonly relevant:

- Would disclosure be in the public interest? This exemption is an absolute exemption, so strictly not subject to the Act's public interest test. However, public interest is the most common defence against breach of confidence actions. Before using the exemption, therefore, authorities need to consider whether there is an overriding public interest in the information being disclosed even if it would breach the provider's confidence.

Section 42: legal professional privilege

Applies to: information which is protected by legal professional privilege, in effect legal advice (and requests for advice) from solicitors, barristers or legal executives (advice privilege), or information brought into existence for the purposes of litigation (litigation privilege).

Considerations:
- Is the information covered by litigation privilege? For example, this could include a report commissioned by a barrister from a safety expert to defend a claim.
- Is the information legal advice? Was it given by a barrister, solicitor or legal executive? Was it commissioned (asked for)? If not, it will not be protected by legal professional privilege.[58]

- Has privilege been waived? This can be done by sharing the advice too widely.[59]
- The format in which the advice was provided is not relevant. For example, presentation slides used to deliver legal advice will still attract legal professional privilege.[60]

These public interest test arguments are commonly relevant:

- 'There is a strong element of public interest inbuilt into the privilege itself. At least equally strong counter-vailing considerations would need to be adduced to override that inbuilt public interest.'[61]
- Arguments in favour of disclosure include the timing of the request (the longer the passage of time since the advice was given, the less the public interest will favour withholding the information); the subject matter (issues relating to individuals and their rights afford more protection than 'civic' issues such as building projects); the level of controversy of a project; and (perhaps related to the last) the expense of a project.[62] In practice, it is difficult to make the case for disclosure of legal advice on public interest grounds.

Section 43: trade secrets and prejudice to commercial interests

Applies to: information that is a trade secret or that would (or would be likely to) affect the commercial interests of any party – including the public body itself. Such information could include documentation relating to procurement activities – contracts, tender submissions, sales figures, an authority's purchasing position – but also details of a public body's marketing activities or products it has developed in a competitive market place (e.g. course documentation in the higher education arena – though see comments below).

Considerations:
- Is the information a 'trade secret'? The first part of s. 43 provides protection for 'trade secrets', but doesn't define them. An example is the secret recipe for Coca-Cola. It is information used in business that is highly confidential, which gives its owner a competitive edge. Others should not be able to reproduce it without having access to the requested information.[63]
- Is the interest that needs protection commercial? One error occasionally fallen into is to confuse commercial interests with financial interests. Commercial interests are those to do with the buying or selling of goods or

services.[64] Prejudice to these interests is protected by the second (and most commonly used) part of s. 43.

- Whose commercial interests would be prejudiced? Section 43(2) states that the interests of 'any person' can be protected, including the public authority. It is therefore necessary to identify whose interests are being discussed.
- Would disclosure prejudice or be likely to prejudice commercial interests? As with other prejudice-based exemptions, it is necessary to follow the three-step test identified in 'The gist: conducting the prejudice test' earlier in this chapter, including identifying what harm is envisaged.

These public interest test arguments are commonly relevant:
- There is a public interest in transparency of public spending – in public authorities being held to account for their decisions. Transparency may stimulate more competition and lower prices. There will be a public interest in the public and companies being able to see that a procurement process has been fair.
- Against that, there is a public interest in a healthy and competitive market place. Such a thing could be threatened by loss of trust (if companies fear public authorities will disclose their commercial secrets), or by undermining the competitiveness of companies (by allowing competitors to gain access to information that gives a company an edge).

The gist: some decisions on procurement and contracts

'Those who engage in commercial activity with the public sector must expect a greater degree of openness about details of those activities' (ICO decision notice FS50063478).

- If arguing that disclosure will prejudice a third party's commercial interests, the third party should be consulted (*Derry City Council v Information Commissioner*, EA/2006/0014).
- The Office of Government Commerce (Civil Procurement) Policy and Guidance (see Chapter 4) provides 'a useful approach to dealing with an information request' for procurement information (*Department of Health v IC*, EA/2008/0018).
- A financial model can be a trade secret (*Department for Works and Pensions v IC*, EA/2010/0073).
- The offering of courses by universities is a commercial activity (*University of Central Lancashire (UCLAN) v IC and Professor Colquhoun*, EA/2009/0034).
- If arguing that prejudice to the authority's or a commercial partner's commercial interests would be likely as other companies would be able to undercut the current pricing arrangements, authorities need to demonstrate that disclosure 'would have "a very significant and weighty chance" of causing prejudice that is "real, actual or of substance"'. It is difficult to do this where an agreement relates to a unique set of

circumstances (*London Legacy Development Corporation v IC and Richard Hunt*, EA/2015/0223).
- A contract might have such longevity that pricing arrangements are of such little use to competitors that it is not possible to demonstrate prejudice (ICO decision notice FS50591864).
- The fact that there is a limited number of suppliers in a particular market can strengthen the argument that disclosure would be likely to prejudice the authority's commercial interests (*Secretary of State for the Home Department v IC and Phil Miller*, EA/2015/0143).
- There is a public interest in public authorities that provide commercial services being able to maintain their income given the financial pressures on the public sector (*Council of the Borough and County of the Town of Poole v IC*, EA/2016/0074).

Section 44: prohibitions on disclosure

Applies to: information the disclosure of which is prohibited by statute or court order.

Considerations:
- Is it possible to point to a legal requirement that prevents disclosure? Applying this exemption requires practitioners to have knowledge of the wider legal environment in which their organisation works.
- Examples include s. 18 of the Commissioners for Revenue and Customs Act 2005 (which prohibits disclosure of tax information that would allow persons to be identified), s. 39(1) of the Statistics and Registration Services Act 2007 (which prohibits disclosure of personal information by the Office for National Statistics), and s. 237 of the Enterprise Act (which prohibits disclosure of certain information about a business).[65]

Public interest test: this is an absolute exemption, so no public interest test is necessary.

Summing up
- The exemptions in the FOIA can be qualified (requiring a public interest test) or absolute (not requiring such a test).
- Many exemptions are subject to a prejudice test, where it is necessary to demonstrate the harm that would, or would be likely, to result from disclosing information.
- Absolute exemptions often prevent the FOIA from conflicting with other legal requirements (such as data protection or confidentiality) and established custom (such as parliamentary privilege).
- It is possible to apply exemptions to the duty to confirm whether information is held,

requiring a refusal notice to spell out why the authority can neither confirm nor deny the existence of information.
- If an exemption is qualified, it is necessary to consider arguments for and against disclosure, and to conclude which arguments are the most convincing and serious.
- Most countries with FOI legislation have exemptions covering similar ground to the FOIA's exemptions.

Chapter 4

The FOI officer's toolkit

Introduction

The last two chapters have explored the FOIA – its key provisions and the exemptions available to justify non-disclosure of information, and highlighted comparable provisions from FOI laws around the world. Wherever an FOI officer plies their trade, the legislation itself is the primary source when establishing their organisation's obligations.

That said, the language used in legislation is not always easy to comprehend without assistance. Few FOI officers are fortunate enough to have benefitted from formal legal training of any kind. Very often even experienced lawyers struggle to interpret legislation that they encounter. The wording can be ambiguous, so that different readers understand the same provision in varying ways. Then there's the difference between the real world that most of us live in, and the world as set out in statute. Very often, situations arise that the drafters of legislation could not possibly have foreseen. With thousands of organisations having to comply with the FOIA in the UK, and millions of people able to use its provisions to make requests, it is inevitable that circumstances emerge that could not reasonably have been envisaged during the passage of the legislation.

Very often applicants disagree with how legislation has been interpreted, and ask ombudsmen (such as the Information Commissioner in the UK) or the courts to decide what should happen. Over (sometimes considerable) time their decisions clarify FOI laws – for the most part. Sometimes the decisions themselves are not easy to understand.

There are many situations that cannot be resolved simply by turning to a battered old copy of the FOI law. This book aims to be a resource that FOI officers can turn to for reliable assistance at times like these, but this chapter identifies where else FOI officers can turn to for help when they are unsure what is expected of them or their employer. Taken together with the relevant legislation, the resources discussed below constitute the FOI officer's toolkit.

Codes of practice

The FOIA requires the government to publish codes setting out good practice. Section 45 of the FOIA requires the relevant secretary of state (currently the Chancellor of the Duchy of Lancaster since machinery of government changes in 2015)[1] to set out best practice for compliance with Part I of the Act in a code of practice. Section 46 of the FOIA requires another code to be issued, originally known as the Lord Chancellor's code, but now the responsibility of the Secretary of State for Digital, Culture, Media and Sport.[2] It deals with management of records. The codes do not have statutory force – authorities cannot be directly penalised or prosecuted for failing to comply with their provisions. However, the Information Commissioner can issue a 'practice recommendation' requiring that an authority adjusts its practices so that it better complies with a code (though nowadays is more likely to issue an 'undertaking' – a less formal and non-statutory sanction). Perhaps more importantly, if a complaint is being investigated, it is hard to see the Commissioner having much sympathy for an authority if its non-compliance with a code has contributed to any failure.

For the first time since 2004, a new s. 45 code was published in July 2018. Its foreword explains its status and what it aims to achieve, namely setting 'the standard for all public authorities when considering how to respond to Freedom of Information requests'. The content of the code is much expanded from the 2004 version, covering:

- the right of access
- advice and assistance
- consulting third parties
- time limits for responding to requests
- internal reviews
- the cost limit
- vexatious requests
- publication schemes
- transparency and confidentiality obligations in contracts and outsourced services
- communicating with requesters
- datasets.

The s. 46 code, most recently updated in 2009, was drafted by TNA's Information Management department. It is in two parts. Part 1 summarises recommended good practice for managing records, and is aimed at all public authorities. Authorities should:

- have organisational arrangements, such as records management programmes, training and governance, in place
- have a records management policy
- know what records they need and ensure that they are kept
- use systems that facilitate storage and retrieval
- know what records they have, and ensure that they are preserved for as long as necessary
- keep records securely
- set out rules on how long to keep records, follow them, and be able to explain why records have been disposed of
- ensure that third parties, especially contractors, that hold records on their behalf, comply with the code
- monitor their compliance and the effectiveness of their records management programme.

Part 2 applies to public records bodies and sets out how they should review and transfer records to TNA or the Public Record Office of Northern Ireland under the provisions of relevant public records legislation.

The s. 46 code of practice is explored in more detail in Chapter 7. Both codes are referred to regularly throughout this book.

Around the world: codes of practice

Section 48 of Ireland's FOI Act 2014 permits, but does not require, the relevant minister to publish a code of practice. A code was published in September 2015. It includes detailed guidance on the role of the FOI officer, describing them as 'the linchpin of a public body's capability in relation to FOI'. It also covers the responsibilities of decision makers to support FOI compliance, training, records management, proactive publication, request handling and the maintenance of FOI statistics.[3]

Section 60 of the Isle of Man's FOI Act requires a code of practice to be issued by the Council of Ministers. The code is very detailed, providing guidance on the interpretation of whether information is held, whether requests are vexatious, how to determine the public interest, as well as many of the other issues covered in the UK s. 45 code.[4]

The States of Jersey's FOI law empowers ministers to issue regulations permitting or requiring the island's Information Commissioner to issue a code of practice. An 'article

44 code of practice' was issued by the Commissioner in December 2014 with an extensive section covering the handling of appeals by the Information Commissioner.[5]

Section 60 of the FOI(S)A requires Scottish ministers to issue a code similar to the FOIA s. 45 code. Section 61 requires ministers to issue a code on records management.

Codes of practice in this form are by no means a common feature of FOI laws internationally. Some empower the Commissioner or ministers to issue guidance to authorities, such as Canada's Access to Information Act, which requires a minister to 'cause to be prepared and distributed to government institutions directives and guidelines concerning the operation of this Act and the regulations'.[6]

The UK Information Commissioner's guidance

One of the Information Commissioner's responsibilities is to raise awareness of the FOIA. Aside from supplying speakers for events and conferences, the main way this manifests is through the provision of guidance on the ICO website (ico.org.uk).

There is a main guide to the FOIA and one to the EIR. These are useful starting points in learning about how the main provisions of the legislation work, but the really useful information can be found in the Guidance Index, which provides access to more detailed guidance on various aspects of the FOIA and the EIR. In particular, the guides to the exemptions provide the Commissioner's current view on their application. These are updated regularly, reflecting the latest case law.

In addition, public authorities are expected to follow a model publication scheme mandated by the Commissioner. The ICO website contains definition documents for each part of the public sector, indicating what information the Commissioner expects authorities to publish proactively under each class of the model scheme. This is discussed in more detail in Chapter 8.

Other published guidance

For many years the Ministry of Justice (and its predecessors) published guidance on FOI, and in particular the application of the exemptions. Since responsibility for FOI in government moved to the Cabinet Office in 2015, such guidance can only be found in the TNA web archive.[7] The guidance includes standard templates designed for use by government departments when responding to requests.[8]

An essential piece of guidance that can similarly be found in the TNA web archive is the Office for Government Commerce's *FOI (Civil Procurement) Policy & Guidance*, vol. 2 (2008).[9] This is a guide to the interaction between procurement and FOI and includes detailed advice on when documents related to the contracting process can be disclosed, and which exemptions are likely to be relevant. It has been cited in ICO and tribunal decisions (e.g. ICO decision notice FS50473543). It should be used with caution as it has not been updated in a decade, but it remains a helpful guide whenever requests touch on the procurement process. Practitioners should also look out for government procurement policy notes on this subject, such as PPN 01/17, an Update to Transparency Principles, and its associated guidance.[10]

ICO decision notices

Decision notices of the UK Information Commissioner are published on the ICO website (ico.org.uk). The relevant page provides a search and filter function, making it easy to sort decisions by date, authority, section (or regulation for decisions relating to the EIR), or sector. This can be very useful if trying to locate a decision which looks at issues that are relevant to a current request that the FOI officer is handling.

The cases are listed in reverse chronological order, and a brief summary of each decision is provided on the main page. Each entry provides name of authority, date of decision, sector, and a paragraph summarising the case (taken from the 'summary of decision' section of the notice itself). The relevant sections and a note of whether the decision upholds the complaint or not are also listed. These case summaries make it easier to scroll quickly through a long list of relevant decisions and quickly identify potentially useful cases. A link under each entry allows the reader to delve deeper by reading the full notice.

The notices take a standard form, and with practice the key components of a decision can very quickly be isolated. A typical decision notice is broken down as follows:

- It starts by providing the date of the decision and the public authority concerned.
- Then the decision is summarised, including a brief description of the request made, how the authority dealt with the request, any exemptions applied, what the Commissioner's decision is – whether the legislation was correctly applied, and whether any steps are required to be taken.
- The request is set out next, together with how the authority responded and a description of what happened from then until the involvement of the ICO.
- The scope of the decision is set out – what the applicant complained about, and what the focus of the Commissioner's investigation has been.

- The reasoning behind the decision is provided. This can include setting out the relevant sections of the Act or EIR, how the Commissioner interprets those sections including referencing any relevant case law, any public interest arguments considered, and how much weight the Commissioner has afforded them, and finally what conclusion they reached.
- Other issues might be set out – if the Commissioner was particularly disappointed with the authority's co-operation, they might say so here.
- The right to appeal to the tribunal and the deadline for doing so is provided with the name of the ICO officer who has approved the decision.

If the summary of the case hasn't provided enough information, it is clearly the reasoning behind the decision that is most of value to the FOI officer. Sub-headings enable FOI officers to navigate to the most relevant comments – for example, they might be most interested in the public interest arguments, and the arguments either way are usually separated out.

Around the world: regulator resources

It is common for regulators and ombudsmen to publish guidance on the legislation that they are responsible for enforcing, along with summaries of their decisions and sometimes notable court cases. All of the below websites contain invaluable resources for FOI officers in the relevant jurisdiction:

- Australia – Office of the Australian Information Commissioner (oaic.gov.au)
- Canada – Office of the Information Commissioner of Canada (oic-ci.gc.ca)
- India – Central Information Commission (cic.gov.in)
- Ireland – Office of the Information Commissioner (oic.ie)
- Isle of Man – Information Commissioner (inforights.im)
- States of Jersey – Office of the Information Commissioner (oicjersey.org)
- New Zealand – Office of the Ombudsman (ombudsman.parliament.nz)
- Scotland – Scottish Information Commissioner (itspublicknowledge.info)
- USA – has no direct equivalent to the UK Information Commissioner at federal level, but the following organisations provide the sort of resources that would normally be provided by such an institution in other jurisdictions:

    - the Office of Information Policy (justice.gov/oip) in the Department of Justice: issues FOI guidance and provides resources for government agencies
    - the Office of Government Information Services (archives.gov/ogis), part of the National Archives and Records Administration: provides a mediation service to assist in resolving disputes between applicants and agencies, publishing its final response letters.

Tribunal decisions and case law

The UK Commissioner's decisions can be challenged, initially to the First-Tier Tribunal (Information Rights). Their decisions are similarly published online (informationrights.decisions.tribunals.gov.uk). Again, the database can be searched, enabling relevant case law to be identified.

Cases at this level are referenced by the parties involved, by case reference and by date. The appellant is the first named party – this might be the original applicant or the public authority, depending on how the Commissioner ruled. At FTT level, they are always appealing the decision of the Commissioner, so the Commissioner is always the respondent. Other parties can apply to be 'joined' to the case. So, for example, if the appellant is the applicant, the case would normally be listed as *Frederick Bloggs v Information Commissioner*. In this case, the Commissioner will have ruled in favour of the authority, and the applicant is appealing. The public authority may though wish to be involved in the hearing, since it has an interest in the outcome. So the case would be listed as *Frederick Bloggs v Information Commissioner and Freedomshire County Council*.

FTT decisions vary in format, but broadly speaking start by outlining the background to the case – the original request, how it was dealt with, and what the Information Commissioner did. Having set this out, the FTT describes the arguments put forward by the various parties and any witnesses who were called. This can be confusing, because quickly scanning through a decision, the reader can see what looks like a useful heading – 'public interest' for example. However, this might just be the arguments put forward by one party or another. A good approach is to scroll through the decision to the very end, then slowly scroll back to the beginning of the tribunal's conclusion. What the FOI officer is really interested in is what the tribunal concluded in this case. Sometimes the conclusion goes into detail, spelling out why the tribunal reached this conclusion (and avoiding the need to read the decision in full). For example, there is usually a summary of why the FTT members believe that an exemption applies (or not); and what public interest arguments they accept (which can be useful if the FOI officer is dealing with a similar scenario) and which they discount. They sometimes criticise one party or another, or explain why they were unconvinced by a particular argument (which can be very useful if an FOI officer is trying to articulate the reasons why similar information cannot be disclosed).

Appeals from the FTT are considered by the Upper Tribunal (Administrative Appeals Chamber). Their decisions are published at www.gov.uk/administrative-appeals-tribunal-decisions. The decisions relating to the FOIA or EIR can be found by selecting 'information rights' from a list of categories on the web page. Further search functionality is available to assist FOI officers in finding the case that they are interested in.

In the rare circumstances that a case is appealed beyond the Upper Tribunal to the Court of Appeal (or, even rarer, the Supreme Court), decisions can normally be found on the British and Irish Legal Information Institute (BAILII) website (bailii.org). Again, there is a search engine to assist in locating particular cases, but as BAILII is not a website dedicated to FOI decisions, it is rather more complicated to navigate, particularly for those not used to legal research. Knowing the parties involved in a particular case, or the case citation, can speed up the process of finding a decision significantly. Supreme Court decisions are also published on the Supreme Court website (supremecourt.uk).

Other online resources

Not that long ago the best way to keep up to date with the latest developments was through discussion groups, mailing lists or listservs. They remain useful, and allow users to ask questions of fellow practitioners. Members can remain silent and 'lurk' if they prefer. Most groups allow users to set preferences, including whether to receive e-mails as they are sent, or, for example, whether to receive a daily digest containing all the e-mail discussion of the previous day. Group members can usually access a web archive containing all past correspondence, which can be a useful resource to search through when struggling to find a solution to an FOI problem, since often topics have been discussed before.

Two discussion groups hosted by JISCMail are useful examples: FREEDOM-OF-INFORMATION and RECORDS-MANAGEMENT-UK. They can be accessed and subscribed to via an alphabetical list at jiscmail.ac.uk. Remember these groups are open to anyone – it is not unknown for journalists or campaigners to join them to follow discussions. Some other groups are private and require an application to be made to join them – several sector-based groups operate in this way.

Blogs and social media provide other means to keep up to date with FOI developments. This book originated in a blog called FOIMan, which can still be found at foiman.com. It provides commentary on developments in FOI and associated legal requirements, alongside resources such as guides to the exemptions. An associated Twitter feed (@foimanuk) highlights useful resources. FOI Directory (foi.directory) is a website aimed primarily at journalists, which highlights news about FOI. Finally, a useful way to keep up to date with the most significant case law is to read the Panopticon Blog (panopticonblog.com), written by barristers from the 11KBW chambers. A list of useful websites and blogs can be found at foiman.com.

Around the world: online resources

India's RTI Foundation of India (www.rtifoundationofindia.com) is a website established by 'a group of professionals who have keenly observed the RTI Act'. It aims to provide 'critical information, analyses, expert viewpoints, editorials and related news on developments related to the Act', including updates on the latest case law.[11]

South Africa's Open Democracy Advice Centre (www.opendemocracy.org.za) is a non-profit company that promotes open and transparent democracy. It does this by assisting people to use South Africa's FOI law (the Promotion of Access to Information Act), and supporting 'effective implementation of the new legislation by assisting public and private institutions to develop policies, procedures and systems'.[12]

Australian lawyer and consultant Peter Timmins (http://foi-privacy.blogspot. co.uk) blogs about FOI and open government developments in Australia. Similarly, Canadian lawyer Dan Michaluk provides useful updates on FOI in Canada in All About Information (allaboutinformation.ca).

Professional associations and other networks

There is no single professional body representing FOI officers in the UK. The following two bodies are most likely to welcome any FOI officers who are looking for a forum in which to discuss their work:

- The Information and Records Management Society (www.irms.org.uk) is a membership body aimed at information professionals. There are no requirements for membership, though in recent years a professional accreditation scheme has been launched. It has an annual conference and regional and special interest groups, which organise regular events hosting speakers on a range of information management subjects, including FOI.
- The National Association of Data Protection and Freedom of Information Officers (NADPO; www.nadpo.co.uk) organises quarterly events with speakers on a range of topics related primarily to data protection but also on FOI.

In addition, there are many regional or sectoral groups that meet regularly to discuss the FOIA and other information governance issues. The importance of having these forums to discuss current issues and practice is recognised in Ireland: 'The FOI networks provide an excellent means of sharing learning and expertise and assist in developing common approaches. The FOI officer should participate in relevant FOI networks to realise such benefits and transfer learning to the body.'[13]

Summing up

- FOI officers rely on a toolkit of resources that helps them carry out their duties.
- In the UK and some other jurisdictions, FOI law requires the government to issue codes of practice setting out how to comply with FOI duties.
- Information commissioners or their equivalents usually publish detailed guidance on the interpretation of the law.
- There is a range of other online resources available, including websites, blogs, social media and more traditional tools such as e-mail mailing lists.
- Decisions of commissioners or their equivalents, tribunals and courts are usually published online and are essential resources for FOI officers.
- Professional associations, networks and sectoral groups provide opportunities to meet fellow practitioners and to develop knowledge and skills.

Part 2

FOI in context

Chapter 5

The Environmental Information Regulations

Introduction

In the UK, the FOIA is not the only law providing access to information held by public authorities. There are many rules requiring authorities to make information available, many of which are described in the following chapters. The most significant of these are the Environmental Information Regulations 2004 (EIR).

The EIR provide a right of access to environmental information held by public authorities. They are the 'Cinderella' right to information – they tend to be ignored in favour of their better known relation. In the UK they were brought into force on the same day as the right of access under the FOIA and, understandably, attention at the time focused on the Act. Indeed for most authorities, the FOIA is much more significant. Government statistics for 2017 show that across all monitored bodies, only 3% of requests were handled under the EIR. However, the EIR is much more significant for some authorities – the proportion of requests dealt with under the EIR by the Department for the Environment, Food and Rural Affairs (DEFRA) was over 31%.[1] Outside central government, a significant proportion of information requests made to local authorities is covered by the EIR, given councils' role in planning, waste disposal and other activities designed to manage local impact on the environment.

The EIR have their origin in a European directive and an international agreement so regulations providing access to environmental information have been adopted in other European countries. Scotland has adopted its own regulations on environmental information just as it has its own FOI Act. Outside Europe, access to this information is normally covered by the main FOI law.

It is important for FOI officers to be able to identify when to apply the EIR rather than the FOIA. There are many similarities, but also significant differences between the two laws. In particular, it is important to apply the right law when information needs to be withheld for any reason.

Why do we have EIR?

Unlike the FOIA, which is purely UK legislation and over which the government had a choice, the EIR had to be implemented as a result of a European directive. This in itself was designed to give effect to a previous agreement called the Aarhus Convention, named after the city in Denmark where it was reached in 1998. The Convention aimed 'to contribute to the protection of the right of every person . . . to live in an environment adequate to his or her health and well-being', through signatories guaranteeing the three 'pillars' of 'the rights of access to information, public participation in decision making, and access to justice in environmental matters'.[2] Access to information was seen as a prerequisite of ensuring the other rights, but 'it is equally important in its own right, in the sense that the public may seek access to information for any number of purposes, not just to participate'.[3]

The relationship between the FOIA and the EIR

There is an exemption at s. 39 of the FOIA for environmental information. Its effect is to remove information falling within the definition of environmental information (as set out in the EIR) from the FOIA. Technically the exemption here is qualified – subject to a public interest test – but in practice this is unlikely to have much effect. The Information Commissioner describes the public interest test at s. 39 as a formality, as 'it is hard to envisage any circumstances where it would be in the public interest for the authority to also consider that information under FOIA'.[4]

In effect, as long as the public authority is subject to the EIR, the public interest favours handling the request under that legislation. The Commissioner also points out that the EIR constitute an alternative means by which information may be accessed. Therefore s. 21(1), the exemption covering information accessible to the applicant through other means, is also relevant when a request is received for environmental information. The Commissioner's pragmatic advice is that 'rather than issuing a s. 21 or a s. 39 refusal notice we would recommend that the public authority simply deals with the request under the EIR'.[5]

Which bodies are subject to the EIR?

For the most part, if a public authority is subject to the FOIA, it will be subject to the EIR. Government departments and most other public bodies listed in schedule 1 of the FOIA are subject to the regulations.[6] Bodies can be added to schedule 1 under s. 4 of the Act and where this happens, they will also become subject to the EIR. However, public bodies that are only partly covered by the FOIA – for example broadcasters like the BBC or Channel 4 – are not subject to the EIR.[7] Bodies added to the FOIA by a s. 5 order will not automatically be subject to the EIR either.[8] Where authorities are 'acting in a judicial or legislative capacity' the regulations will not apply.[9] The same is true for each House of Parliament to the extent required to avoid an infringement of their privileges.[10]

Bodies that are under the control of public authorities that carry out functions relating to the environment have to respond to EIR requests.[11] This will include publicly owned companies in line with the FOIA.

There are some circumstances where the EIR will apply even though the FOIA doesn't. The special forces, such as the SAS, are excluded from the FOIA's coverage, but are subject to the EIR, though obviously it is likely that exceptions will apply to much of their information.

The regulations also specify that any body carrying out functions of public administration will be covered.[12] Having consulted the European Court of Justice (CJEU), the Upper Tribunal explored this and established that the test for whether a body is carrying out such functions will be whether they have special legal powers to carry out services of public interest.[13] According to the Information Commissioner, such powers might include compulsory purchase, being able to obtain access to property without the owner's permission, or powers to propose new laws to government.[14] Water companies,[15] and even energy companies,[16] have been found to be subject to the EIR on this basis.

What is environmental information?

Environmental information 'has the same meaning as in Article 2(1) of the Directive, namely any information in written, visual, aural, electronic or any other material form on…'. A list of categories is provided in the regulations to assist in deciding whether information falls under them.

Information in a 'material form',[17] such as hard copy letters, e-mail, drawings, sound recordings and CCTV footage, is covered,[18] as long as it is 'on' one or more of a list of categories. The definition should be interpreted broadly.[19] The Aarhus

Convention implementation guide states that the 'clear intention of the drafters
... was to craft a definition that would be as broad in scope as possible, a fact that
should be taken into account in its interpretation.'[20]

The categories listed at regulation 2(1)

The definition at reg. 2(1) lists six categories of information that constitute
environmental information.

Category (a)

Category (a) covers 'the state of the elements of the environment, such as air and
atmosphere, water, soil, land, landscape and natural sites including wetlands,
coastal and marine areas, biological diversity and its components, including
genetically modified organisms, and the interaction among these elements'.

This includes water and air quality data,[21] as well as information on land use
(including maps), or even ownership.[22] Information on a specific species – animal
or plant – is not environmental information, but information on a species'
interaction with other species or elements of the environment is.[23] For example,
a request for correspondence on hedgehogs would not automatically be handled
under the EIR. A request for the number of hedgehogs that were killed by road
vehicles would be, since it relates to the interaction between humans and
hedgehogs.

Category (b)

Category (b) is 'factors, such as substances, energy, noise, radiation or waste,
including radioactive waste, emissions, discharges and other releases into the
environment, affecting or likely to affect the elements of the environment
referred to in (a)'. These can include radio waves (even though the scientific
evidence in this regard is inconclusive), and domestic drainage.[24]

Category (c)

Category (c) covers 'measures (including administrative measures), such as
policies, legislation, plans, programmes, environmental agreements, and
activities affecting or likely to affect the elements and factors referred to in (a)
and (b) as well as measures or activities designed to protect those elements'.

Very commonly, where a public authority finds that requested information is
environmental, it is because it falls within category (c). Public authorities take
measures which very often have an impact on their environment.

A 'road map' for establishing whether information falls under category (c) is set out in Figure 5.1.

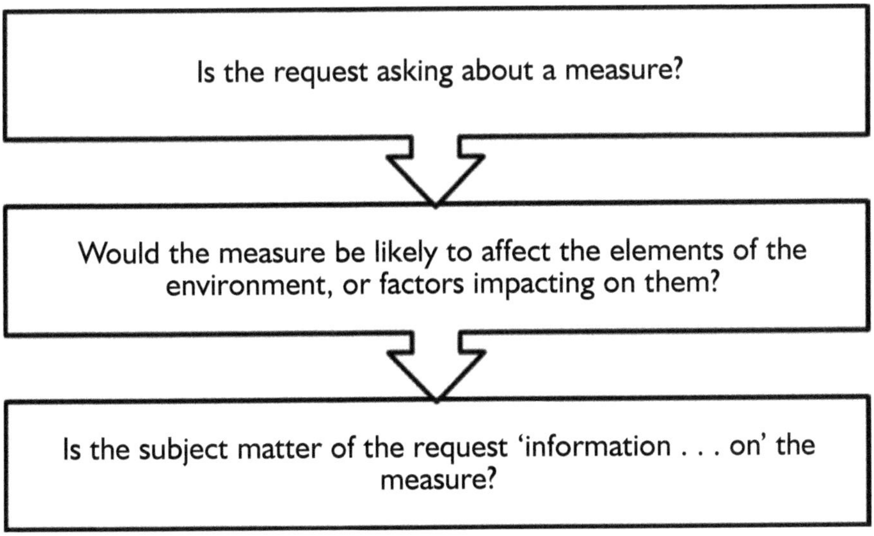

| Is the request asking about a measure? |

| Would the measure be likely to affect the elements of the environment, or factors impacting on them? |

| Is the subject matter of the request 'information . . . on' the measure? |

Figure 5.1 A road map to establish whether information falls into category (c) of reg. 2(1) of the EIR[25]

This roadmap was usefully applied in one case involving a council's refurbishment of a housing estate as follows:

- The future development of a housing estate is a *measure*.
- The external features of houses subject to planning controls are part of the *landscape*.
- A document summarising options for the development of the estate is *information on* the measure.[26]

Information might still fall within category (c) where the process the information describes is not itself environmental, but is part of a wider programme that is. So an equality impact assessment on the erection of a monument was environmental information because the monument was a measure affecting the landscape.[27] A project assessment review of the data and communications component of a smart meter programme designed to reduce carbon emissions is environmental information because the data and communications component was an integral part of the smart meter programme, and the programme in question is a measure (c) designed to reduce a factor (b) that impacts on an element of the environment (a), namely the atmosphere.[28] It is important not to take this too far, however. A Porsche motor car has an impact on the environment, but that doesn't mean that anything to do with the car is environmental information.[29]

Information on internal alterations to properties is not normally environmental, because while they are a measure, in most cases they do not (sufficiently) affect any of the elements of the environment.[30]

Category (d)

Category (d) consists of 'reports on the implementation of environmental legislation'. The scope of category (d) is self-explanatory, though there may be dispute over when legislation is 'environmental', especially given that no definition is offered for that word in the regulations, the directive or the convention.

Category (e)

Category (e) covers 'cost-benefit and other economic analyses and assumptions used within the framework of the measures and activities referred to in (c)'. This 'ensures the definition of environmental information extends to information about the economic and financial implications of environmental measures and activities'.[31] There is often overlap between category (e) and category (c). In *Southwark v IC & Lend Lease*, the redevelopment of Elephant & Castle was found to be a measure falling under category (c), while an assessment of the financial viability of the development was found to fall under category (e) – it was an economic analysis used within the framework of the overall measure.[32] In other cases, similar analyses were found to be a measure under category (c), and the tribunal found it unnecessary to conclude whether it also fell under category (e).[33]

Category (f)

Finally, category (f) is:

> the state of human health and safety, including the contamination of the food chain, where relevant, conditions of human life, cultural sites and built structures inasmuch as they are or may be affected by the state of the elements of the environment referred to in (a) or, through those elements, by any of the matters referred to in (b) and (c).

Category (f) does not cover everything to do with human health. It focuses on environmental factors that *affect* human health.[34] An example is information on contamination of the food chain.[35] Information on the health effects of coal mining or asbestos exposure could fall within this category.[36]

Similarities between the EIR and the FOIA

In many respects the EIR are very similar to the FOIA. They are both pieces of legislation designed to facilitate access to information held by public authorities. The EIR impose the same duties. While there is no mention of publication schemes in the EIR, there is a duty to 'progressively make the information available to the public', taking 'reasonable steps to organise the information . . . with a view to the active and systematic dissemination to the public of the information'.[37] This can plainly be met by including environmental information in an authority's publication scheme. This is discussed further in Chapter 8. Those subject to the EIR are also required to provide information in response to requests that they receive.[38]

Requesters can specify the format they want to receive information in, just as at FOIA s. 11.[39] For the most part requests have to be answered within 20 working days or sooner if possible.[40] Fees can be charged, but only where listed in a schedule.[41] Advice and assistance has to be provided to applicants.[42] A code of practice has to be issued by the Secretary of State for the Environment, Food and Rural Affairs.[43] Complaints can be made to the Information Commissioner, who has the same powers to enforce the regulations as she has to enforce the FOIA.[44]

Differences between the EIR and the FOIA

Although there are these significant similarities, there are some differences, some of which are described below.

Holding information

For the purposes of these Regulations, environmental information is held by a public authority if the information—

(a) is in the authority's possession and has been produced or received by the authority; or
(b) is held by another person on behalf of the authority.

This definition does not mention information held on someone else's behalf. The Information Commissioner's guidance acknowledges that this could be interpreted to mean that information is held in a wider range of circumstances than under the FOIA.[45] However, it concludes that in practice information won't be in the authority's possession unless it is held for the authority's own purposes.

Around the world: the Environmental Information (Scotland) Regulations 2004
The Scottish regulations on environmental information are very similar to the UK regulations. These are some of the differences:

- The list of information that public authorities are expected to make proactively available is transposed from the directive (making it easier to see at a glance what must be published).
- Scottish authorities have to explain why they believe information to be complex and voluminous when extending the deadline to 40 working days.
- The regulations specify that exceptions are to be interpreted in a restrictive way in addition to the requirement to apply a presumption in favour of disclosure.
- The 'adversely affect' exceptions are worded 'would, or would be likely to, prejudice substantially' – in other words, they borrow the wording used in prejudice-based exemptions in the FOI(S)A.
- Internal reviews must be considered within 20 working days.
- The Scottish Information Commissioner considers appeals.

Answering requests

Unlike the FOIA, there is no definition of what a 'request' is. One implication of this is that requests do not have to be made in writing – they can be made orally. While in practice most requesters submit requests for environmental information in writing, it is appropriate to adopt procedures to cater for requests made over the telephone or in person.

Requests must be answered 'as soon as possible' and, just like the FOIA, no later than 20 working days after receipt.[46] As with the FOIA, the Commissioner views the 20th working day as a limit and not a target.[47] On at least one occasion, the Commissioner has found a public authority in breach of the regulation because even though staff had responded to the request within 20 working days, there had been an administrative error in its processing which resulted in a failure to respond 'as soon as possible'.[48]

Public authorities can extend the deadline for responding to a request from 20 working days to 40 working days.[49] This can be done where they reasonably believe that it would be impracticable to comply with the request within the normal timeframe because of the complexity and volume of the requested information. They must inform the applicant that they need longer than the original 20 working days.

Charging for information

A 'reasonable' charge can be made for information under the EIR and calculation of this can include staff time searching for information.[50] Public authorities can only charge 'the costs attributable to the time spent by staff of the public authority concerned on answering an individual request for information'. Any charges must not have a deterrent effect on those wishing to access environmental information.[51] In an early decision, it was viewed that 10p a sheet was a reasonable charge for photocopying,[52] though the Information Commissioner has noted that what is considered a reasonable charge depends on the circumstances at the time.[53] Charges can only be made at all if listed in a published schedule[54] – an authority's publication scheme being the best way to meet this requirement.

There is no 'appropriate limit' in the EIR. Neither do the FOIA regulations on fees and cost limits apply to environmental information. Burdensome requests can be dealt with by either extending the deadline as outlined above, or by refusing them as 'manifestly unreasonable'.[55]

Refusing requests

Just as with the FOIA, a refusal notice must be issued whenever information is not going to be provided.[56] In the EIR, there is even an exception (the EIR version of an exemption) to cover situations where the information is not held.

Except for personal information, all the exceptions are subject to a public interest test (in theory, if not in practice – it is very difficult to see how the public interest could possibly favour disclosing information that is not held, for instance). Public authorities are also explicitly required to 'apply a presumption in favour of disclosure',[57] something not stated in the FOIA. One of the reasons why public authorities often resist the interpretation of a request as being about environmental information is that as this 'presumption' suggests it can be harder to justify withholding information under the EIR. 'Grounds for refusal should be interpreted in a restrictive way', says the directive which the EIR implements.[58]

The exceptions at reg. 12(5) illustrate this well. They are similar to the prejudice-based exemptions in the FOIA. In this case they allow information to be withheld if disclosure would adversely affect the interests covered by the exceptions. Note though the absence of the option to argue that disclosure 'would be likely' to adversely affect those interests. Taking the rules outlined in the guide to the FOIA exemptions in Chapter 3, this means that to be able to demonstrate that one of these exceptions applies, it is necessary to show that there would 'more likely than not' be an adverse effect (i.e. the risk is more than 50%). Showing that there is a 'real and significant risk' would not be sufficient.

Table 5.1 lists the exceptions available in the EIR and notes the factors to consider in applying them.

Table 5.1 *Exceptions in the EIR*

Regulation	Notes
5(3)	Equivalent to s. 40(1) in the FOIA – applies if the applicant is asking for information relating to themselves.
12(3)/13	Equivalent to s. 40(2) in the FOIA – applies where disclosure would breach the data protection principles, conflict with a data subject's objection under the GDPR or the DPA 2018, or the information would be exempt from disclosure to the data subject under the GDPR or the DPA 2018.
12(4)(a)	Applies where the information is not held according to the definition at reg. 3(2).
12(4)(b)	Equivalent to the vexatious provision at s. 14(1) of the FOIA (the difference between the two is 'vanishingly small').[59] It can also be used where the cost of compliance would be excessive. While it is appropriate to use the FOIA fees regulations as a guide (the ICO in particular suggest that staff time can be estimated on the basis of £25 an hour in line with the fees regulations), it isn't necessarily the case that a request costing more than £450 or £600 is 'manifestly unreasonable'. The authority needs to argue this on a case-by-case basis.
12(4)(c)	Where a 'request is formulated in too general a manner'. Similar to s. 1(3) in the FOIA in that it will apply where the request requires clarification. Can only be applied if advice and assistance is provided in line with reg. 9.
12(4)(d)	Protects 'material which is still in the course of completion . . . unfinished documents [and] incomplete data'. Similar to s. 22 of the FOIA. Can be applied to drafts, even once the final version of a document has been published; conversely, it won't apply to completed documents just because they relate to a wider project that is still ongoing. With 12(4)(e), a 'safe space' type exception.
12(4)(e)	This exception protects 'internal communications'. 'Internal' covers communications across government (between government departments and executive agencies), but not communications between government and other public authorities. It does not cover communications from external consultants, unless they are 'embedded' within the authority (they are effectively a 'temp'). Nonetheless, potentially very broad, but the difficulty is always to demonstrate that the public interest favours withholding the communication.

(continued)

Table 5.1 *Continued*

Regulation	Notes
12(5)(a)	Adversely affects international relations, defence, national security and public safety. Covers similar ground to ss. 27, 26, 24, 31 and 38 of the FOIA. A minister can sign a certificate to verify that national security would be adversely affected and the public interest favours withholding the information (as with the s. 25 certificates that apply under ss. 23 and 24 of the FOIA).
12(5)(b)	Adversely affects 'the course of justice, the ability of a person to receive a fair trial or the ability of a public authority to conduct an inquiry of a criminal or disciplinary nature'. Can cover matters such as legal advice (s. 42 FOIA), criminal proceedings (s. 30 FOIA), but also disciplinary proceedings within a public authority.
12(5)(c)	Adversely affects 'intellectual property rights'. Very difficult to make the case for this exception – the UK ICO has never upheld its application in any relevant decision. For an example of its successful use in Scotland, see Chapter 9.
12(5)(d)	Adversely affects the confidentiality of a public authority's proceedings. Only covers the most formal proceedings of public bodies – such as closed council committee meetings or information disclosed to an ombudsman as part of an investigation. Cannot be used to withhold information about emissions.
12(5)(e)	Adversely affects 'the confidentiality of commercial or industrial information where such confidentiality is provided by law to protect a legitimate economic interest'. Often seen as equivalent to s. 43(2) of the FOIA, it is really a sort of hybrid of the exemption for commercial interests and the exemption at s. 41 covering information provided in confidence. The following questions must be addressed: ● Is the interest commercial or industrial? ● Is the confidentiality protected in law (this might be through a contract, statute or common law)? ● Is a legitimate economic interest being protected? ● Would disclosure (more likely than not) adversely affect the economic interest? ● Does the public interest in withholding the information outweigh the public interest in disclosing it?[60] Cannot be used to withhold information about emissions.

Table 5.1 *Continued*

12(5)(f)	Adversely affects the interests of someone who provided the information voluntarily in circumstances where the authority would not otherwise than under the EIR be entitled to disclose it. Seeks to avoid individuals and others from being inhibited in responding to public consultations and the like, but it can also apply to commercial arrangements. Cannot be used to withhold information about emissions.
12(5)(g)	Adversely affects 'the protection of the environment to which the information relates'. An example is the revelation of the location of a protected species where that would lead to that species being further threatened. Cannot be used to withhold information about emissions.

In a further illustration of the difficulty of applying exceptions under the EIR, it is only possible to neither confirm nor deny whether information is held in relation to the personal information exception at reg. 12(3) and reg. 13, and the exception that applies where disclosure would adversely affect international relations, defence, national security or public safety (reg. 12(5)(a)). The last four of the 'adversely affect' exceptions cannot be applied to information about emissions. Unhelpfully, emissions are not defined in the EIR or in any precedent-setting case law. The ICO define emissions as 'the by-product of an activity or process, which is added (or potentially added) to and affecting the elements of the environment, over which any control is relinquished'.[61] In a case involving genetically modified crops, the FTT ruled that such crops were not emissions as they are deliberately placed in the environment.[62] Chemicals leaking from a damaged pipeline is an example of an emission.

> **Around the world: protecting environmental information in the Isle of Man**
> Outside the European Economic Area (EEA), it is unusual to find exemptions designed explicitly to protect information relating to the environment (although the USA's FOI Act, somewhat bizarrely, provides explicit protection for data concerning oil wells!). The Isle of Man, perhaps because of its proximity to the EEA, has sought to address the issue within its version of the FOIA.
> Section 37(2) of the Act provides a qualified exemption where disclosure 'would, or would be likely to, prejudice the well-being of . . . a cultural, heritage or natural resource . . . a species of flora or fauna; or . . . a habitat of a species of flora or fauna'.

Complaints and enforcement

The EIR, unlike the FOIA, set out a process for consideration of internal reviews by authorities. This is summarised in Chapter 14.

Once complaints reach the Information Commissioner, the process is much the same as for the FOIA. A couple of differences remain though. Ministers are not able to veto the disclosure of environmental information[63] because the use of such a power contradicts the underlying directive, which states, 'Applicants should be able to seek an administrative or judicial review of the acts or omissions of a public authority in relation to a request.'[64]

Another difference is that UK courts, such as the tribunals, for the time being can still request an opinion from the European Court of Justice on tricky EIR issues. This is not a facility open to them for the FOIA.

Summing up

- The EIR are the legislation that applies when dealing with requests for environmental information.
- They are based on a European directive, which is why they are separate from the FOIA.
- Most organisations subject to the FOIA are also subject to the EIR, but there are some bodies that have to answer EIR requests even though they are not FOIA public authorities.
- Interpret 'environmental information' broadly to include information on the elements of the environment, factors that affect them, and measures taken that impact on these factors.
- Most of the rules in the EIR are the same as the FOIA, but there are some significant differences.
- Requests under the EIR do not have to be made in writing.
- The deadline for meeting requests is broadly the same, but it can only be extended for complex and voluminous requests (not for consideration of the public interest, as with the FOIA).
- Requests can be charged for in limited circumstances as long as the charges are published in a schedule – it makes sense to use a publication scheme to achieve this.
- There is no cost limit under the EIR, though there are alternative ways to deal with burdensome requests.
- There are exceptions instead of exemptions which must be applied when refusing requests.
- There is a presumption to disclose in the EIR, and the exceptions are more difficult to apply.
- The EIR specify deadlines for the consideration of complaints by public authorities.

Chapter 6

The FOIA, personal information and the GDPR

Introduction

The right to know and the right to privacy are inextricably linked. Many people believe they are in conflict, and certainly there are times when observing the rights of individuals prevents information about them being disclosed. However, the right to privacy often depends to some extent on transparency, since individuals cannot defend their right to privacy if they do not know what information is held about them, and what it is used for. There are times when an absolute approach to privacy would be damaging for society, and potentially individuals. What is necessary is a mechanism to balance the two rights.

As Figure 6.1 on the next page illustrates, the most commonly used exemption in the FOIA by far by UK central government bodies in 2017 was the exemption for personal information at s. 40. This demonstrates how important the relationship between these two rights is, and how often it needs to be considered in practice. Whatever an applicant may be interested in, very often personal information is interspersed within documentation. Names, addresses, telephone numbers, signatures – all can be found among documents that may not be primarily about an individual. As personal information is so prevalent across public authorities it is essential that FOI laws provide protection for it.

In the UK protection of personal information is provided by the exemption at s. 40 of the FOIA, and in the EIR by regs 5(3), 12(3) and 13. These provisions seek to avoid a conflict between FOI and the GDPR and the DPA 2018, the laws that govern the use of personal information in the UK. Internationally, many FOI laws incorporate data protection rules, recognising the close link between the two rights.

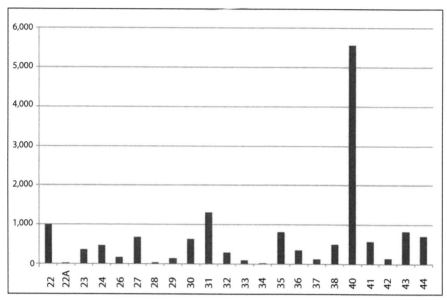

Figure 6.1   *The use of exemptions by monitored UK government bodies in 2017* [1]

Around the world: personal information exemptions
Given that the GDPR applies across the whole of the EEA, and even countries outside
that area have adopted, or are intending to adopt, compatible laws on handling
personal information, pretty much every European state has mechanisms in their FOI
laws to manage the relationship between the GDPR and the right to know.

Scotland's FOI(S)A has an exemption at s. 38 which is broadly the same as the FOIA s.
40 exemption. Like the UK's Act, the FOI(S)A and the Scottish EIR have been amended by
the DPA 2018 to take account of the GDPR. The most significant difference is that it
includes protection for 'personal census information' and 'a deceased person's health
record'. In the UK Act, there is no explicit protection for any information relating to the
deceased (see 'The gist: the FOIA and the dead' at the end of this chapter). The Isle of
Man's FOI Act reproduces this approach in its absolute personal information exemption
(there is a separate qualified exemption covering personal information in the Isle of
Man, covering the same aspects that are subject to a public interest test in the UK – see
the section 'Third party personal information' later in this chapter).

The Irish FOI Act (s. 37) requires a request to be refused if it would involve the
disclosure of personal information – and notably 'including personal information
relating to a deceased individual'. Authorities can disclose personal information in
specified circumstances, such as with the individual's consent.

The USA's federal FOI Act ((b)(6)) includes an exemption for 'personnel and medical
files and similar files the disclosure of which would constitute a clearly unwarranted
invasion of personal privacy'. The Canadian Access to Information Act (s. 19) includes an
exemption for 'any record that contains personal information as defined in section 3 of
the Privacy Act'. It goes on to allow disclosure with consent of individuals, if the

information is already public, or if it meets criteria set out in the Privacy Act. India's Right to Know Act (s. 8(1)(j)) provides protection for 'information which relates to personal information the disclosure of which has no relationship to any public activity or interest, or which would cause unwarranted invasion of the privacy of the individual', though allows for this to be overridden if 'the larger public interest justifies the disclosure'.

What is personal information?

The GDPR defines personal information (or strictly 'personal data') as 'any information relating to an identified or identifiable natural person ("data subject").'[2]

A natural person just means an individual, as opposed to a company (which can be described as a legal person). The important phrase above is 'identified or identifiable' – information is personal information if it is possible to identify a particular individual, even if that is only with the assistance of other records, or even the knowledge of individual employees within an organisation. It can still be personal information even if the name of the person is not known; the GDPR lists other valid identifiers such as identification numbers, location data and online identifiers.

The format the information is in is largely irrelevant, especially for public authorities. Information held in automated (IT) systems is captured, but also that kept in manual filing systems accessible according to specific criteria. This excludes manually recorded information stored in unstructured form – a note taken by a manager about an employee added to a random pile of papers in their desk drawer, for example. However, the DPA 2018 addresses this specifically and ensures that such unstructured information held by public authorities is subject to most of the obligations that the GDPR applies to information stored in other formats.

The upshot of the above is that if it is possible to identify the individual to whom information held by a public authority relates, it is personal information, no matter what form it is in. Examples of personal information include someone's name, telephone number and such obviously identifiable information, but also what they get paid, how they perform in their job, what complaints have been made about them, or they have made, their opinion, or someone's opinion of them.

One important exclusion from the definition of personal information has not

The gist: examples of personal information
These are some examples of personal information:

- names – unless they are so common that it isn't possible to distinguish individuals (*Edem v Information Commissioner & Financial Conduct Authority* [2014] EWCA Civ 92)
- addresses – where they can be linked to individuals, perhaps through the electoral roll (*Exeter City Council v IC and Nicola Guagliardo*, EA/2012/0073)

- job title – especially when there is only one employee filling the role (*Yiannis Voyias v IC*, EA/2013/0003)
- statistics – where numbers are so low that they might allow individuals to be identified (*Smith v IC and Devon and Cornwall Constabulary*, EA/2011/006; *Beckles v IC*, EA/2011/0073 & 0074)
- information on work carried out by the owner of a house (*Henderson v IC*, EA/2013/0055)
- salaries paid to individuals (*M.B. Dicker v IC*, EA/2012/0250)
- expenses claimed by individuals (*Corporate Officer of the House of Commons v IC and Leapman, Brooke and Thomas*, EA/2007/0060 and others).

yet been mentioned. Information relating to the deceased is not personal information. This can have important ramifications for some FOI requests (see 'The gist: FOI and the dead' later in this chapter).

FOI and subject access

Article 15 of the GDPR gives individuals the right to access personal information about themselves held by organisations (or 'data controllers' in GDPR-speak) by making a 'subject access request'. This is not a new concept since the right of subject access in some form dates back to the first Data Protection Act in 1984. The DPA 2018 extends the right of subject access to information held for law enforcement purposes (which is excluded from the GDPR's coverage) and the 'manual unstructured data' held by public authorities.

In order to avoid a conflict between the FOIA and the GDPR (and DPA 2018), s. 40(1) of the FOIA provides an absolute exemption for information about the applicant. This doesn't mean that they cannot access the information – but that it should be accessed through the GDPR or DPA 2018 instead. An exception provided in the EIR at reg. 5(3) has the same effect when the personal information is also environmental information.

Where a request is received from an applicant and it appears that they are asking for their own information, the technically correct approach is to issue a refusal notice citing s. 40(1) and provide advice and assistance directing them how to make a subject access request. Nonetheless, if it is possible to answer the request without referring back to the applicant, this should be done. The deadline for answering subject access requests is 'one month', similar to the 20 working days for a FOI request. In many cases, though, it is still necessary to go back to the applicant to obtain proof of their identity.

Third-party personal information

When personal information relating to individuals other than the requester is captured by a request, the exemption at s. 40(2) may be considered. It applies if one of the conditions set out at ss. 40(3A), (3B) or (4A) is met. These conditions are:

- s. 40(3A) disclosing the information would contravene one of the data protection principles set out in article 5 of the GDPR
- s. 40(3B) the affected individual has objected to disclosure under article 21 of the GDPR
- s. 40(4A) the affected individual would not be entitled to the information if they made a subject access request due to an exemption in DPA 2018.

Where a public authority is relying on the last two of these conditions, a public interest test must be carried out. It has proved very rare that an authority relies on either of these two conditions to justify non-disclosure.

It is the first of the conditions, s. 40(3A), that is most often used to protect personal information. There are six data protection principles listed in the GDPR article 5(1), but only the first is relevant when considering an FOI request. It requires that personal information shall be: 'processed lawfully, fairly and in a transparent manner in relation to the data subject'.

Fairness in the data protection context means both that the use of the information is fair in the generally understood sense, and that individuals have been told, or have a reasonable expectation, that their information will be used in a particular way. Taken together with the word 'transparency' it is about ensuring that there are no nasty surprises for individuals.

Lawfulness means that any processing of information will not contravene other legal requirements. Primarily, though, in this situation it means that it must be possible to identify a lawful basis for the disclosure from the list of conditions set out at article 6. Furthermore, if the information is 'special category data' – it relates to racial or ethnic origin, political opinions, religious or philosophical beliefs, trade union membership, an individual's health or sex life, or is biometric or genetic data about them – it is also necessary to find a condition from article 9 to make the disclosure lawful.

In summary, if disclosure would be unfair (or even in theory if it is fair, but a lawful basis cannot be found) then the exemption at s. 40(2) can be applied, and the information can be withheld.

The same criteria are used to decide whether to confirm the existence of information. The exemption from the duty to confirm or deny is set out at s. 40(5A and B) (there is an example of where it would be used in Chapter 3).

Under the EIR, reg. 12(3) provides that personal information relating to third parties will not be disclosed unless conditions at reg. 13 are met. The conditions listed there are the same as those set out from s. 40(3A) through to s. 40(5B), so in effect personal information is handled the same way under the EIR as under the FOIA.

The process of considering whether personal information is exempt from disclosure is summarised in Figure 6.2.

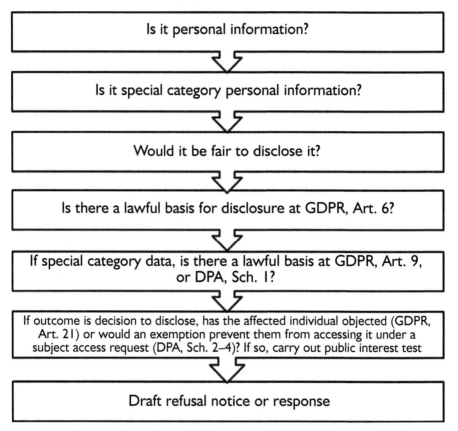

Figure 6.2 *How s. 40(2) operates and its interaction with the GDPR and the DPA 2018*

Judging fairness

There is no requirement to consider the elements of the first principle in any particular order. The ICO usually takes the approach of considering whether disclosure would be fair first.[3] The argument is that it will not be necessary to go on and consider whether disclosure would be lawful if it has already been established that disclosing the information would be unfair. It suggests that the following four considerations are relevant in deciding on fairness:

- whether the information is sensitive (or special category in GDPR terms) personal information
- the possible consequences of disclosure
- the reasonable expectations of the individual
- whether there is a legitimate interest in the disclosure, balanced against the rights of the individual.[4]

The reason for the first point is that if the information is special category data, it is highly unlikely that disclosure will be either fair or lawful. If the information falls within this definition, therefore, it is rarely necessary to go any further.[5]

The gist – the relationship between transparency and fairness
Shaw v Information Commissioner, EA/2015/0069, 5 August 2015

Mr Shaw asked the London Borough of Southwark for copies of the objection letters received in relation to a planning application. The FTT was shown a 'neighbour consultation letter' sent to addresses in the local area. It had stated that identifiable information would not be made public. Mr Shaw pointed out that the council's website had at one stage asserted that names of those who submitted comments would be made public. However, the statement on the website had later been changed to be consistent with the letters that had been sent out. The message given to local residents was confusing, to say the least.

Given this 'unhappy lack of clarity', the FTT agreed with the Information Commissioner that it would have been unfair to disclose the identities of those who had objected to the application, as at least some of them would have assumed that their identities would not be made public. They upheld the council's use of the exception at reg. 12(3) of the EIR, since disclosure would have breached the first data protection principle.

The article 6 conditions and legitimate interests

These are the conditions of article 6 of the GDPR under which processing personal information is lawful:

- The data subject has given consent.
- It is necessary for performance of a contract.
- It is necessary for compliance with a legal obligation.

- It is necessary to protect vital interests.
- It is necessary for performance of a task in the public interest or in the exercise of official authority.
- It is necessary for the purposes of legitimate interests except where those interests are overridden by the interests or rights of the data subject.

A public authority only ever needs to consider two of these in a FOIA context. The first is consent. However, as there is often an imbalance between public authorities and those whose information they are processing, it may be difficult to obtain valid consent to disclose personal information.[6] Therefore, more often than not it is the last condition – legitimate interests – that is relevant. Public authorities cannot normally rely on this lawful basis for activities related to their public task, but the DPA 2018 amends the FOIA and the EIR to specifically permit its use when considering disclosures of personal information in response to requests.[7]

Figure 6.3 shows the process for considering whether a legitimate interest justifies disclosure.

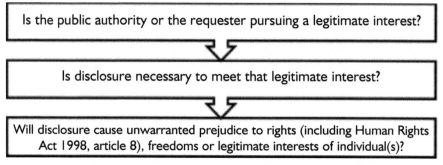

Figure 6.3 The process for considering whether disclosure can be justified on legitimate interests grounds[8]

First the authority needs to consider whether a legitimate interest is being pursued. This is one of those situations when the 'purpose and applicant blind' rule can be cheerfully tossed aside. It is often necessary to know who is asking, and why, in order to decide whether a legitimate interest is being pursued. In most cases, the legitimate interest is that the disclosure is in the public interest. The most famous example of that was when the FTT ruled that MPs' expenses should be disclosed.[9] Sometimes, though, the legitimate interest may be a private matter,[10] though the Information Commissioner is still somewhat reluctant to accept this.[11] It is important to consider specific cases on their merits.

The gist: a private legitimate interest
Henderson v IC, EA/2013/0055, 16 September 2013

Mr Henderson owned a house which he let to tenants. The house next door had been bought by another landlord for letting, and was being refurbished in preparation. The works included the removal of a chimney breast, and a lot of noise was caused in the process. Mr Henderson's tenants complained about the noise and reported that cracks had appeared in the party wall. Worse than that, a steel girder had emerged through it. Unsurprisingly, Mr Henderson wanted to know more about what was going on. He asked the council for details. The council explained that it had a policy of not releasing information about building regulations applications.

When the case reached the FTT, they were not impressed by the application of a blanket policy. They agreed with the Information Commissioner that the information was personal information. The Information Commissioner had suggested that although Mr Henderson had an interest in the information being disclosed, it didn't count as a legitimate interest because it was a private interest. The FTT disagreed – a private interest can be a legitimate interest.

The second consideration is whether disclosure is necessary to meet the legitimate interest identified. This often boils down to deciding whether there is another way to meet the interest. For example, when the FTT considered requests made by journalists for access to MPs' expenses claims, they noted that 'the extent of information published is not sufficient to enable the public to know how the money is spent. Nor is the system sufficient to create public confidence that it is being spent properly'.[12] It was therefore necessary to disclose the detailed claims, and not just the overall annual figures that had previously been made available.

The final stage is to consider whether the rights of individuals affected by the disclosure override the legitimate interests of the applicant.

The gist: when legitimate interests are overridden
Dr Dubey v IC and Bournemouth University, EA/2015/0163, 31 December 2015

A complaint had been made against Dr Dubey, which the university had not upheld. Dr Dubey was unhappy with the handling of the complaint, however, and wanted to find out more about the university's processing of grievances. He asked for details of all complaints made against university employees within a 17-month period. This was refused by the university on the grounds that the individuals would be identifiable from the information.

The FTT agreed that Dr Dubey had a legitimate interest in the information being disclosed given the seriousness of the complaint made against him. It agreed that it would be necessary for the information to be disclosed in order to meet that interest. However, it concluded that disclosure would cause unwarranted prejudice to the rights of the individuals affected. It was unwarranted because there was a clear policy regulating the process of complaint handling, the complaint against Dr Dubey had not been upheld (so there was no 'miscarriage of justice' to be established), and it was important to ensure that people would have no doubts about the confidentiality of the complaints process and wouldn't be put off making complaints in the future where necessary.

Looking at the process of considering whether there is a legitimate interest in disclosure, and balancing any interest against any unwarranted prejudice to individuals, it could be argued that the process duplicates the consideration of whether disclosure would be fair. This point was made by a judge in one Upper Tribunal case.[13] If a practitioner is struggling with the concept of fairness, they are unlikely to go far wrong if they start by following the process illustrated in Figure 6.3 to establish whether there is a legitimate interest in disclosure.

If special category or criminal record data is involved, the practitioner needs to be able to find another condition in article 9 of the GDPR (or one of the associated public interest conditions set out in Schedule 1 of DPA 2018). As noted above, it is unusual, though not impossible, for such data to be disclosed.

Employees and elected officials

Given their unavoidable involvement in the work of public authorities, employees' personal information is a key test ground for the s. 40 exemption. In establishing whether employees' personal information can be withheld, the Commissioner primarily focuses on fairness, and specifically what employees might reasonably expect. The ICO identifies the following relevant factors:

- Does the information relate to their private life or their public (work) life? Employees might have more expectation that information about their pay or work performance would be disclosed, but would expect information about where they live or their family to be withheld.
- How senior is the employee? Contrary to common belief, there is no blanket protection for junior employees, but it is certainly the case that the more senior an official, the more likely it is that it will be fair to disclose information about them.
- Is the employee in a public facing role? For example, employees who are press officers should probably expect that their name will be disclosed to those outside the organisation.
- Does the organisation have a policy on disclosures of employee information or is it common practice in the sector to disclose or withhold the information?[14]

The gist – different kinds of personal information about employees
Names of employees
A junior FOI officer was allowed to remain anonymous.[15] The name of the head of a housing department who ordered staff to allow police access to a council house had to be disclosed, but the names of the junior staff following their instructions didn't.[16] Officials at the MoD who speak to the media might expect their names to be disclosed, but junior staff who only corresponded with the public were entitled to remain anonymous.[17]

Salaries
There are specific rules in some sectors requiring publication of remuneration. For example, local authorities in England have to publish the job title and salary of those earning over £50,000.[18] It is common practice to publish salaries within £5,000 bands or at least pay scales.[19] In this context, it is difficult to justify a blanket refusal of such information. The ICO suggests that account should be taken of any consequences of disclosure when deciding whether to disclose salary information.

Termination of employment
There are legal requirements to publish how much is paid to employees on termination of their contract where the sums exceed £50,000.[20] However, employees have a reasonable expectation of confidentiality of agreements reached in most cases – it depends on the circumstances. If there was evidence of malpractice being covered up, for example, there might be a legitimate interest in disclosure of severance terms.[21]

Elected officials – councillors, MPs – can expect less protection than others in some circumstances. The most obvious example of this was the order to disclose MPs' expenses.[22] More recently, the name of a councillor who had defaulted on their council tax was disclosed. The Upper Tribunal took the view that a journalist had a legitimate interest in seeking this information, and that its disclosure was not unwarranted due to councillors' role in making decisions on council spending. The tribunal stressed that elected officials were in a unique position and should therefore expect more information about themselves to be disclosed.[23]

The gist: the FOIA and the dead
'This Regulation does not apply to the personal data of deceased persons' (GDPR, rec. 27).
   Since information about the dead is not covered by the GDPR, the personal information exemption cannot be used to protect it. That said, often it would be inappropriate to disclose information about the dead. Other options must be found.

Section 21
If there is information in the public domain about the deceased, s. 21 is likely to apply. A

response can be issued providing advice and assistance pointing to the location of the available information.

One circumstance where s. 21 may apply relates to health records held by a healthcare body. Where the applicant is the 'personal representative' of the deceased, their executor or they have a claim resulting from the death of the individual, they may be entitled to access the records through the provisions of the Access to Health Records Act 1990.[24]

Furthermore, certain details of those who died intestate (without a will or known family) in England and Wales are published by the *Bona Vacantia Division* (BVD) of the Treasury Solicitor's Department. The BVD publishes a daily Unclaimed Asset List of unclaimed estates which have been referred to them. If an individual is listed there, the information published is otherwise accessible, so other authorities can rely on s. 21 for this information. If an authority has passed on information to the BVD itself and knows the details will be published, they will be able to rely on s. 22 (the exemption for future publication) until the details are published.[25]

Section 41
Information provided by the deceased in confidence to medical professionals, social workers or others may be protected by s. 41, as long as the disclosure would be actionable.[26] This exemption was successfully used to protect information about the tax affairs of James Bond creator Ian Fleming over 50 years after his death.[27]

Section 38
It may be that disclosure would, or would be likely to, endanger the mental health of a living individual if the information is sufficient to cause them significant distress, particularly if it can be shown that disclosure would exacerbate an existing condition (e.g. depression, anxiety). However, the FTT has shown a reluctance to accept this argument in the absence of specific evidence.[28]

Section 31
Disclosure might facilitate the commission of a crime in some circumstances. For example, if a person has recently died, disclosure of their address might assist criminals or squatters to identify an empty property, or assist those perpetrating identity fraud.[29]

Section 40
While the personal information exemption cannot be used to protect information specifically about the deceased, it can be used to protect any information about relatives and other living individuals that may be found in their records.[30] If there is doubt about whether someone is dead, s. 40 may still apply – as was found to be the case following press reports of the death of 'Jihadi John'.[31]

Summing up

- The personal information exemptions in both the FOIA and the EIR are designed to prevent a conflict between the right to access information and the GDPR (and the DPA 2018).
- The exemptions apply where the information meets the definition of personal information in the GDPR (or the DPA 2018).
- Handle requests about an applicant for their own data under subject access rules in the GDPR and the DPA 2018. The data is exempt from disclosure under the FOIA and the EIR.
- The most common way to refuse requests for third-party data is to argue that disclosure would be unfair and/or unlawful.
- In assessing fairness, it is appropriate to consider the reasonable expectations of the affected individual(s).
- In assessing lawfulness, it is necessary to consider the legitimate interests of the applicant and whether the rights of individuals override those legitimate interests.
- Information about the deceased is not covered by the personal information exemptions, but can often be protected using other exemptions.

Chapter 7

Records and archives

Introduction

As discussed in previous chapters, s. 46 of the FOIA requires that the secretary of state at the Department for Digital, Culture, Media and Sport (DCMS) issue a code of practice on managing records. At the time of the Act's passage, this duty fell to the Lord Chancellor, and the preface to the s. 46 code contains his explanation as to why such a code was felt necessary:

> Freedom of information legislation is only as good as the quality of the records and other information to which it provides access. Access rights are of limited value if information cannot be found when requested or, when found, cannot be relied upon as authoritative.[1]

In many authorities, this link between records management and the FOIA has been recognised in the bringing together of the corporate responsibilities for both in one person or team: the FOI officer may also be the authority's records manager, or at least work alongside them. As well as these obvious connections between records management and the FOIA, the latter has implications for historical archives and vice versa. In many cases, exemptions can only be applied until the point that a record becomes a 'historical record'.[2] Records preserved for future historical research remain subject to the FOIA, and archivists responsible for their care need to understand the implications of that for their work.

FOI officers need to understand their authority's approach to records management. They may even be responsible for it, or involved in developing it. They also need to know whether records are likely to be retained in historical archives preserved by their authority, and what the implications are for FOIA compliance.

What is a record?

The official definition of a record can be found in the international standard on records management, ISO 15489. A record is: 'information created, received and maintained as evidence and as an asset by an organisation or person, in pursuit of legal obligations or in the transaction of business'.[3]

In essence though, most of those words could be deleted. One word in that paragraph sums up what a record is: evidence. Records are evidence of the fact that you paid for a service; that you fulfilled your part of a contract; that your boss told you to do something; or that you did it.

In Chapter 2, the definition of 'information' was discussed. As noted there, the FOIA does not provide a right to access documents or records (though many FOI laws around the world do), but to information. However, there is a close relationship between records and the information that they contain, and as was also demonstrated in Chapter 2, it is often impossible to separate the two.

Records need to have the qualities of reliability, authenticity, integrity and usability. They are no use if they can't be accessed whenever they are required, or if there are suggestions that they may have been faked or tampered with, or if nobody can actually read or understand them. The process of ensuring that records have these qualities is described as records management. As the quotation in the introduction to this chapter suggests, there is an important link between records management and the FOIA, and this link is formalised by the s. 46 code of practice.

The section 46 code and enforcement

The current code was drafted by staff of TNA in 2009. The first part of the code describes the essential components of a records management programme. The second part provides a guide for public records bodies as to how they should fulfill their obligations to transfer records to TNA under the Public Records Act 1958 (PRA) or the Public Record Office of Northern Ireland under the Public Records Act (Northern Ireland) 1923. The following sections summarise and explain the code's requirements. For brevity's sake, the rules in Northern Ireland are not described here; they are broadly similar to those for the UK.

Like the s. 45 code, the s. 46 code of practice is not a statutory code as such – failure to comply with its provisions does not constitute a breach of the Act, though the Information Commissioner can issue a practice recommendation to an authority identifying how it is in breach of the code (s. 48). This has only been done twice in relation to records management, both times in 2009, when the

Department of Health and Nottingham City Council received one each following audits carried out by TNA staff at the request of the Commissioner. Since then, the ICO has moved to using 'undertakings' to highlight bad practice by public authorities. The Commissioner has agreed to consult TNA before issuing either a practice recommendation or an undertaking relating to records management.[4]

What Part 1 of the code requires

Organisational arrangements

The code recommends the identification of records management as 'a core corporate function' – something to which resources need to be allocated. That might be a dedicated records manager or records management team, or – particularly for smaller authorities – adding records management to the responsibilities of another team. Roles, responsibilities and records-management-related risk should be identified. The code suggests that records management could be linked organisationally with FOI, data protection and re-use compliance. It also calls for an individual at board level to be identified as a 'records management champion'. Guidance and procedures should be published and managers made aware that they are responsible for ensuring that their teams maintain adequate records. New IT systems should be designed with good records management in mind, for example by providing appropriate security measures and audit trails. Staff should be trained to keep good records and a sufficiently resourced records management programme should be in place.

Records management policy

There should be a policy setting out the authority's approach to records management, endorsed by senior management. At a minimum it should include:

- a commitment to create, keep and manage records
- an outline of the role of records management and how it links to other corporate priorities
- an explanation of the relationship between records management and other policies
- details of roles and responsibilities
- details of how compliance is monitored.

The code and the Information Commissioner recommend that records management policies should be published (in the Commissioner's case, specifying that it should be included in an authority's publication scheme guide).

Identify records needed

Given the current absence of any 'duty to document' in UK law,[5] the closest we come to this is the requirement in the code that public authorities should identify what records are needed for 'business, regulatory, legal and accountability purposes', and ensure that such records are kept. Business rules should identify:

- what records to keep
- who should keep them
- when to keep them
- what they should contain
- where to store them.

Around the world: a duty to document in Australia

Shortly after taking up her role as UK Information Commissioner in July 2016, Elizabeth Denham gave a speech proposing a 'duty to document' for the UK.[6] This would require public authorities to keep specified records – essentially placing the requirement to identify records set out in the s. 46 code on a statutory footing.

One example of such a law in practice can be found in the Australian state of Queensland, where s. 7 of the Public Records Act 2002 requires:

Making and keeping of public records

(1) A public authority must—

   (a) make and keep full and accurate records of its activities; and

   (b) have regard to any relevant policy, standards and guidelines made by the archivist about the making and keeping of public records.

(2) The executive officer of a public authority must ensure the public authority complies with subsection (1).

Records systems for storage and retrieval

Records should be retained in appropriate storage systems that facilitate their ready retrieval. At one time there was a trend towards moving records from the system they were created in into an electronic records management system.

Nowadays the favoured approach is to keep records within the system that they were created in, but ensure that those systems are designed to assist with their mid- to long-term management. For example, they might provide for the automatic deletion of data in line with retention policies. They should record metadata about records such as file title, author, date created or closed. It should ideally be possible to track who has accessed, amended or deleted a record and when.

Retention and disposal policies

The more records are retained, the more work is involved in answering FOI requests, and the more uncontrolled risk an organisation is exposed to. It is good practice to adopt a retention schedule, outlining the kinds of records that are retained by an authority, how long to retain them, and what to do with them at the end of that period. Some records may be of permanent value as a historical resource, and records managers should make arrangements for them with an archivist or record office. The vast majority of records will need to be deleted or destroyed once their original purpose has expired. Importantly, from a FOIA perspective, retention schedules assist a public authority in proving to applicants, and the Information Commissioner, that records are no longer held as a result of a carefully thought out policy, rather than as a response to fears of disclosure through the FOIA.

Retention schedules need to be supplemented by procedures or systems that ensure their implementation. An annual review of paper files can help identify those records that are due for disposal. As suggested earlier, digital systems may facilitate automatic deletion of records in line with an automated retention schedule, or simply flag records that are due for review. At the very least they should allow for records to be deleted manually.

Records should be disposed of securely. In particular, paper records should be shredded or removed by a contractor under strict conditions for secure destruction. Old computer equipment should similarly be disposed of with care. In 2012, Brighton & Sussex University Hospitals NHS Trust received a monetary penalty of £325,000 from the Information Commissioner after a contractor auctioned off their old computers, which were found by purchasers still to hold information about patients.[7]

Metadata – data about the records – should be retained to indicate what was destroyed and when. This might be a record in a database or on a file list for paper records. For digital records, it is good practice to design systems so that a record 'stub' is retained including basic details of the record, including when and why it was destroyed.

Third-party records management

If services are outsourced, it is necessary to ensure that contractors maintain records to the same standards. Contractual provisions should include requirements for record keeping.

Monitor compliance and effectiveness

Progress with the records management programme should be monitored and reported to senior management. TNA provides a self-assessment tool to assist with the task of monitoring compliance with the code.

The gist: does the FOIA need – or lead to – good records management?
The preface to the s. 46 code makes the link between FOIA compliance and records management, and many records managers believed that the FOIA was an opportunity to improve records management in their authorities. The reality hasn't always lived up to expectations though.

If the FOIA requires good records management, it might be expected that the Commissioner and the courts would penalise failures in this area, particularly if they prevent individuals from accessing information. As mentioned earlier, the Information Commissioner did in fact issue two practice recommendations in 2009, calling on the Department of Health and Nottingham City Council respectively to improve their records management. None have been issued since, though several decision notices have criticised poor record keeping.

Imagine if an authority explained that it was refusing an FOI request because its poor records management made it impossible for staff to answer a request within the cost limit. Surely this would not be accepted as an explanation by the courts?

In fact, cases that have reached the tribunals have found that there is no obligation to keep or manage records – only to provide what is held and can be found within the cost limit, as explained by a judge in the Upper Tribunal: 'The fact is that the FOIA is about the citizen's right to information. . . . It is not a statute that prescribes any particular organisational structure or record-keeping practice in public authorities.'[8]

In practice, many FOI officers have found that they rely more on the knowledge of colleagues than on efficient filing systems, as discussed in Chapter 12.[9]

At the same time, as a result of the resources devoted to answering FOI requests less time is available to work on improving records management, especially as often the same person or team is responsible for both.[10] There are even historians, such as Peter Hennessy, who believe that fewer records are kept as a result of the FOIA: 'FOI, to be candid, is not an unmixed blessing for scholars because it has led to greater caution in what is written down.'[11]

Therefore, despite the claims of the Lord Chancellor in the s. 46 code's preface, the relationship between the FOIA and records management is not entirely positive.

The Public Records Act 1958 and Part 2 of the code

The PRA (and its Northern Ireland equivalent, the Public Records Act (Northern Ireland) 1923) established the framework for selection and transfer of (primarily at least) central government records to a permanent repository to facilitate future historical research. Schedule 1 of the PRA identifies 'public record bodies' as government departments, their agencies and arms-length type organisations like the ICO, as well as NHS bodies, and the courts. Public record bodies then are not the same as the much wider range of organisations that are described as 'public authorities' in the FOIA.

Public record bodies are expected to appraise and select records before transferring them to TNA or a 'place of deposit'. TNA operates an inspection regime under which certain repositories, such as record offices run by local authorities, hospitals or universities, can be authorised to act as such places of deposit.

Part 2 of the s. 46 code sets out the procedure that public record bodies are expected to follow when selecting and transferring records in line with their PRA obligations. The inclusion of these rules within the s. 46 code was a recognition that the FOIA eroded conventions around public records selected for permanent preservation. In particular, the code advises public record bodies to 'ensure that public records become available at the earliest possible time in accordance with the Act and the EIR'.

The code requires public record bodies to put in place arrangements for the selection of records for permanent preservation. Those records that are selected must normally be transferred to TNA or a place of deposit by the time they become 'historical records'. A process exists whereby public record bodies can apply to TNA to delay transfers to their custody. In these cases, a body called the Advisory Council on National Records and Archives (ACNRA) decides whether to allow this (technically, ACNRA advise the secretary of state, but in practice it is their decision). Public record bodies can also ask for records to remain closed on transfer to TNA or places of deposit. In the case of transfers to the TNA, the public body has to submit a schedule for consideration by ACNRA setting out why the records should be closed and which exemptions would be relevant if a request for access were to be received.

Staff in public record bodies are responsible for preparing materials for transfer, and ensuring that they are transferred securely. Records that are transferred as 'open' are deemed available to the public, as are records whose 'closure' period has expired. FOI requests for information held by TNA or places of deposit are always handled on a case-by-case basis – so even 'closed' records might be disclosed if an exemption is found no longer to apply, or the public interest favours disclosure at the time of the request.

Around the world: FOI and records management in Scotland

As with the FOIA, FOI(S)A requires a code of practice to be issued on managing records (s. 61). Just as with the UK code, it is split into two parts, with the first part setting out good records management practice. As might be expected, this covers very similar ground to the s. 46 code, with a very familiar nine 'key elements' (like those listed in 'What Part 1 of the code requires' earlier in this chapter). Part 2 is also similar, but applies both to public records bodies that are required to transfer records to the Keeper of the Records of Scotland at the National Records of Scotland, and to other public authorities transferring historical records to a public sector archive.[12]

In 2007, an inquiry into historic abuse in Scotland's children's homes reported that its work had been impeded by poor records management. The same issue had also prevented former residents of these homes from accessing records about their care. The report resulted in a review of the existing public records laws in Scotland, and ultimately in the Public Records (Scotland) Act 2011.

Specified Scottish public authorities, including the Scottish Government, local authorities, the police and NHS bodies, are required to seek approval from the Keeper of the Records of Scotland for a 'records management plan', which they must implement. The plan has to identify the authority's functions and what records they keep to support them, and include policies on storage, retention, disposal and security of their records, as well as arrangements for selection and transfer of historical records. In the same way that the UK ICO has introduced a model publication scheme under the FOIA, the Keeper has produced a model plan and advises authorities on what they expect to see in records management plans.

The FOIA and 'historical records'

When the FOIA was passed, s. 62(1) of the FOIA made clear that a record 'becomes a "historical record" at the end of the period of 30 years beginning with the year following that in which it was created'. That period of 30 years was reduced to 20 years by the Constitutional Reform and Governance Act 2010.[13] In order to manage the transition from 30 to 20 years, a further ministerial order set out when a record will become a historical record between 2013 and 2022 (Table 7.1 opposite).[14]

Aside from dictating when to transfer records selected for permanent preservation by public record bodies to TNA and places of deposit, there are serious implications for all public authorities of records becoming 'historical'.

Table 7.1 *Transitional arrangements for move from 30-year to 20-year rule for public records in the UK*

Year record was created	Year record becomes 'historical record'
1984	2013
1985	2014
1986	2014
1987	2015
1988	2015
1989	2016
1990	2016
1991	2017
1992	2017
1993	2018
1994	2018
1995	2019
1996	2019
1997	2020
1998	2020
1999	2021
2000	2021
2001	2022

How long do exemptions last?

Several exemptions in the FOIA cease to have effect once a record becomes 'historical':

- s. 30(1) – criminal investigations and proceedings
- s. 32 – court records
- s. 33 – audit functions
- s. 35 – policy formulation and development by government departments
- s. 36 – effective conduct of public affairs (outside Northern Ireland)
- s. 42 – legal professional privilege.

If a request covers information that might at one time have been covered by one of these exemptions, it is necessary to identify an alternative exemption, or to disclose the information.

Other exemptions survive longer, but no exemption is eternal. The lifespan of some other exemptions is specified in the FOIA:

- s. 28 – relations within the UK (30 years)
- s. 31 – prejudice to law enforcement etc. (100 years)
- s. 37(1)(a)–(ac) – communications with the sovereign, their two closest heirs, and other members of the royal family (5 years after the death of the individual(s) in the royal family involved in the communication or 20 years after the information was created, whichever is latest)
- s. 37(1)(ad) – communications with the royal household (5 years after the death of the sovereign reigning when the information was created or 20 years after the information was created, whichever is the latest)
- s. 37(1)(b) – honours or dignities conferred by the Crown (60 years)
- s. 36 – effective conduct of public affairs (in Northern Ireland) (30 years)
- s. 43 – trade secrets and commercial interests (30 years).

Even where no time limit is specified, the effectiveness of exemptions inevitably fades over time. For the most part, where an exemption is prejudice-based, it is likely that any potential for prejudice will decline over time, making it more difficult to justify the exemption the longer it is since the events in question. Similarly, in the case of qualified exemptions, the public interest in withholding information will decline over time. Since the exemption relating to s. 40 only applies to personal information, and the GDPR specifically excludes the dead from its coverage, the efficacy of the exemption has the same lifespan as the individual affected. Confidentiality obligations do not last forever, either; as Wadham and Griffiths put it, exemptions such as ss. 30(2), 41 and 43(1) are 'subject to an inherent trend towards obsolescence'.[15]

Archivists and the FOIA

TNA is not the only destination for records selected for permanent preservation in the public sector. A significant proportion of local authorities provide archive services, for example, and many universities and hospitals also house record offices. Some of these are PRA places of deposit, and archivists should note the requirements of Part 2 of the code in these circumstances.

Not all records transferred to record offices are subject to the FOIA's obligations. Records 'deposited' by private sector bodies may not automatically be subject to the FOIA (it depends on the terms of the deposit, as the records may be held 'on behalf of' the depositing body). TNA have published guidance to assist archivists in assessing whether privately deposited records are subject to the FOIA (www.nationalarchives.gov.uk/documents/information-management/guidance_private_archives.pdf).

Records that have been 'gifted' or 'donated' to a public authority's record office are normally subject to the FOIA, whatever the original source. In addition, records that have been transferred by the record office's own authority are subject to the FOIA.

Records deposited by another public authority are subject to the FOIA, and it is necessary therefore for the deposit agreement to include instructions for how to handle requests in these circumstances.

Managing FOIA obligations in an archive

Effectively, all the tools that are normally available to public authorities in the FOIA are at the disposal of archivists when it comes to handling FOI requests. The biggest challenge for archivists is when requests are received for information contained in uncatalogued material. If records have been transferred in a well ordered state, indexed or listed, it may not be difficult to identify and locate requested information. However, if it is poorly organised, there are obvious problems. In these circumstances, the archivist can use the cost limit or other mechanisms set out in the Act (or indeed in the EIR) to manage requests. If it would cost more than the appropriate limit to establish whether information is held, to locate it, to retrieve it or to extract it, the request can be refused. If the problem would be the necessity of reading through a significant quantity of material to establish whether exemptions apply to it, it may be possible to use the provisions set out at s. 14 of the FOIA (or reg. 12(4)(b) of the EIR).

If a cataloguing plan is in place, this could be used as evidence that records are intended for future publication, allowing the use of the exemption at s. 22 of the FOIA. According to the Information Commissioner's guidance on the exemption, as long as record office facilities meet the following requirements, an intention to make records available there can count as 'publication':

- clearly advertised
- readily available
- accessible, and
- easy for the public to use (e.g. by providing catalogues and indexes).[16]

Similarly, once records have been made available for public access, the exemption for information that is reasonably accessible (s. 21) is often available. This is not the case for records in TNA, but other public authorities and record offices can use it. For example, Wark Parish Council used it when an applicant requested access to parish council minutes that had been transferred to the county record office.[17] Section 21 does not apply, however, if a record office is not readily accessible to the applicant, for example, if the records are only accessible by physically attending the record office, and the applicant could not reasonably be expected to do so.

Until the point that they cease to have effect, as described earlier in this chapter, other exemptions may apply to transferred records. Where this is the case, a refusal notice has to be issued as in other circumstances. One particular issue for archivists is the existence of personal information within records in their custody. Once a person dies, this problem usually comes to an end, but in many cases, data is retained on large numbers of individuals, and it is practically impossible for archivists to know for sure when each one dies.

It is therefore necessary for archivists to make assumptions, and the Code of Practice for Archivists and Records Managers under s. 51(4) of the Data Protection Act 1998,[18] provides some assistance with this. It suggests the following:

- Assume a lifespan of 100 years.
- If the age of an adult data subject is not known, assume that he was 16 at the time of the records [*sic*].
- If the age of a child data subject is not known, assume he was less than 1 at the time of the records.[19]

If an individual could still be alive based on these criteria, archivists can continue to apply the personal information exemption. Even if someone is likely to have died, it is possible that certain information about them may remain confidential for a period, such as:

- details of infirmity or other health-related information;
- information about family relationships which would usually have been kept secret, for example: information that a child who was being raised as the child of the head of the household was in fact the offspring (perhaps illegitimate) of another family member;
- information relating to very young children who were born in prison and whose birthplace is not recorded on their birth certificate.[20]

There may be circumstances in which it would be appropriate to allow access to information that would be exempt under the FOIA outside the FOIA regime. For example, the Code of Practice for Archivists and Records Managers suggests that researchers should be asked to sign an agreement to comply with the DPA 1998 (now replaced by the GDPR) in relation to any personal information that they find in a collection. The important point here is that the data is not being disclosed through the FOIA, and exemptions continue to apply to it.

Summing up
- Records are evidence, and records management is the process of putting in place controls to ensure the reliability, authenticity, integrity and usability of this evidence.
- Section 46 of the FOIA links good records management to FOIA compliance.
- Part 1 of the records management code of practice outlines a framework for a good records management programme.
- Part 2 of the code sets out how public records bodies should comply with their obligations to select and transfer records to TNA or places of deposit.
- The FOIA established the concept of 'historical records' in law for all public authorities.
- The point at which records become historical is in transition, but will be 20 years after the last record on a file was created from 2022.
- Exemptions do not last forever; the FOIA specifies a lifespan for many of them.
- The terms on which records are transferred to a record office determine whether they are subject to the FOIA.
- Archivists may face challenges due to the state of some records transfers – they should use the provisions available in the FOIA to manage their obligations effectively.
- Making records available in a record office can count as 'publication' for the purposes of ss. 21 and 22 of the FOIA.
- Other exemptions may apply until the point that they expire.
- Archivists should be particularly careful about requests for access to records containing personal or confidential data.

Chapter 8

Publication schemes and proactive disclosure

Introduction

> If Publication Schemes are still the Cinderella of the freedom of information
> regime, only the Information Commissioner has the magic wand to make a
> dazzling transformation.[1]

There are two main duties under the FOIA, but one tends to get neglected.
Originally the concept of the publication scheme was intended to be central to
the FOIA's workings, but in practice it has tended to be overshadowed by the
duty to provide information on request. 'Pull' has predominated over 'push'.

Despite this, publication schemes are an important part of the FOIA, and if
anything their role is expanding. They are increasingly seen as a tool to meet
other requirements under the EIR and re-use rules. From the FOI officer's
perspective, if nothing else, they can assist in managing the burden of FOI
requests.

Indeed there is renewed emphasis on proactive disclosure. The UK
Information Commissioner has spoken of the need to 'augment the request-
based, and, frankly, reactive model of openness that exists under our FOI laws'.[2]
In March 2016 the UK's Independent Commission on Freedom of Information
recommended there should be more proactive publication and that the
government should give the Information Commissioner 'responsibility for
monitoring and ensuring public authorities' compliance with their proactive
publication obligations'.[3] The new s. 45 code of practice for the first time contains
a section on publication schemes.[4]

At the same time, there has been a rise in other duties to publish proactively.
While FOI officers may not be directly responsible for compliance with other

legal requirements, they need to be aware of them, and publication schemes need to refer to information made available through other transparency laws.

What the FOIA says about publication schemes

The requirement to adopt a publication scheme is set out in Part I of the Act, at s. 19. It requires that public authorities 'adopt and maintain a scheme', publish information in line with their scheme, and keep it under review. Publication schemes must specify the classes of information that they publish, make clear how they will be published, and state whether they are subject to charges.

Authorities are also expected to review their schemes regularly with 'regard to the public interest' in 'allowing public access to information held by the authority' and 'in the publication of reasons for decisions made by the authority'.

Section 19 goes on to set out the Commissioner's powers to review and approve schemes. Amendments made by the Protection of Freedoms Act 2012 added the responsibility to list datasets that have been disclosed under the FOIA in authorities' publication schemes unless it is not appropriate to do so.

Section 20 of the Act enables the Information Commissioner to adopt a model publication scheme for particular classes of public authority. The Commissioner has to give six months' notice if she wishes to withdraw approval for a scheme.

The model publication scheme

In 2009, the then UK Commissioner took advantage of his powers under s. 20 of the FOIA and adopted a model publication scheme, mandating it for the whole public sector. Every public authority now has to adopt the Commissioner's scheme and needs special permission to depart from it.

The Commissioner's model publication scheme consists of seven classes:

- who we are and what we do
- what we spend and how we spend it
- what our priorities are and how we are doing
- how we make decisions
- our policies and procedures
- lists and registers
- the services we offer.[5]

Public authorities work differently and create different information. Therefore the ICO publishes a 'definition document' for each part of the public sector outlining what information to publish under each of the above headings. FOI officers should regularly review their publication schemes against the relevant definition document to ensure they are publishing the right information.

Publication scheme guides

Technically the model publication scheme is an authority's publication scheme, but the ICO expects public authorities to publish a publication scheme 'guide to information', preferably on their website.[6] This takes the headings from the model scheme and supplements them with the categories set out in the relevant definition document. Under the relevant headings, FOI officers should provide links to the documents that can be found on their websites. If any information is not available via the website, the guide should explain how applicants can obtain it, for example, they might advise applicants to complete a form or visit the authority's premises.

Importantly, the guide needs to spell out whether information is only available for a fee. Any charges must be justified, clear and transparent. Examples include where there is a statutory requirement to make charges, and printing, copying and postage charges. If an authority makes information available commercially (for example, TNA has a bookshop, and public sector museums commonly publish books and make them available for purchase), it needs to describe these in its publication scheme guide and make clear what charges are made (which might be by linking to a catalogue of publications). If information has been collected and analysed for commercial purposes, using professional time and skill, this could be charged for (see 'The gist: the reasonable charge of £1550').

The gist: the reasonable charge of £1550
Matthew Davis v Information Commissioner and the Health and Social Care Information Centre, EA/2012/0175, 24 January 2013

Matthew Davis, a journalist, asked the Health and Social Care Information Centre (HSCIC) for data on drug dependent mothers. The HSCIC refused the request under s. 21 on the basis that details of their charges for statistics were provided in their publication scheme. They had adopted the ICO's model publication scheme so, in effect, the scheme – and by extension the charges made under it – had been approved by the Information Commissioner. The HSCIC operated a system of cost recovery for providing data analysis services and in this case quoted £1550 to provide the data that Mr Davis was interested in. Despite this high cost, the FTT drew the following conclusions:

- The data was reasonably accessible by virtue of being listed in HSCIC's publication scheme.

- Therefore it was up to the ICO to decide whether a cost was reasonable under FOIA provisions that applied to publication schemes, not those relating to requests.
- Even if it was within the FTT's jurisdiction to rule, their view was that it was reasonable to seek to recover the cost of such extensive analysis from private members of the public rather than the taxpayer.

Datasets rules

The Protection of Freedoms Act 2012 amended the FOIA to the effect that an applicant was able to specify that a requested dataset be disclosed in a re-usable format. These changes also required that disclosed datasets be made available for wider use through the authority's publication scheme. It was now required that the published dataset be kept up to date (unless it was 'not appropriate' to do so). In practice, few public authorities appear to have judged it 'appropriate' to keep datasets up to date (most likely for logistical reasons), but many have provided dataset repositories on their websites.

The new s. 45 code of practice and publication schemes

The original s. 45 code of practice was silent on publication schemes. The new code, published in July 2018, reinforces that authorities should use the Commissioner's model publication scheme and adopt a publication scheme guide.[7]

More radically, following a recommendation in the report of the Independent Commission on Freedom of Information in March 2016, the code now specifies that certain information be published via the publication scheme guide. First, public authorities with more than 100 full-time equivalent employees should publish the following data each quarter:

- the number of requests received
- the number of requests received during the period that have not yet been processed
- the number of requests processed in full within the period, including:
  - the number of requests answered within 20 working days
  - the number of requests where the deadline was extended to consider the public interest test
  - the number of requests that were answered late
- the number of requests where information was granted in full
- the number of requests where information was refused in full
- the number of requests where the information was partially refused
- the number of internal reviews (which can be reported annually).

The code goes on to state that it 'is for individual public authorities to decide whether they wish to publish more detailed information', such as a breakdown of the exemptions applied or outcomes of internal reviews.

Second, data on senior executive pay, expenses and benefits in kind should be published. The code does not strictly define 'senior executive' but indicates that at a minimum it should include those at management board level. It suggests that pay and benefits should be published annually, and expenses published quarterly. Local authorities in England are already expected to publish much of this sort of information under the Local Government Transparency Code, and government departments also already publish it. The s. 45 code is effectively extending those expectations to other public authorities.

The EIR

The EIR don't refer to publication schemes, but reg. 4 states that a public authority shall:

(a) progressively make [environmental] information available to the public by electronic means which are easily accessible; and

(b) take reasonable steps to organise the information relevant to its functions with a view to the active and systematic dissemination to the public of the information.

This sounds a lot like a publication scheme. Indeed, the Information Commissioner recommends that public authorities fulfill the obligations at reg. 4 by including environmental information within their publication schemes. Regulation 4 even spells out what to include: 'facts and analyses of facts which the public authority considers relevant and important in framing major environmental policy proposals'.

Information referred to in article 7(2) of directive 2003/4/EC (the Environmental Information Directive underlying the regulations) should also be published: texts of treaties; policies, plans and programmes; progress reports on their implementation; reports and data on the state of the environment; authorisations with a significant impact on the environment; and environmental impact studies and risk assessments.

If an authority wants to charge for environmental information, it must publish a schedule giving the relevant costs. The publication scheme is an obvious candidate for this schedule.

Around the world: publication schemes and proactive disclosure

A similar approach to the UK is taken in Ireland and Scotland, where publication schemes are mandatory and, just as with the UK, a model scheme has been mandated by the regulator or the government. The model schemes are similar to the UK's but a little more detailed.

Scotland's scheme has nine classes of information, including 'How we manage our human, physical and information resources', 'How we procure goods and services', 'Our commercial publications' and 'Our open data'. The Scottish Commissioner provides detailed guidance on its implementation, with the *Model Publication Scheme: guide for Scottish public authorities* fulfilling the same role as the ICO's definition documents in the UK, spelling out what to publish as a minimum under each class. It also sets out six principles of the model publication scheme:

- Information should be available online where possible or alternatives offered.
- Information covered by the model publication scheme can be exempt from disclosure, but refusals to provide it must be explained.
- The conditions applying to copyright and re-use of disclosed information must be explained.
- Any guide to information must include a schedule of charges.
- The guide must include contact details for enquiries and to obtain advice and assistance.
- Once published, information should be available for at least two years.[8]

In the Isle of Man, the FOI Act does not require authorities to adopt a publication scheme, but they are encouraged to do so, and the Manx code of practice provides guidance on what should be included if one is adopted.

The European Union's access to information law, Regulation 1049/2001, does not specifically require EU institutions to adopt a publication scheme, but certain documents have to be published, including a register of documents.

Maltese government departments do not have to adopt a publication scheme but have to publish details of their structure, categories of documents held, and details of how to make a request, including the contact details for the department's FOI officer.

Australia's FOI Act requires the publication of an information publication scheme. The Act itself outlines what must be published, including details of the organisation's structure, information which is routinely made available in answer to requests, and operational information (policies and procedures in relation to the work of the body concerned). New Zealand's Official Information Act (which only covers central government) requires the Ministry of Justice to publish information about the structure of government departments, what information they hold and how to make requests.

In the USA, the federal FOI Act requires government agencies to publish similar information to New Zealand's Official Information Act. An amendment to the FOI Act in 1996, known as 'E-FOIA', required the creation of 'electronic reading rooms'. Documents that have been requested more than three times are expected to be made available in these online repositories.

India's Right to Information Act lists a whole range of information that must be published by public authorities, including the sorts of information held, details of their responsibilities and manuals, policies and procedures that are followed in the execution of them, directories of their employees, monthly remuneration of employees, and contact details for making requests.

Publication schemes and the FOIA exemptions

Section 21 of the FOIA allows public authorities to refuse requests if the information is reasonably accessible to the requester. Sections 22 and 22A can be applied in circumstances where the authority intends to publish information in the future.

These provisions provide an incentive to publish information proactively. Doing so not only benefits those with an interest in the matter, but also helps public authorities to manage resources effectively. If there are statistics which are published annually, not only can the applicant be referred to those already available (technically refusing to provide them under s. 21), but any request for more recent figures can be turned down on the basis that they will be published later under s. 22. There is a public interest in public authorities being able to manage their resources effectively and not being rushed into preparing statistics earlier than planned.

Section 11 of the FOIA requires information to be provided in a form specified by the applicant if it is reasonably practicable to do so. The same is true of reg. 6 of the EIR. However, if the information is already reasonably accessible, e.g. through a publication scheme, the authority does not need to do this.[9]

The exemptions at ss. 21 and 22 apply even when the information is published by other organisations (though the information must also be held by the authority itself for s. 21 to be a valid means of refusal). Environmental information that another body is working on but has not yet completed at the point that a request is received may similarly be refused under reg. 12(4)(d) of the EIR. Developing a knowledge of the wider sector's publishing patterns can assist in reducing the amount of work involved in answering commonly received requests.

Remember that s. 21 even applies where the information is only available for a charge (see 'The gist: the reasonable charge of £1550' earlier in this chapter). Public authorities can charge for information as long as it is listed in their publication scheme.

Other proactive transparency requirements in the UK

On top of transparency requirements in the FOIA and the EIR, there are other requirements, sometimes affecting only certain types of public sector bodies. The most notable examples are discussed below.

Open data

There has recently been an emphasis on 'open data' from the UK Government and internationally. The UK Government has sought to identify itself as a leader in this area, particularly through its involvement in the Open Government Partnership (opengovpartnership.org). The most tangible representation of this in the UK has been the growth of datastores. Central government has led the way with data.gov.uk, but there are now many such repositories, for example data.london.gov.uk (maintained by the GLA) and data.police.uk (providing access to data about policing across the UK). Some authorities even publish their FOI performance statistics and disclosure logs via these datastores.

Central government corporate transparency commitments

A series of consultations and announcements during the coalition government of 2010–2015 sought to open up government through a more proactive approach to transparency. Leadership on this issue was originally with the Cabinet Office, and it was famously championed by the Minister for the Cabinet Office, Francis Maude MP. Enthusiasm appeared to have waned under Prime Minister Theresa May's government, and responsibility for these policies was moved to the DCMS in April 2018.[10] Nonetheless, government departments are expected to publish the following information:

- civil service sickness and absence data (published centrally by the DCMS)
- ministers' interest declarations (published centrally by the DCMS)
- ministers' salary data (published centrally by the DCMS)
- senior civil servants' names, grades, job titles and annual pay rates (published centrally by the DCMS)
- special advisers' names, grades and annual pay (published centrally by the DCMS)
- central government contracts over £10,000
- central government spending over £25,000
- government major projects portfolio data
- senior responsible owners of government major projects portfolio data
- ministerial gifts, hospitality, travel and meetings
- monthly payment card data over £500

- non-consolidated performance related pay
- organograms
- prompt payment data
- senior civil servants' business appointment applications
- senior officials' business expenses, hospitality and meetings
- single departmental plans
- special advisers' gifts, hospitality and meetings
- spend control data
- trade union facility time
- workforce management information.[11]

The Equality Act 2010 and the Equality Act 2010 (Gender Pay Gap Information) Regulations 2017

Organisations with 250 or more employees have to publish certain information on their gender pay gap. This requirement attracted a lot of publicity in early 2018 when the first deadline for publishing information was reached, prompting a rush of disclosures.[12]

The INSPIRE Regulations (SI 2009/3157 and SI 2012/1672)

The Infrastructure for Spatial Information in the European Community (INSPIRE) Regulations implement European directive 2007/2/EC and apply to any organisation that is subject to the EIR, and anyone who holds data on behalf of one of those organisations. They cover spatial data, which according to the Information Commissioner is 'any data with a direct or indirect reference to a specific location or geographical area. Spatial data is often referred to as geospatial data or geographic information.'[13] The regulations require that certain standard metadata (or 'data about the data') be created about the relevant datasets, and that specified spatial data be made available to the public in a consistent format. The regulations are enforced by the Information Commissioner.

The Local Government Act 1972 and the Local Government (Access to Information) Act 1985

The original 1972 Act required certain records to be kept of council meetings and councillors' interests. The 1985 Act amended the earlier Act to require councils to allow the public access to meeting agendas, papers and minutes, and introduced exemptions to cover the specific circumstances in which these should not be disclosed. Later amendments brought these exemptions into line with the FOIA.

The Local Audit and Accountability Act 2014

The latest in a series of Acts requiring councils to allow inspection of their accounts by 'any persons interested', which is usually interpreted to mean local council tax payers, at the time of audit. The Local Audit (Public Access to Documents) Act 2017 adds that 'any journalist' including 'citizen journalists' should be allowed access. 'Accounts' are described in the legislation as 'the accounting records for the financial year to which the audit relates and all books, deeds, contracts, bills, vouchers, receipts and other documents relating to those records', and case law has reinforced that the right to inspection applies to a broad category of information.[14] There are protections for commercial confidentiality and personal information built into the Act.[15]

The Local Government Act 2000 and the Local Authority (Executive Arrangements) (Meetings and Access to Information) (England) Regulations 2012

The Local Government Act 2000 introduced new arrangements for local authorities in England, including the options of allowing directly elected mayors or a leader and cabinet of elected councillors to direct the operations of the council. As part of these changes, the same papers that had to be published about other council meetings were required of new executive meetings. The later regulations require public notice of executive meetings and 'key decisions' to be given 'on the relevant local authority's website, if it has one', specific records to be kept of decisions, and even copies of relevant documents to be supplied on request as long as the applicant pays the 'necessary charge for transmission'.

The Openness of Local Government Bodies Regulations 2014

The rules on giving public notice, providing copies of documents on websites and on request were extended to other council meetings. In addition, those attending council meetings were now allowed to film meetings, make audio recordings of them, and report on proceedings through social media. The following details of 'delegated decisions' (certain decisions taken by officers under delegated authority) must be published on the website and made available at council offices:

- the date the decision was taken
- a record of the decision with reasons

- the details of alternative options considered
- the name of any member who has declared a conflict of interest
- the background papers on the decision.

The Local Government Transparency Code

The Local Government Transparency Code,[16] first published by the Department for Communities and Local Government in 2014, requires English local authorities to publish certain information. Part 2 has statutory force: councils must publish the information listed in it. Each quarter they must publish:

- details of expenditure exceeding £500
- details of government procurement card transactions
- procurement information.

Each year they must publish details of:

- local authority land
- all grants to community organisations
- their organisation chart
- trade union facility time
- their parking revenues
- their controlled parking spaces
- their constitution
- their social housing assets.

They must give the following information on employee pay:

- the pay multiple (difference between lowest and highest earning staff)
- details of salaries of all staff earning over £50,000 in £5k bands, with job titles and responsibilities
- the names of those earning over £150,000.

The Police Reform and Social Responsibility Act 2011 and the Elected Local Policing Bodies (Specified Information) Order 2011 (as amended by the Elected Local Policing Bodies (Specified Information) (Amendment) Order 2012)

An elected local policing body (police and crime commissioners in most of the country) must publish information specified by the Home Secretary and other information to allow the public to assess the performance of the body and the relevant chief officer of police, including:

- the police and crime commissioner's name and contact details, salary, allowances, register of interests, and complaints brought to their attention
- numbers of staff, equalities data, organogram, details of senior staff, gifts and hospitality register
- information on income and all expenditure over £500
- contracts let by the police and crime commissioner or police force, including copies of those with a value exceeding £10,000
- date and time of public meetings, agenda, minutes and records of decisions made
- policies on conduct, records management and data sharing, decisions of significant public interest and qualifying disclosures
- copies of reports required from local authorities
- information on operation of arrangements for independent custody visitors.

Disclosure logs

A disclosure log is a published list of requests received and responded to by public authorities. These logs are not required by the FOIA, but they are considered good practice. The ICO recommends adopting them through their definition documents.[17] The Independent Commission on Freedom of Information recommended that they be made mandatory for public authorities with 100 or more full-time equivalent employees.[18] Notably this requirement was omitted from the s. 45 code of practice published in July 2018.[19]

Disclosure logs can take various forms. Sometimes authorities publish just a simple list of requests received (without the responses). An example of this approach can be seen on the House of Commons website, where annual lists of requests received are published in .pdf and .csv formats.[20] This is easy to prepare, but requires the potential applicant to make a request for the response if they are interested. Therefore it has limited value from the point of view of applicants, and FOI officers still have to process requests that might not have been necessary had the response been published.

A more useful disclosure log lists the questions asked together with the response provided, though any information that might allow an individual applicant to be identified should be redacted from the published request and response. A good example can be seen on the GLA website.[21] Requests can be sorted by category or by date. Clicking on a specific request leads to a page setting out the request itself and providing links to a redacted response and any disclosed documents.

Some FOI officers are sceptical of the value of disclosure logs, arguing that they are time consuming to produce, and that in any case applicants invariably ask for information in such a way that published responses cannot satisfactorily answer them. There are significant benefits to publishing responses in disclosure logs, however. It may prevent a request being made if the prospective applicant is able to find a previous response online before they submit a request for the same information. Even if it doesn't, s. 21 applies to information that is already published, and the request can be answered straightforwardly by providing a link to the previous response. Most public authorities have particular subjects that come up again and again in requests, so if they publish responses it is likely to save the FOI officer a lot of time.

If the disclosure log is difficult to search, the advantages to FOI officers and applicants may be lost. It should be structured in a logical fashion – usually by date of disclosure, with most recent disclosures at the top of the list – and ideally include some search functionality. HTML web pages are preferable to pdf documents in order to facilitate searches.

Summing up

- Publication schemes are a legal requirement under the FOIA and in many other jurisdictions.
- The ICO mandates a model publication scheme, made up of seven standard information classes, for all UK authorities.
- Definition documents flesh out the information that the ICO expects to see published by different kinds of public authority.
- Public authorities are expected to adopt and maintain a publication scheme guide, usually on their website, which provides access (either directly via links, or through instructions on how to access information not available online) to the information that they make available proactively. Structure the guide by referring to the model scheme and the relevant definition document.
- The publication scheme guide must set out any charges that will be made for information such as publications.
- Include links to disclosed datasets in publication scheme guides.
- The EIR require information to be made available proactively, and the publication scheme guide provides the obvious means to do this.
- Proactive publication of information may be required under other laws and public sector practices. This information should be included in an authority's publication scheme guide.
- It is considered good practice for public authorities to adopt disclosure logs as they can be a useful tool for FOI officers and applicants alike.

Chapter 9

Copyright and re-use of information

Introduction

Public authorities are subject to many obligations to make information available proactively. The FOIA's requirement to adopt a publication scheme is just one of these. Together with the duty to respond to requests under the FOIA, there are wide-ranging rights of access to public authority information.

However, access to information is just the start of the story. The next thing to consider is what people are allowed to do with the information they can access, whatever route they access it through. Intellectual property law, most notably copyright, applies to any use that recipients want to make of all this information.

Public authorities usually retain copyright in information that they or their employees have created, so in theory they have some control over what people do with disclosed information. In practice, there are limitations on this control.

Recent years have witnessed the rise of open data. Open data is partially about giving people access to more information through FOI and transparency laws, but also about giving them more freedom over how that information can then be used. Changes to the law such as the RoPSI Regulations 2015 have sought to do this.

Many FOI officers include standard text in responses warning applicants that they must seek permission before re-using disclosed information. Some have sought to use copyright as a means to constrain the effect of the FOIA. Developments in recent years have limited what FOI officers and their colleagues can do in this regard.

This chapter explores how copyright affects what people can do with information that they access from public authorities, what limits public authorities can place on this, and how the growth of open data is affecting FOI and transparency more generally. It aims to help FOI officers to better understand the relevance of copyright and re-use laws to their work.

Copyright

Copyright protects the rights of those who create original works. Articles, books, photographs, paintings, sculptures and even computer databases can attract copyright protection. Information disclosed by public authorities under the FOIA and other laws is often (though not always) protected by copyright.

Under UK law it is not necessary to take any specific action for copyright to apply. Most will be familiar with the copyright symbol and the statement '© Paul Gibbons 2018' or similar. However, providing this statement is not legally required for copyright to apply – it applies instantly when a document or other work is created. Normally the author of a work retains the copyright in it. If an individual takes a photograph, that person retains the copyright in that photograph and has a degree of control through the law over who can use it.

Unless otherwise stated in contracts of employment, it is usual for the copyright in work completed in the course of employment to belong to the employer. Therefore the copyright in e-mails, reports and other documents that may be created by public authority staff is the authority's copyright. Documents written by civil servants attract crown copyright, and those written or commissioned by officials of the House of Commons or House of Lords are protected by parliamentary copyright.

Not every piece of information disclosed by public authorities attracts copyright. Copyright only applies if:

- the (legal or natural) person claiming it created the information
- it is an original piece of work
- the information is recorded.

One expert comments that 'the author must have contributed quite a lot of their own ideas or skills to the making of the work'.[1] In addition to this, copyright can only be used to protect 'substantial' parts of a work. This doesn't necessarily mean a lot of the work, as it can cover significant (or important) parts of a document, even if they only make up a small proportion of the text. However, it can't be assumed that all disclosures of public authority information are protected by copyright.

If a public authority discloses a report written by its own officials it is protected by copyright, but copyright does not prevent the recipient reproducing a short extract from the report. For example, an authority may report annually on its performance against set performance indicators, including the proportion of FOI requests answered within 20 working days. If a member of the public writes a blogpost and quotes that figure, they will not breach the authority's copyright, since this figure will not be a 'substantial' part of the work.

There are limitations and exemptions on copyright. In some circumstances, it is possible for a work to be copied without it damaging the author, and it may well be in the wider interests of society that copying is allowed, which is known as 'fair dealing'. It covers non-commercial use, quotation, criticism and review, and news reporting. What is fair to reproduce differs from case to case. A commonly applied rule of thumb is that the reproduction of 5% of a work is fair in these circumstances.

Just as with the FOIA, the concept of public interest is important. It is hard to see a public authority taking successful action against a journalist for breach of copyright if the document they have reproduced exposes malpractice or a public safety risk.

Certain aspects of copyright protection can be assigned to others (a publisher perhaps), and copyright holders can also license use of works they have created, stating on what terms they are prepared to allow the re-use.

The key point here is that while copyright may apply to information disclosed by public authorities, it is not always the case. Sometimes the information is not substantial enough to attract copyright protection. Even if it does, in many cases it is entirely permissible for others to re-use a proportion of disclosed information without permission from the authority, depending on what they are doing with it. If there is a public interest in the dissemination of the information, it may be difficult to do anything about any breach of copyright. Any statement given to FOIA applicants, or on a public authority website, should reflect this reality.

Open data

Open data is defined as 'data that can be freely used, re-used and redistributed by anyone'.[2] In other words, it is not just about having access to data, but also being able to use it with as little restriction as possible. Placing limitations on the use of data, such as 'non-commercial use only', means that it cannot be open data.

Governments have embraced the concept of open data. While FOI laws have been hard won across the globe, it has been relatively easy to obtain political support for open data initiatives. This is perhaps because campaigners have made an economic case for open data successfully. Studies for the European Commission have suggested that open data could be worth billions of euros in growth across the European Union. Some studies suggest it could be worth US$ trillions in growth globally.[3]

Consider it this way. A commercial provider wants to create an app that helps the public to navigate public transport. A public authority has the dataset that would facilitate this, including timetables and real-time bus and train arrival data. The public want better information about available services. If the public authority were to create its own app, it costs money. If it allows the company to have access to the data and gives them permission to re-use it, then it is created at their cost. The public authority has not spent any more than it needed to for its own purposes, the company can charge the public for the app and hopefully thrive, and the public benefit by having better quality tools to help them get around. From a government's point of view this is a win-win-win situation.

> **The gist: the five-star open data rating system**
> The inventor of the world wide web, Sir Tim Berners-Lee, is a long-term promoter of open data. He developed a rating system for it. The UK Government has encouraged publication of data in line with the three-star rating, for example in its datastore at data.gov.uk and in transparency requirements such as the Local Government Transparency Code:
>
> - 1 star – available in any format (e.g. pdf) on the web (but with an open licence)
> - 2 stars – available as machine-readable structured data (e.g. Excel spreadsheet)
> - 3 stars – as for 2 stars but in a non-proprietary format (e.g. .csv)
> - 4 stars – all the above plus using open standards to identify individual records within the data so that it can be linked to by others
> - 5 stars – all the above plus the data is linked to data elsewhere to provide context.

Dataset rules

In 2012, the FOIA was amended by the Protection of Freedoms Act 2012 to the following effect:

- If an applicant asked for a dataset (raw data) in a re-usable form, the authority had to allow this as long as it was reasonably practicable to do so.
- If the authority or the Crown held the copyright in the dataset, it had to allow re-use under licence.
- If a dataset was requested, it had to be included in the authority's publication scheme, together with details of the conditions for its re-use.

A code of practice was issued under s. 45 covering how to approach these new rules. In particular, it identified three possible licences, developed by TNA, for re-use:

- a non-commercial re-use licence
- a charged use licence
- the Open Government Licence.

These rules now only apply to public authorities not subject to the RoPSI Regulations 2015.

The Open Government Licence

The Open Government Licence is the most widely used licence for permitting re-use across the public sector, and its use is encouraged by the Information Commissioner, among others. If a public authority adopts it, the licence effectively allows anyone to re-use specified information. It is simple for authorities to provide and all applicants have to do is acknowledge the public authority that created the information by using their preferred attribution statement (or one provided in the body of the licence itself), and if possible, provide a link to the licence.[4]

The Re-use of Public Sector Information Regulations 2015

Having an easy way to license re-use is handy, as for the most part UK public authorities are now required to do so. The RoPSI Regulations 2015 apply to UK public sector bodies (as with the FOIA and the EIR, the Scottish Government has adopted its own, very similar, regulations), and for the most part encapsulate the same authorities that are subject to the FOIA. The authorities must allow re-use if requested to do so unless affected documents were created by broadcasters, educational or research establishments, cultural establishments (other than libraries, museums and archives), are logos or crests, or consist of personal information. Information created by third parties (e.g. where the copyright is held by a contractor) and information exempt under the FOIA or EIR is also exempt.

Requests for re-use must be answered within 20 working days, just as with FOIA and EIR requests. Public bodies can charge for re-use but normally only the marginal costs of reproduction, production and dissemination of documents (trading funds, libraries, museums and archives are allowed to make a reasonable return on investment and cover costs and overheads). The RoPSI Regulations also require that a schedule listing information available for re-use be made available, together with guidance on how to make a complaint.

In practice, it appears that it may be difficult to justify charging for re-use in most circumstances. The Information Commissioner regulates the RoPSI Regulations. At the time of writing only two decisions have been made in relation to the regulations (FS50630368 and FS50619465), but in both cases the Commissioner ruled against the authority for unnecessarily restricting the re-use of the information concerned. This was because they had chosen not to use the Open Government Licence and had been unable to convince the regulator that alternative (more restrictive – including charging for re-use) terms were necessary.

Can FOIA provisions be used to protect copyright?

The Commissioner is not generally sympathetic to arguments that disclosure of information leads to breaches of copyright. The routine argument here is that if a person breaches a public authority's copyright once information is disclosed, the law provides mechanisms for authorities to seek redress. So, for instance, the ICO was unimpressed when the House of Commons sought to argue that it was not reasonable to disclose information via the website WhatDoTheyKnow (https://www.whatdotheyknow.com/) since the ensuing automatic publication of the disclosed information would breach parliamentary copyright (FS50276715). The Commissioner's argument was that copyright law provides a mechanism for the authority to pursue those who breach copyright, and that this can therefore be dealt with afterwards through the courts. It is not a reason to place limits on access to information.

This approach can also be seen in the regulator's consideration of a specific exception protecting intellectual property rights in the EIR. Searching decision notices on reg. 12(5)(c) on the ICO website, of 16 notices, not one use of the exception has been supported by the Commissioner.

The key to using the FOIA or EIR provisions to protect copyright is to demonstrate that the disclosure of information will not only breach copyright, but by so doing cause prejudice to a specific interest – normally a commercial one. The Scottish Commissioner upheld the use of reg. 12(5)(c) in one case, but this was where damage to such an interest had been proven. The Ordnance Survey and the Centre for Ecology and Hydrology had provided data to the Scottish Environmental Protection Agency, which together with submissions from the other authorities was able to demonstrate that the disclosure of a dataset would be likely to result in mass breaches of the agencies' copyright that would be impractical to enforce. Importantly, the Ordnance Survey is a trading fund, which relies on licensing of its data to finance its operations.[5]

The UK Commissioner has shown similar understanding of the damage that breaching copyright might do to commercial interests of third-party suppliers. An obvious example is where the requested information consists of materials that a particular supplier uses to deliver its services. For instance, the regulator accepted that the disclosure of training materials that had been developed by a training provider would be likely to prejudice their commercial interests, since their competitors would be able to gain insight into their success.[6]

Practical issues

What does all this mean for FOI officers? It is a good idea to meet colleagues and agree a copyright and re-use policy. This should outline the approach that the authority takes to licensing and enforcement. It should be considered whether re-use could be charged for in certain circumstances, and whether this is desirable. If not, a policy could be adopted that the Open Government Licence will be used to license all re-use of information that the authority retains copyright in. Decisions should be documented, since any decision not to adopt the Open Government Licence may need to be justified to the Information Commissioner.

The publication scheme can be used as the authority's re-use schedule, setting out what information is available for re-use. In practice this may be simply a matter of stating at the beginning of the scheme that all information listed is available for re-use under the terms of the Open Government Licence unless otherwise specified.

When responding to FOI and other access requests, an authority can insist that applicants seek permission to re-use the information being disclosed, but it is more efficient for all concerned to give permission proactively through the terms of the Open Government Licence. FOI officers do not want to spend unnecessary time answering re-use requests, especially if it is highly unlikely that the authority would ever take legal action against anybody that failed to ask permission to re-use information. It is sensible to warn applicants that they will need to ask third parties for permission to re-use information that was not authored by the authority, but authorities can be more permissive about other information.

TNA suggest some standard wording for use in responses. The example below can be used where the authority is disclosing information in which it retains the copyright, and is content for the applicant to use the information freely (it is using the Open Government Licence):

Using information under this licence

Use of copyright and database right material expressly made available under this licence (the 'Information') indicates your acceptance of the terms and conditions below.

The Licensor grants you a worldwide, royalty-free, perpetual, non-exclusive licence to use the Information subject to the conditions below.

This licence does not affect your freedom under fair dealing or fair use or any other copyright or database right exceptions and limitations.

You are free to:

- copy, publish, distribute and transmit the Information
- adapt the Information
- exploit the Information commercially and non-commercially for example, by combining it with other Information, or by including it in your own product or application.[7]

If the authority wishes to place limited restrictions on re-use, the following text can be adapted:

Most of the information that we provide in response to Freedom of Information Act 2000 [or other access legislation as appropriate] requests will be subject to copyright protection. In most cases the copyright will be owned by [insert name of public sector organisation]. The copyright in other information may be owned by another person or organisation, and this will be indicated on the information itself.

You are free to use any information supplied for your own non-commercial research or private study purposes. The information may also be used for any other purpose allowed by a limitation or exception in copyright law, such as news reporting. However, any other type of re-use, for example by publishing the information in analogue or digital form, including on the internet, will require the permission of the copyright owner.

For information where the copyright is owned by the [insert name of public sector organisation] details of the conditions on re-use can be found on our website at [insert link].

For information where the copyright is owned by another person or organisation you must apply to the copyright owner to obtain their permission.[8]

Summing up

- Copyright protects the rights of creators of documents, artworks, databases and other original creations.
- It applies to much of the information disclosed through the FOIA or EIR – but not all.
- To benefit from copyright protection, information disclosed by public authorities must be original.
- It is only a breach of copyright if a person copies a substantial part of disclosed information.
- Fair dealing permits some re-use of information in specific circumstances.
- Journalists can often justify reproducing disclosed information under fair dealing and public interest rules.
- The RoPSI Regulations 2015 require public authorities to allow re-use of disclosed information in most circumstances where they own the copyright.
- The Open Government Licence is the recommended licence for permitting re-use of public sector information.
- Departing from the Open Government Licence may be seen by the ICO as being unnecessarily restrictive.
- Publication schemes can be used to fulfill obligations in the RoPSI Regulations to publish a schedule of re-usable information.
- Applicants still need to be warned that they need permission to re-use information that originated with third parties.

Part 3

FOI in practice

Chapter 10

The FOI officer

Introduction

It seems obvious that FOI laws cannot work without administrative support. The quotation that opens the introduction to this book highlights the important role that public employees play in ensuring that FOI laws work in practice. In particular, there are those who oversee the day-to-day management of FOI obligations – the FOI officers. Their job is crucial, since however an organisation chooses to manage its compliance, someone has to establish policies and procedures, provide advice to colleagues, and monitor progress in the handling of requests. FOI cannot function without some sort of central resource to maintain it.

Yet despite their central importance to the delivery of FOI laws, not much has been written about FOI officers. This limits our understanding of how FOI works in practice, and leaves those in this essential role without the support they need to do the job well. This chapter seeks to address this, looking in detail at what an FOI officer is, and indeed what they should be.

What does the FOIA say about FOI officers?

As Chapter 1 demonstrated, the journey to the adoption of the FOIA in the UK was long, with the legislation receiving significant scrutiny. Following its passage, the government allowed over four years for full implementation. As a relatively late adopter of an FOI Act, the UK was also able to benefit from others' experience. It would be reasonable to expect in these circumstances that thought would have been given to how the legislation would work in practice, and – more to the point for present purposes – who would be responsible for delivering it. Yet the FOIA is silent on its own resource implications. There is no requirement to identify an officer with lead responsibility for FOIA implementation, or who applicants should contact to make their requests.

The preface of the original s. 45 code of practice referred to the need to appoint staff to support FOIA compliance, but even then it was fleeting and of limited application: 'Larger authorities should ensure that they have a central core of staff with particular expertise in Freedom of Information who can provide expert advice to other members of staff as needed.'[1] The 2018 version of the code doesn't even go this far.

Even subsequent government or parliamentary inquiries have stayed curiously silent on the human resources dimension of the FOIA. The post-legislative scrutiny of the FOIA, undertaken by the House of Commons' Select Committee on Justice in 2012,[2] devoted a significant portion of its time to considering the cost of the FOIA, as did the Independent Commission on Freedom of Information in 2016.[3] Yet neither devoted any attention to the resources provided to support compliance. The post-legislative scrutiny report's only significant reference to FOI officers appears in their eighth recommendation, which explains why they are not recommending the inclusion of reading and consideration time in estimating the cost of answering requests: 'Such activities are overly dependent on the individual FOI officer's abilities, introducing an element of inconsistency into the process that undermines the fundamental objective of the Act, that everyone has an equal right to access information.'[4]

Officially there is very little recognition in the UK of the fact that the success of the FOIA depends on FOI officers and other staff. This is concerning as resource allocation 'is central to the success or failure of a policy regime'.[5] Though the legislation is silent on the need for supporting staff they will still need to be appointed, but the omission makes it harder to argue for appropriate resources, and is likely to lead to inconsistency across the public sector.

How widespread are FOI officers?

Despite the lack of official recognition, it is clearly necessary to have at least one member of staff in a public authority with lead responsibility for FOIA compliance. Someone has to receive, log and allocate requests (even if they don't answer them), someone has to maintain publication schemes, and someone has to advise colleagues. Whether the people who carry out these activities see themselves as FOI officers is perhaps irrelevant – the outside world does.

One of the problems is that, again, there are very few sources available to assist in understanding the role of FOI officers. A few studies have looked at the resources available to support FOIA compliance, but not many, and very often they are difficult to interpret.

In preparing this book, the author sent an FOI request to 70 English local authorities asking them questions about how they manage their obligations under the FOIA (referred to in the rest of this book as the 2017 council survey). Appendix 1 has a description of the methodology of this survey. This and the next chapters in this book draw on this research, supplemented by other sources, to examine how FOI works in practice in the UK.

One question was:

> Do you have an individual member of staff and/or team with lead responsibility for FOI (e.g. FOI officer or Information Governance team)?

There were responses from 64 councils, 56 of which claimed to have an individual or team with lead responsibility for FOI. This is in line with research in Scotland a decade ago, which suggested that the vast majority of authorities had made some organisational adjustment to accommodate the FOIA.[6] It is also consistent with data collected from UK higher education institutions, which suggests that most universities have some sort of central resource to support information compliance including the FOIA.[7] UK government departments have central FOI units whose staff allocate, monitor and advise on the handling of requests.[8] It is common practice to identify a central resource to manage FOIA obligations, and it is hard to see how it would be possible to manage without one. Having an FOI officer or team, whatever it is called in practice, is essential.

Which begs the obvious question – why did eight councils claim not to have such a resource? Previous studies have noted the difficulty in understanding the use of resources in relation to FOI compliance, in particular because:

- staff involved in FOI compliance activities are commonly involved in other activities as well
- it is rare for staff to record how long they spend on FOI activities.[9]

Very few of the individuals or teams with responsibility for FOI were solely responsible for compliance with its obligations. In most councils the teams leading on FOI were also responsible for managing a range of other matters from data protection and records management through to monitoring performance and providing legal advice (see below). This may explain why some of the councils responded that they did not have a central FOI resource, since FOI work is seen as simply incidental to other work.

Where do FOI officers fit in?

In an attempt to understand where FOI responsibilities are commonly allocated, the 2017 council survey asked:

> What other responsibilities do staff in this team have? (e.g. data protection, records management, etc.)

The responses suggest that FOI officers or teams can end up almost anywhere in a local authority. Unsurprisingly, information governance or records management units were common hosts for FOI responsibilities. This was the case with nearly two-thirds of the responses received. Beyond that, FOI work was dealt with alongside performance and risk management in nine councils. In seven councils legal teams provided leadership on the FOIA, and it is not hard to see why this might be thought appropriate. In another seven councils customer services staff co-ordinated FOI work, and in three councils FOI work was considered a 'democratic service', sitting alongside support for councillors.

The councils involved in this study were at the top tier of English local government (county, borough, metropolitan and district councils). Very small authorities, such as parish councils, have to add FOI work to the duties of their very few clerical staff, often with predictable consequences.[10]

An interesting phenomenon picked up in the local government research is the emergence of shared services. Eight separate authorities (over 10% of those that responded) reported that FOI requests were co-ordinated by a service that they shared with one or more other authority. Six of these arrangements were between district councils. As such councils are in the lowest tier of English principal local authorities, it is not surprising to see them working together to seek efficiencies. However, two of the eight London boroughs that responded had chosen this approach (so at least four out of the – often sizeable – 32 London boroughs are operating this kind of arrangement).

The NHS reorganisation of the last decade has resulted in some even more complex arrangements among the many resulting NHS bodies. Clinical commissioning groups, which replaced primary care trusts in England, are able to use commissioning support units for legal and other services. Some of these provide the FOIA administration services for clinical commissioning groups. A decision notice of November 2017 records that the Information Commissioner 'has been disappointed by the lack of engagement' from a commissioning support unit which was providing this service for the clinical commissioning group to which the request had been directed.[11] This is an isolated example, but perhaps it demonstrates that such fragmented arrangements do not assist with FOIA compliance.

How many FOI officers?

Perhaps the most important question is how much resource is allocated for FOI compliance. For the reasons explained above, it is a difficult question to answer. The 2017 council survey asked:

> How many FTE staff are there in [the team with lead responsibility for FOI]?

Some respondents answering this question worked out (presumably roughly) how much time staff spent on FOI, others how many staff there were in the team that managed compliance with the FOIA (though those staff may in fact spend most of their time on other activities). Many were at pains to stress that dealing with FOI was only a small part of their job: 'No members of staff are currently employed solely to carry out functions in respect of the Freedom of Information Act. Corporate support for Freedom of Information is handled within Corporate Services, with the following officers working on Freedom of Information as part of wider duties' (response 58).

As some councils operate in a shared service arrangement, the 64 responses submitted provide data on central FOI resources for 69 authorities. Between these 69 councils, approximately 166 FTE employees were involved in the central management of FOIA obligations. This works out as on average about 2.4 FTE per council. A few authorities reported relatively large numbers (as many as ten in one London borough [response 33]) but stressed that only a small percentage of their time would be spent on the FOIA. Others were clear that about 50% of one person's time was spent on FOIA co-ordination [response 3]. Well over half of the councils had two or fewer FTE employees with FOIA co-ordination as part of their job. If outliers with more than five employees (such as the London borough mentioned) are excluded, the average is reduced to 1.9 FTE. As these employees are usually involved in many other tasks, the average central resource dedicated to FOIA compliance is no more than one FTE in practice.

These figures are similar to those found in previous studies of UK local government. The Constitution Unit of University College London (UCL) carried out a series of surveys of councils between 2005 and 2010. In this research respondents were asked about the staffing of work related to the FOIA, though unfortunately the published results do not distinguish between central FOI teams and time spent on FOIA compliance by staff in departments. The results across all the studies suggest there was an average of just over two FTE employees per council.[12] As this figure includes the time of staff collating information across the council, it again seems reasonable to conclude that any dedicated central FOI resource will on average be in the region of one FTE employee at most.

A Joint Information Systems Committee (JISC) survey of higher education in 2016 found that 93% of the UK universities that responded employed at least one member of staff with responsibility for information compliance (including compliance with the FOIA). Only 11% employed more than two people for this purpose.[13]

What can we conclude from all this about being an FOI officer in the UK? All (or the vast majority of) authorities appear to recognise that they need someone to lead on the FOIA. Some, notably in central government, are in a position to appoint teams of people to fulfill this function. More commonly, though, FOIA work has had to be added to the duties of existing teams. Sometimes this has been accompanied by additional resources, but not routinely. Those we call FOI officers in the UK often do not see themselves that way, and even if they do they are likely constantly to be distracted by other duties.

Around the world: FOI officers

FOI laws around the British islands – those of Scotland, the Isle of Man, the States of Jersey, and of Ireland – contain no requirement to appoint FOI officers.

However, the Irish government has much to say about FOI officers in its code of practice (discussed later in this chapter).[14] The Scottish Commissioner also recognises the importance of having one person or a team with day-to-day responsibility for FOI in their guidance.[15]

Elsewhere, many laws specify that an individual be identified by public authorities to whom requests may be addressed. The Maltese FOI Act requires authorities subject to the Act to publish 'particulars of the officer or officers to whom requests for such access should be sent'.[16] Online guidance supporting the Maltese FOI Act states that every 'Public Authority has appointed an FOI officer who shall handle requests for documents submitted by the public and represent the Public Authority on all matters related to the FOI Act'. It provides a list of all authorities and their FOI officers.[17] The Australian FOI Act similarly requires that public authorities include contact details for an officer (or officers) who can be contacted by people wanting to make a request for information in their 'information publication scheme'.[18]

In India, the Right to Information Act 2005 requires that public authorities designate public information officers and assistant public information officers to receive and deal with requests.[19] Heads of Mexican agencies subject to their FOI law must designate a 'liaison section' responsible for proactive publication of information, processing requests, providing advice to applicants, recording requests and training colleagues. The head of the liaison section is required to be a member of an information committee that has oversight of the agency's FOI obligations.[20]

The USA's FOIA Improvement Act 2016 amended the federal FOI Act. Among the changes were requirements to 'beef up' the role of the chief FOI officer in each government agency, 'who shall be a senior official of such agency'. Their role includes taking overall responsibility for the agency's FOI Act compliance, offering training to staff, monitoring compliance and appointing 'FOIA Public Liaisons'. The latter effectively have day-to-day oversight of compliance with the FOI Act and try to resolve disputes with applicants. Requests are initially handled by requester service centres. If applicants are unhappy with the service they receive from the staff of these centres, they can contact the FOIA Public Liaisons.[21]

FOI officers in Ireland

The Irish code of practice, issued under the Freedom of Information Act 2014, gives particular prominence to the role of the FOI officer. Arguably it provides a template for what FOI officers should be, wherever they might be fulfilling those duties.

It stresses that management boards in public authorities are expected to promote the aims of the FOI Act, ensure that policies and procedures are established, and that organisational structures including 'assignment of operational responsibility to an FOI officer' are in place. They should receive 'the requisite training to enable them to undertake these roles competently'.[22] It goes on to explain the importance of the FOI officer's role: 'While the Board's leadership role in relation to the delivery of FOI as described above is critical, the FOI officer, as the gatekeeper for the public body's FOI requests and conduit both to the requester and decision maker, is the linchpin of a public body's capability in relation to FOI.'[23]

The code specifies that FOI officers should:

- be given appropriate administrative support, depending on the size of the authority and the number of requests they receive
- have sufficient expertise and experience of handling FOI requests
- have sufficient expertise in how the FOI Act applies to the information created by the authority

- have leadership skills and be in a position to raise significant issues with senior management or the board
- report to senior management at least bi-annually on FOI performance
- not allow other responsibilities to encroach on their ability to perform their duties as the authority's FOI officer.[24]

FOI officers advise on the application of exemptions, redaction and other issues related to the handling of FOI requests. They are able to access assistance from the government's FOI Central Policy Unit or wider FOI networks. The code stresses the importance of maintaining anonymity of applicants when specific requests are discussed by these networks.[25]

In addition, FOI officers are responsible for maintaining their knowledge of decisions of the regulator and courts, raising awareness and providing regular (suitably tailored) training for colleagues.[26] They should be in a position to advise members of the public on how to submit valid requests, and have enough knowledge of other access regimes to be able to direct them to alternative routes as necessary.[27]

Their role includes monitoring compliance, in particular by collecting statistics. They should use the evidence they build up in this way to advise senior management on whether and how procedures can be improved. They are the contact point for applicants, the Information Commissioner, central government, as well as their colleagues internally, and are expected to maintain good relationships with them. They are also responsible for maintaining and promoting the means by which requests can be made.[28]

It is hard to think of a better description of the work of an FOI officer than that set out in the Irish code.

Data protection officers

Those in organisations throughout Europe and beyond who have had to employ data protection officers (DPOs) under the GDPR will have found some of the description in the Irish code familiar. In particular, the GDPR requires that:

- organisations support DPOs in performing their tasks and involve them in issues relating to personal information
- DPOs have expert knowledge of data protection and how the GDPR applies to their organisation
- DPOs are able to do their jobs independently, can't be penalised for doing

their jobs, and are able to report directly to the highest management level
- DPOs can carry out other tasks as long as they don't result in a conflict of interests with their role as a DPO
- DPOs are a contact point for individuals, the Information Commissioner (or other supervisory authorities), and for colleagues within their organisation
- DPOs also have to advise individuals and colleagues on rights and responsibilities under the GDPR
- DPOs have to monitor compliance.[29]

Much of this mirrors the content of the Irish code of practice and two points arise:

- Taken together with the Irish code, the GDPR provides public authorities with the basis for a person specification and job description for an FOI officer.
- Given the similarities, perhaps it is appropriate to appoint a DPO as an FOI officer, or vice versa. It is mandatory for public authorities to appoint DPOs, and in the UK this means those authorities that are subject to the FOIA (with the exception of parish councils and certain similar bodies).[30] It would make some sense to link these two responsibilities.

One objection to appointing FOI officers as DPOs in practice has been the suggestion that FOI officers may have a conflict of interest, since making decisions about the disclosure of information would constitute processing of data that a DPO may be asked to advise on. An answer to this is that the FOI officer's role is very often simply to advise on whether information should be disclosed. The information is disclosed because of a legal obligation in the form of the FOIA, and any decision about whether to apply exemptions would be taken by others under the FOI officer's advice. In any case, the UK Information Commissioner does not see a problem with appointing an FOI officer as an authority's DPO, and considers them suitable persons to appoint to the role if their GDPR guidance is any indication.[31]

Recruiting FOI officers

It is a common misconception that answering FOI requests is a basic administrative task that can be performed by anyone. Reading the requirements set out in the Irish code – which accurately captures the range of activities that

FOI officers are expected to perform - it is clear that this is not the case. Consider some of the tasks involved in answering a request:

- analysis of requests to identify what is being asked for and how best to provide it
- being able to read and interpret legislation and case law and apply it to specific situations
- advising colleagues, at all levels in the organisation
- negotiating with colleagues at all levels
- liaising with officers from other organisations of all types, from local businesses to the Royal Household
- understanding and articulating arguments in favour of withholding information.

These are just some of the activities that an FOI officer might have to engage in. Clearly this is a job that requires excellent analytical, communication, and negotiating skills. FOI officers need to be capable of quickly building up a good understanding of their authority and where information will be found. This need for information literacy perhaps explains why many FOI officers come from an information management background, and why the 2017 council survey shows FOI oversight very commonly being placed within information governance and records management units. Records managers, archivists and librarians are experienced at gaining a swift understanding of organisations, and the way that information flows through them. Of course, they can also support connected activities such as delivering a records management programme.

Similar benefits can be gained by appointing employees as FOI officers that have worked in the authority for a long time. One respondent to the 2017 council survey asked to explain their success in meeting the 20 working day deadline, replied that they and their assistant had worked for the council for over 50 years between them:

> 'This is perhaps unusual but it does mean we know whether the Council is likely to hold the information and if so, to whom the request should be directed, with a high degree of accuracy.'[32]

Other professionals can bring different strengths to the role. Those with legal qualifications will be experienced at interpreting the law and arguing a position. Ultimately, whoever is recruited will bring particular strengths with them, and there will be areas of their skill set that they will want to develop.

Authorities should be cautious of overloading a job role that is intended to support compliance with the FOIA. It is tempting to justify a new post by bringing together several areas of responsibility that are looking for a home. The problem with this is that the appointed individual may end up with a job description that sets them up for failure. If the same person is in charge of the FOIA process, data protection, records management and maybe other tasks, and is not sufficiently resourced, it will be virtually impossible for them to succeed in all areas. As well as exposing the authority to compliance risks, such a set up will often result in low morale.

As with so much else in life, authorities will get what they pay for. If an FOI officer is recruited on a low salary, such as the £15-16,000 offered by one council,[33] the authority cannot expect that person to do much more than provide basic administrative support. The burden, presumably, will be taken up by their colleagues, so such a decision may be a false economy.

The FOI officer's development

The very fact that the FOIA is still something of a novelty presents a problem for FOI officers, especially those whose main job is to manage FOIA compliance. There is no established career path for them. Yet career development has many advantages both for the individual and for their employer, including increased confidence, credibility and productivity.[34]

How can FOI officers best be developed? Development goes much further than training:

> Training is . . . about people learning how to carry out a particular task in order to do a job. It has its place in developing staff, particularly in terms of meeting legal requirements such as health and safety considerations, but it is not the only aspect to consider. Development is much broader. It is about developing the whole person.[35]

The trick is to use a range of methods to develop. There are certainly training courses that FOI officers can attend, but these should be seen as part of the individual's development jigsaw.

First, FOI officers should develop their knowledge and skills in the subject matter. The more they know, and the better they learn to apply their knowledge, the better they will be at their job (and the less stressful it will be).

If FOI officers are not sufficiently educated about how to do their work, it can prove embarrassing and sometimes expensive for an authority. In April 2018, the Royal Borough of Kensington and Chelsea received a monetary penalty notice for £120,000 after accidentally disclosing personal information about landlords in the borough. The information was hidden in a pivot table within a spreadsheet. The Information Commissioner described the contravention that led to the penalty as follows:

(a) The Council did not provide the FOI team with any (or any adequate) training on the functionality of Excel spreadsheets or possible alternatives.
(b) The Council had in place no guidance for the FOI team to check spreadsheets for data hidden in any pivot table before they are disclosed under FOI.[36]

FOI officers can develop their abilities by learning from those with more experience, including managers and colleagues. The Irish code of practice highlights the importance of building professional networks and these provide valuable opportunities to learn from others.

Chapter 4 of this book lists several resources that help an FOI officer to build and maintain their knowledge. In particular it is essential to keep up to date with the latest case law.

Training plays a part. There are several providers of FOIA training in the UK (see list under 'Training providers' in Chapter 11). The main providers publish details of external courses on their websites. There are one-day courses that give overviews of the subject or focus on specific aspects, such as the exemptions. There are also longer courses leading to a qualification. The most widely recognised award is the British Computing Society's Certificate in Freedom of Information. Most of the providers offer this qualification. It usually involves four or five days' study of the FOIA (either intensively over a week or one day a week over a month), followed by a three-hour exam. Some providers offer their own certificate after a course studying the FOIA with a similar format. For those interested in an even more in-depth exploration of the subject, Northumbria University offers a certificate, diploma or master's degree in information rights, law and practice by distance learning, which as well as covering FOIA, looks at data protection, information management, intellectual property and other related subjects.

A cost-effective way to train a whole team is to hire an external trainer to deliver training on the authority's premises. If the team isn't big enough to make this viable on its own, collaborating with other authorities may be an option. As well as generally being cheaper than sending several employees on an external course, such in-house training has the advantage that the trainer can be asked to tailor the course to address the authority's particular needs.

FOI officers may want to consider other aspects of their development, particularly if they wish to pursue other opportunities in their later career. If they are interested in information rights or information governance more broadly, they might consider developing knowledge, skills and experience in data protection and related matters. With the advent of the GDPR, demand for those with data protection knowledge is high, and it can be a lucrative area to move into.

FOI officers who are part of a larger team may be able to take on other roles temporarily to gain experience. Sometimes managers encourage staff to take on projects to stretch themselves and learn new skills.

Beyond this, it is always sensible to develop management and interpersonal skills. Employers may offer opportunities such as supervisory skills or project management courses, or be prepared to fund staff who want to attend them. FOI officers are often expected to deliver presentations and training to their colleagues, so train-the-trainer-type courses are beneficial. All of these skills are transferable, so are useful however long an individual remains an FOI officer.

Supporting FOI officers

The job of an FOI officer can be challenging. As the gatekeeper to the authority's information, those fulfilling this role can find themselves caught between determined FOI applicants, who see them as blocking their access to information, and angry colleagues, often in positions of power, who view them as the enemy within. FOI officers won't always find their efforts dissected by their colleagues in a public forum,[37] or raised in Parliament,[38] but nonetheless their situation can at times be stressful.

It is essential that those responsible for managing FOI officers recognise the challenges they face, and are ready to support them. Chapter 11 examines the importance of having FOI champions at a senior level within public authorities.

The attitude of FOI officers

It is up to FOI officers to provide leadership with a small 'l'. If they regularly bemoan the FOIA and having to answer requests, this will bolster resistance when they are trying to do their job in the future. Cynicism is a strong force, easier to fall in with than confront. Despite its challenges, the FOIA is the reason that many FOI officers have a job. If they are heard to query its importance, or even seen tacitly to agree with others doing so, they may end up out of one.

Arguably, FOI officers are there to challenge the status quo, and to promote the principles underlying the legislation. In practice, they must therefore not just accept requests from colleagues to refuse requests, but ask the difficult questions:

- Why can't this information go out?
- What harm will result from its disclosure?
- How likely is it that harm will occur?
- Will it really exceed the appropriate limit to provide the information?
- Have we considered the public interest in disclosing it?
- Can some of the information be disclosed?

Standing up to colleagues who want to cross a request off their to-do list can be difficult, but time spent considering these questions when a request is first being dealt with can save an authority time and expense in the long run. If these questions aren't considered now, they may have to be discussed with an expensive barrister when preparing the authority's case for a tribunal appeal.

Emphasising messages such as 'anything you write down might be disclosed' and 'beware of "smoking guns"' in training sessions is meant to encourage colleagues to take the FOIA seriously, but can result in unintended consequences. If colleagues are taught to fear the FOIA, this can breed scepticism of its requirements, which often makes FOI officers' jobs so difficult. It is important to stress that the legislation provides mechanisms to assist with difficult situations, and that the role of the FOI officer is to provide advice at those times. There are plenty of positive messages to give about the FOIA:

- *Openness is a good look*. Organisations that are less than open about the way they make decisions often have a very poor public image. The FOIA may not often improve trust, but the very fact that people can ask questions about their concerns makes public authorities look better than some of their private sector comparators. The FOIA acts as a pressure valve for unhealthy secrets.
- *Transparency can help to identify improvements*. In the process of answering FOI requests, public authorities often find problems that they were unaware of. A request to police resulted in them identifying a murder witness.[39] Several examples were provided to the Justice Select Committee in 2012 of situations where FOI requests resulted in savings of thousands of pounds being made after it was found that some public officials were being paid through companies.[40] Requests made through FOIA provide spot

checks on the performance of public authorities in random areas, highlighting issues that might otherwise have gone unnoticed.

- *The FOIA focuses the mind.* Officials and politicians are likely to think more carefully before making decisions if they know that the public will be able to find out about them. For example, in one Scottish council councillors had been funded to visit flower festivals around the world, including Tokyo and Barcelona. After this was made public through the FOI requests made by a local journalist, the council clamped down on such activities.[41]

How do others see FOI officers?

FOI officers and the teams they sit within have been rightly described as 'FOI's engine room'.[42] It should be clear how crucial FOI officers are to the proper functioning of FOI laws.

Even those who regularly grumble about the shortcomings of the FOIA in the UK can appreciate the work that FOI officers carry out. Journalists are among the biggest users of the FOIA, and despite the frustrations with it that they often describe, many see FOI officers and their role positively. A journalist from the Financial Times told a colleague that 'the FOI officers in a public authority are usually your best friend'.[43]

This is echoed by Rob Edwards, another journalist who makes regular use of the FOIA and the EIR, who says that FOI officers are often 'the ones who are trying to persuade the bureaucracies, in which they operate, to comply'.[44]

FOI officers carrying out their role politely and professionally will find supporters inside and outside their organisation.

Summing up

- The FOIA does not include a requirement to appoint an FOI officer.
- Nonetheless, to comply with the FOIA it is usually necessary for public authorities to appoint an individual or team to oversee its operation.
- FOI officers are commonly linked to other information governance activities such as data protection and records management.
- Most public authorities appoint one or two people in this role, though they may well have a range of other responsibilities.
- Other FOI laws around the world include requirements to appoint individuals as FOI officers.
- There are lessons to be learnt from other jurisdictions and legal requirements about the role of FOI officers.
- FOI officers require knowledge and skill to do the job well – answering FOI requests is not a simple administrative task.

- Authorities should take care to recruit the most suitable individuals to carry out the role of FOI officer.
- The most suitable candidates for FOI officer roles are information professionals (e.g. records managers, archivists and librarians), lawyers and employees with significant knowledge of the authority.
- Managers should support FOI officers and give them development opportunities.
- FOI officers should seek out opportunities for their own development.
- FOI officers have an important role in championing FOI within their authority, and should be careful not to encourage cynicism.
- FOI officers are most likely to be successful if they perform their role politely and professionally.

Chapter 11

Embedding FOI

Introduction

An FOI officer's job is to ensure that their authority is in a position to comply with its obligations under the relevant FOI laws. Those obligations include answering requests, ensuring that the infrastructure is there to enable that to happen, and meeting additional requirements to publish information proactively.

In order to achieve this, FOI officers need help. Contrary to popular belief, they do not have instant access to every record in their authority, nor are they omniscient. They rely on others to identify relevant information and provide it. In many authorities, colleagues across the organisation may even respond to requests directly. Those people need to know what is expected of them. If they don't co-operate, FOI officers may need support from senior managers, who also want to know how the authority is performing, and whether there are any issues with compliance that need to be addressed.

More and more public authorities outsource services, with implications for FOIA compliance. With an increasing emphasis on proactive disclosure, practitioners need to consider how to promote a more open culture within their authority.

This chapter looks at what public authorities need to put in place to ensure they are in a position to comply with their obligations under FOI laws.

Senior level commitment

It is no good appointing an FOI officer and assuming that will ensure FOI requirements will be met. Public authorities need to ensure that responsibility for FOI compliance goes all the way to the top. The Irish code of practice discussed in Chapter 10 stresses that the management board of an authority is responsible for ensuring that the 'necessary structures' and 'effective governance' are in place.[1] The Scottish Information Commissioner recommends that a senior member of staff is made accountable and responsible for compliance with FOI legislation. Other managers should also be responsible for ensuring that policies and procedures are in place and that their staff are trained.[2] The Irish code states that senior managers are responsible for promoting the idea that FOI is part of the core work of the authority.[3]

This idea that senior managers should take responsibility for FOI is important. Leadership from the top is essential if an organisation is to implement FOI legislation successfully. If senior or elected officials are heard to complain about its implications, it is not surprising that FOI officers encounter resistance from other colleagues. Research looking at local government from UCL's Constitution Unit in 2011 found that hostility from a chief executive or council leader can 'percolate an organisation and embolden resistance and create nervousness'. Conversely, if they talk positively about FOI and provide support to their FOI officer, it makes a 'tremendous difference'.[4]

As discussed in Chapter 10 and at the end of this chapter, FOI officers can find themselves in a difficult position, since their job involves them providing advice which may not be welcomed by colleagues. It is essential that they feel supported by senior managers.

The senior manager with lead responsibility for FOI, or 'FOI champion', needs to be regularly updated on FOI performance and current issues. It is good practice for this to happen at a minuted meeting. This might be a committee dedicated to FOI, or one that has oversight of information governance more broadly. It can even be a one-to-one meeting with the 'FOI champion'. Typically, this body will agree the authority's FOI strategy, approve relevant policies and procedures, and review monitoring reports. Its activities may then be reported to the authority's main decision-making body from time to time. In this way senior managers remain aware of, and if necessary engage with, the day-to-day management of FOI.

Performance monitoring

The Irish code suggests that senior managers should review the authority's capability and capacity to handle requests annually in the light of the number of requests that are being received and the success in responding to them in a timely manner.[5] This seems a sensible approach. Many FOI officers in the UK produce annual reports summarising performance and issues that have arisen during the year, and such a report can be used to inform the FOI champion, and if necessary other senior managers, in conducting such a review. As the Scottish Information Commissioner observes: 'Senior level commitment can often be demonstrated by how well managers monitor the organisation's FOI performance and react to lessons learned.'[6]

Data on the volume of requests being received and the performance of the authority in handling them can assist in demonstrating to managers and budget holders when resources are hard pressed, and help make the case for more support.

The 2017 council survey asked about performance monitoring:

Who is FOI performance (e.g. request volumes and timeliness) reported to internally?

and

How often are such reports made?

In reply to the second question, the responses showed that most FOI officers reported regularly on performance. A few only reported annually, but most commonly they reported monthly or quarterly. In only four authorities was there no report on performance at all.

In over half of the councils FOI performance was reported to the senior or corporate management team, typically made up of the chief executive and directors of an authority. In the rest of the councils performance was reported to either a particular director or service head – presumably their FOI champion – or to a committee, often an information governance or audit committee. In a handful of councils performance was also reported to the relevant cabinet member (an elected member of the authority with an executive role). This response [response 3] from one council illustrates the way that FOI performance reports can find their way up the reporting structure:

> There are FOI timeliness indicators for each department in the Council's perform-
> ance management system. The Chief Executive is provided with this and other
> performance information for use in his monthly one-to-one meetings with the . . .
> heads of each department. FOI timeliness is included in the Council's Corporate
> Scorecard. Performance against the Corporate Scorecard (for the Council as a whole)
> is included in our quarterly performance bulletins which are reported to Management
> Team and Audit & Governance Committee and are then published [on the council
> website].

One council which performed well in meeting deadlines was asked how they were able to do this. One of their explanations was that performance is logged and 'repeated incidents' of 'non-conformance . . . would lead to disciplinary action being taken'.[7] It is valuable to make clear to employees across the authority that FOI compliance is part of their job and can affect how their work is assessed. It can help keep FOI performance on track.

Given the FOIA's aim to promote transparency, it might be expected that performance statistics would be routinely made public. This is true for central government, which publishes these online on the gov.uk website quarterly.[8] In Scotland, all public authorities have to report on performance to the Scottish Information Commissioner whose office publishes these statistics, again quarterly, on their website.[9] The data recorded by UK central government departments and the Scottish Commissioner far exceeds simple figures on requests received and responses provided within 20 working days. It includes use of exemptions, numbers of internal reviews and complaints to the regulator, and much more. In the rest of the UK, some sectors have published statistics in the past, but coverage is very patchy.

This may change. As discussed in Chapter 8, the 2018 version of the s. 45 code of practice proposes that authorities with more than 100 FTE employees should publish statistics on FOIA compliance and make them available via their publication scheme guides. At the time of writing it remains to be seen how consistently UK public authorities will comply with this new requirement.

FOI policies and procedures

An important part of an FOI officer's role is to document their authority's policy and procedures in relation to the FOIA.

FOI policies set out in broad terms the organisation's approach to how it complies with the FOIA. A typical policy includes:[10]

- a statement that the authority is committed to the principles of the FOIA
- a commitment to make information proactively available in line with the Information Commissioner's model publication scheme
- a commitment to process requests in line with legal requirements and best practice
- a brief outline of the authority's approach to applying exemptions (e.g. that consideration is given to disclosing information even if an exemption applies)
- reference to handling and complaints procedures

- an undertaking to ensure that staff are trained
- an outline of responsibilities of various groups within the authority
- the date the policy was adopted and when it will next be reviewed.

An FOI policy should be approved at the highest level as it constitutes the authority's commitment to comply with the FOIA. The policy can then be used by FOI officers to reinforce their authority as required. Like all policies, it should be reviewed regularly, perhaps every two years or so.

Procedures are important as they provide a single reference point for all employees on how they should be handling requests. The process of drafting or reviewing procedures is a valuable opportunity for FOI officers to take a step back and consider how best to embed the authority's duties under the FOIA within the organisation. Well-drafted procedures can be used to resolve disputes that arise when handling particularly complex FOI requests, and can assist those conducting internal reviews to judge whether requests have been handled properly. They can ensure consistency, particularly when there is a high turnover of staff involved in dealing with FOI requests.

There should be procedures covering every aspect of compliance with the FOIA, bringing together legal requirements with technical and practical necessities. In particular, procedures need to cover how:

- to identify an FOI request
- to distinguish FOI requests from business as usual
- requests are logged
- requests are allocated
- searches for information are conducted
- requests are transferred to other authorities (and in what circumstances)
- (and when) third parties are consulted
- the cost of fulfilling a request is estimated
- exemptions are applied
- to draft a response
- to conduct an internal review.

Procedures may be supplemented by templates for acknowledging and responding to requests, examples of which are provided in Appendix 2. The Information Commissioner suggests that policies and procedures the authority has developed in order to comply with the FOIA should be made available as part of its publication scheme.[11] Therefore it is generally appropriate for them to be set out for staff and public alike on the website, rather than on an authority's intranet.

Contractors

In the FOIA and most other FOI laws, the duty to provide information held by a public authority covers information that has been provided by third parties. This includes private companies that have given information to authorities, perhaps as part of a procurement process.

The original 2004 s. 45 code of practice highly recommended that authorities 'take appropriate steps to ensure that such third parties . . . are aware of the public authority's duty to comply with the Freedom of Information Act, and that therefore information will have to be disclosed upon request unless an exemption applies'.[12] Although this isn't addressed in the 2018 version, it remains good advice.

The 2018 code does address what should happen when a request is received for information that was supplied by a third party or which affects their interests. In these circumstances, the third party should be consulted – in many cases there will be a contractual obligation to do so, but in any case it is likely that the supplier of information will have a better idea of the sensitivity of information than the FOI officer or their colleagues.[13] Where the argument is being made that a third party's interests will be prejudiced, it is necessary to show that they have been consulted.[14]

The code also advises that authorities be cautious about agreeing to confidentiality obligations in contracts, considering carefully whether they are compatible with their FOIA obligations. They should only be accepted when there is good reason – when exemptions could potentially and justifiably be applied.[15]

FOI officers need to liaise with colleagues responsible for procurement in their authority. It is good practice to incorporate text in procurement documentation such as invitations to tender to inform those tendering for work of the implications of the FOIA for information they may supply. Procurement procedures should require those procuring services to consult FOI officers if companies request confidentiality clauses, so they can advise whether it is likely that such information could be protected using the exemptions in the FOIA.

If companies are providing public services on behalf of the authority, there are circumstances in which information they hold about those services is subject to the FOIA, even where the information is in the physical possession of the companies. This is an area of considerable controversy, since it is not always entirely clear whether information is held for the purpose of delivering the service or for the company's internal processes. This is one reason why there are regular calls for the FOIA to be extended to cover information held by private companies providing public services in the UK (as referred to in Chapter 1).

The UK Government has so far resisted these calls, but the 2018 s. 45 code has a chapter called 'Transparency and confidentiality obligations in contracts and outsourced services'. This recommends that contracts for outsourced services include a schedule setting out what information will be considered held for the purposes of answering FOI requests. Arrangements for handling requests for such information should be set out either in the contract or a separate memorandum of understanding. It should include details of:

- how and when to approach the contractor, and who the contact points in each organisation are
- how quickly the contractor should provide the information (a common timeframe is five working days)
- how any disagreement about disclosure will be resolved
- how complaints and appeals will be dealt with
- the contractor's responsibility to maintain adequate records
- the circumstances in which the authority will consult the contractor where it holds relevant information.[16]

The responsibility for answering requests under the FOIA remains with the public authority, but where services are outsourced, companies should assist with the processing of requests affecting their work. This is such an issue for some companies that they have designated employees to take the lead on FOI issues – in effect appointing their own FOI officers.[17] The London Borough of Barnet is renowned for outsourcing many council services, earning it the nickname 'easyCouncil'. It has had to give special consideration to the way it handles requests for information in these circumstances. The response is drafted by the 'commissioned service' (provided by, for example, Capita), before being checked and sent out by the 'commissioning group' (the in-house team with oversight of the commissioned service).[18]

Transparency by design

The GDPR mandates 'data protection by design', and just as the role of the FOI officer can be modelled on that of the data protection officer, this provides a template for how to manage obligations under the FOIA. In the GDPR, data controllers are expected to adopt organisational and technical measures to ensure compliance with the regulation. In some cases, organisations have to conduct data protection impact assessments to ensure that data protection concerns are identified at the design stage of introducing new procedures or technology.

The FOIA does not require such an assessment to be carried out, but the UK's Information Commissioner has suggested that 'access impact assessments' should be conducted to assess the impact any developments might have on an authority's openness.[19] At the very least, authorities should consider ways to build FOI and openness into the way they work wherever possible.

This might include specifying IT systems so they facilitate the extraction of data in whatever format might be required to meet a FOI request. In the early days of the FOIA, it was commonly a problem that systems were inflexible in the way that data could be reported. This kind of problem is avoidable. Such systems should also be designed to allow data to be readily searched when processing FOI requests.

Committee papers and other decision-making records can be designed so that reserved business is recorded separately to open business, enabling the prompt publication of the latter. Figure 11.1 shows an extract from a mayoral decision form, used to document decisions of the Mayor of London. Officials seeking approval for significant expenditure or novel or contentious decisions must complete these forms. The section shown allows officials to defer publication of Part 1 (the 'open' part of the form) in certain circumstances, but normally this

Public access to information
Information in this form (Part 1) is subject to the Freedom of Information Act 2000 (FOI Act) and will be made available on the GLA website within one working day of approval.
If immediate publication risks compromising the implementation of the decision (for example, to complete a procurement process), it can be deferred until a specific date. Deferral periods should be kept to the shortest length strictly necessary. **Note**: This form (Part 1) will either be published within one working day after approval or on the defer date.
Part 1 Deferral: **Is the publication of Part 1 of this approval to be deferred? NO**   If YES, for what reason: Until what date:
Part 2 Confidentiality: Only the facts or advice considered to be exempt from disclosure under the FOI Act should be in the separate Part 2 form, together with the legal rationale for non-publication.   **Is there a part 2 form – NO**

Figure 11.1 *Extract from a mayoral decision form* [20]

part is published online within one working day of the Mayor signifying their approval. Matters that are considered confidential are provided in Part 2 of the form, but the officials must justify this by reference to FOIA exemptions. If a request is received for the information in Part 2, the application of exemptions still needs to be reviewed at the time, but the documentation of the reasoning in the form often assists in making a swift assessment. Many public authorities have adopted similar approaches to the records of their board or similar bodies. In this way, FOI and transparency requirements can be designed into decision-making processes.

It might even be the case that information relating to specific processes is routinely published online unless there is a reason to hold it back. Some public officials have proposed publishing everything their authority creates unless an exemption applies.[21]

Organising FOIA administration

Procedures for managing FOI requests vary from authority to authority, but in broad terms there are two ways to manage FOI requests: a centralised approach or a devolved approach. Figure 11.2 illustrates the two options.

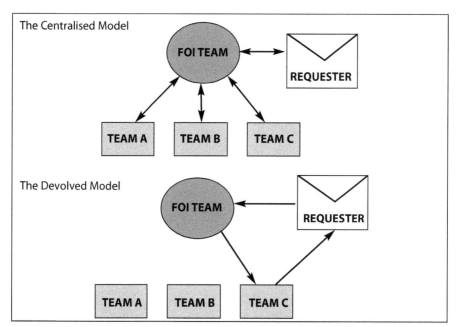

Figure 11.2 *The centralised and devolved models for managing FOI requests*

The devolved approach usually still involves a central co-ordination point. Requests are received by the FOI officer or team who will typically acknowledge and log them, then allocate them to the service area they believe is best placed to answer the request. Once the request is allocated, the rest of the process is in the hands of staff in the chosen service area. There is usually a liaison officer or team that oversees compliance within the service area. They are responsible for collecting information from colleagues, discussing whether exemptions apply, carrying out redaction, and drafting and sending the response. The central FOI officer or team may provide advice and monitor progress, perhaps sending reminders at regular intervals, but otherwise responding to requests is left in the hands of the service area staff. This approach is used in central government (see 'FOI liaison officers' below),[22] and commonly in many large authorities such as Manchester City Council (an authority serving a population of over half a million).

In the alternative centralised approach FOI officers and teams are responsible for the whole process of answering a request. They ask colleagues in service areas to provide relevant information and to inform them of any concerns with disclosure. Once information is provided, they draft the response and ensure it is sent out. This approach is commonly used in smaller authorities and those that provide direct services such as universities and NHS trusts.

There are benefits to both. Devolved arrangements ensure that responses are drafted by the people with the greatest knowledge about the subject area, and that staff with most expertise in interpreting the FOIA focus on the most difficult requests. The centralised approach gives FOI officers more control over the way that requests are answered, enabling them to ensure that responses are compliant. Where request handling is devolved it is harder to maintain consistency in the way that the authority answers requests.

The 2017 council survey asked:

> Are responses to FOI requests normally drafted by the central FOI officer/team, or are they drafted by staff in the department with lead responsibility for the subject matter of the request?

The answers to this question cast light on whether councils were operating the centralised or devolved model, and the local authorities surveyed used both approaches. There were 64 responses to the survey; 24 councils appeared to be operating the centralised model (38%), with the rest using the more devolved model. However, when the councils were grouped according to their performance against the 20 working day deadline in 2016, an interesting pattern emerged: 45% of the best performing authorities (those whose staff answered requests within 20 working days more than 90% of the time) used a more centralised approach in administering requests. Only 18% of poorly performing authorities (those achieving compliance against the same measure in 80% or less of cases) used this approach. One authority even commented that it was moving to a centralised approach 'to ensure consistency' [response 36].

There may be other causes of this variation of performance. As noted above, larger authorities are more likely to adopt a devolved approach, and the size of the council could well explain delays in responses to requests. Nonetheless, the apparent differences in performance between authorities operating the centralised and the devolved model are striking.

Sometimes a 'hybrid' approach is taken. Several of the responses indicated that even though requests were normally answered by departments (devolved), if the information asked for was held by more than one department, the process would be managed centrally by the FOI officer or equivalent. Some councils varied the approach depending on the complexity of the response required, for example, where exemptions were being applied: 'Routine responses are drafted by department staff. Any responses requiring exemptions under the Act or any responses that require assistance are drafted by the Information Governance officer' [response 53].

The case studies below are based on the author's experience.

CASE STUDY 1   GREATER LONDON AUTHORITY (DEVOLVED APPROACH)

In 2003, a correspondence management system was used to manage correspondence sent to the Mayor of London. Correspondence was received by the GLA's Public Liaison Unit (PLU), whose staff allocated correspondence to specific teams. The relevant team would then draft responses and, where relevant, workflow functionality built into the system ensured that draft responses were directed to the Mayor's Office for approval or signature.

To prepare for the administration of FOI requests, the developers added a category of correspondence called 'FOI'. PLU staff merely had to tick a box and a specific FOI workflow would be set off. This included automatic e-mail reminders to staff who had been allocated requests after 10, 15 and 20 working days.

Guidance was provided to assist PLU staff in identifying FOI requests. Procedures on the intranet (and a training programme) helped staff to understand how to process requests, and templates ensured they gave consistent responses. The FOI officer (known as the Freedom of Information and Records Manager), based in the Research Library, provided advice, training and guidance to staff, drafted more technical elements of responses, such as when an exemption was required, and monitored and reported on performance. Performance was reported to the Director of Corporate Services, who occasionally intervened directly if requested to. Where necessary, the FOI officer was able to seek advice from the legal services team.

CASE STUDY 2   AN NHS HOSPITAL (CENTRALISED APPROACH)

FOIA compliance was among the responsibilities of the Information Governance Manager, based in the finance directorate, who was supported by a team of three staff, two of whom were occupied full time in processing the hundreds of subject access requests received each month. The other member of the team maintained a spreadsheet in which FOI requests were logged on receipt. Each request (with the applicant's identity removed) was e-mailed to the relevant contact(s) in each department, who was asked to provide relevant information and/or state whether they had any concerns with disclosure. Where necessary, reminders were sent. Once information had been provided or concerns discussed, a response would be drafted by the Information Governance Manager or another team member, and sent for the relevant director to approve. Once agreed, the response would be sent out. Performance was reported to the Information Governance Board fortnightly.

CASE STUDY 3   A UNIVERSITY (CENTRALISED APPROACH)

The Information Compliance Manager was based in the Directorate, effectively the Vice Chancellor's department. Requests were logged on a Microsoft Access database designed for the purpose. An administrative assistant logged and acknowledged requests, circulated (anonymised) requests to relevant departments, sent out reminders, and drafted straightforward responses where the information was being disclosed. They also published responses in an online disclosure log. The Information Compliance Manager provided advice, discussed the more contentious requests with colleagues, and drafted responses that required exemptions to be applied. Draft responses were sent to the relevant professional services director or dean (if information came from an academic department) for approval. Performance was reported quarterly to the Information Services Committee.

FOI liaison officers

However an authority administers processes relating to its compliance with the FOIA, FOI officers can rarely fulfill their duties without a broad eco-system of support. If a centralised model is in place, FOI officers still need to ask colleagues in other departments to provide information. If a devolved model is used, there need to be individuals in departments around the authority in a position to collate information and draft responses.

Hazell, Worthy and Glover describe the situation in a typical central government department. The central FOI Unit staff allocate requests, monitor progress and provide advice. They rarely answer requests directly, but instead allocate them to 'an official in the appropriate business area'. Business areas may have a 'designated intermediary', perhaps referred to as a 'focal point'. These officials either deal with the request themselves or allocate it to other officials in their business area with expertise in the subject concerned.[23]

This constitutes a 'devolved' approach to complying with the FOIA, but the concept of developing a network of contacts across an authority able to assist with processing requests is common whichever model is used. The responses from English councils described similar arrangements.

Many respondents to the 2017 council survey referred to information being supplied by the 'staff in the relevant area', the 'services themselves' or simply 'departments'. Some councils used specific terms to describe staff in departments who assisted with requests, suggesting there was a degree of formality to their role, similar to that described in central government. These are some of the titles used to refer to these staff:

- FOI link officers
- nominated 'information champions'
- FOI reps (and the even more desirable 'trained FOI reps')
- FOI champions
- FOI co-ordinators
- departmental information guardians
- team FOI officers.

Manchester City Council's FOI procedures refer to their liaison officers as 'decision makers' [response 46], borrowing the terminology used in the Irish code of practice.[24] Another council alluded to 'FOI reps' in teams providing guidance on request handling, with 'information owners' responsible for collating the information [response 68]. In fact this happens in most authorities, since it is rare that even the liaison officer has the knowledge to answer requests without input from other colleagues.

Liaison officers need suitable training to be effective (see section 'Training' below) and it is desirable for such officers to meet the FOI officer or team regularly to discuss current issues and trends. The response from one district council illustrates the importance of developing liaison officers' knowledge of and commitment to complying with the FOIA: 'We believe that keeping FOI responses to a small number of staff ensures consistency and builds expertise, and the [FOI officer] and FOI link officers take pride in providing a good service in responding to requests' [response 3].

Around the world: FOI liaison officers
There is a need for a network of colleagues to support compliance and meet the requirements of any FOI law, not just the FOIA. There must be co-operation between a number of employees across public authorities.

The Irish code of practice, mentioned several times in this and the previous chapter, includes a section setting out the responsibilities and tasks of 'decision makers'. They are responsible for liaising with applicants to clarify requests, overseeing the search process, and work closely with the FOI officer, especially on complex requests. Decision makers are expected to have received at least a basic level of training in their duties under the FOIA.

In the USA, federal agencies have developed a range of roles to support FOIA compliance beyond that of the chief FOI officer (see Chapter 10). Guidance given to applicants states that requests will be handled by 'FOIA Professionals' and 'FOIA Contacts'; chief FOI officers are expected to ensure that 'FOIA Public Liaisons' are in place.[25]

Academic Alasdair Roberts described the processing of FOI requests to government agencies made under the Access to Information Act 1985 (ATIA) in Canada in 2003. Giving the example of an agency called Citizenship and Immigration Canada, he describes how requests are received by the central ATIA office, before being directed to the 'Office of Primary Interest' (the office most likely to hold the relevant information). The Office of Primary Interest assists the ATIA office in finalising the response, before seeking approval as necessary.[26]

Training materials released under New Zealand's Official Information Act 1982 have provided an insight into the various roles involved in answering requests made to the New Zealand Treasury – and it is a complex arrangement. Aside from the Minister and the Secretary to the Treasury, who have overall responsibility for compliance, a whole range of officials is involved. Managers with oversight of the request appoint an 'Assigned Analyst', who is responsible for 'leading the preparation' of the response (and a 'Game Plan' – a plan for the processing of the request, setting out who is doing what, and when). The Assigned Analyst has to ensure a 'QA Analyst' is in place to assess the quality of the game plan, the response and any other materials produced in the handling of the request. A 'Research Analyst' will 'provide a project manager overview', conduct redaction, and review the response. A 'Formatting PA' has the job of formatting the response letter and any materials that will be provided with the response. Finally, 'Records Advisors' can assist with searches for records.[27]

Raising awareness options

Unless colleagues understand their obligations under the FOIA, and how they are affected by its requirements, it will be difficult to comply with the Act. However, a one-size fits all approach rarely works. Staff can be usefully split into three main groups, each of which requires different levels of awareness of the FOIA:

- *practitioners* – FOI officers and others directly involved in responding to requests
- *information co-ordinators* – those who are regularly called on to collate information for requests

- *other staff* – those who are rarely directly involved with matters relating to the FOIA, but are nonetheless affected by it on occasion.

We might add to this list those who are called on to conduct internal reviews, who may not be involved in the day-to-day handling of requests, but nonetheless need practitioner-level knowledge. FOI liaison officers fall into either the 'practitioner' or 'co-ordinator' levels, depending on which model of administration is used, and what level of involvement they have in preparing responses.

Those at 'practitioner' level need a detailed awareness of the FOIA and its obligations, including knowledge of the authority's procedures, technical matters such as the application of exemptions, how to conduct the public interest test, and how to develop their expertise (such as by reading ICO guidance and decision notices). They also need to know how to spot an EIR request, be aware of personal information issues, and what to include in a response.

Those at 'co-ordinator' level should know enough about the technicalities to be able to flag up when a request is likely to exceed cost limits, or when an exemption might need to be applied. They need to know how to conduct a search and when to stop. They may need to know how to prepare information for disclosure including redaction techniques.

Most staff only need to know a minimal amount about the FOIA: how to recognise a request if it arrives in their inbox, and what to do with it (forward it to the FOI officer or team). They should be prepared for the possibility that their work may be subject to an FOI request, and that they may have to supply information to a practitioner or a co-ordinator on occasion.

Methods of raising awareness include:

- in-house newsletters
- FOI officers attending team meetings
- poster and leaflet campaigns (for example, the 'Get it right first time' poster published by the Scottish Information Commissioner)[28]
- guidance on intranet pages
- presentations and training courses.

Training

Training also plays a part in raising awareness. It must be suitable for the audience.

For most staff, the simple messages described above can best be communicated through induction or short, briefing-type sessions. Training on an authority's duties under the FOIA might well be part of a wider session covering data protection or similar issues. Such a session should be no longer than about an hour, depending on how many other subjects are being covered. An alternative might be to provide e-learning to staff. The advantage of this is that staff can complete modules at a time to suit themselves, and a log can be maintained as evidence that members of staff have completed the module. Some suppliers of e-learning products are listed below.

Co-ordinator level training needs to be more detailed, and preferably carried out face to face in sessions of 1–3 hours, depending on the level of knowledge required.

Practitioners and FOI officers might need a full-day or more of training as they need to know a great deal about the subject to be able to do their job well. The section 'The FOI officer's development' in Chapter 10 and the box 'The gist – using a training provider to deliver in-house training', opposite, provide some assistance in planning training for practitioner-level staff.

Face-to-face training allows for more complex messages to be delivered, and allows opportunities for discussion and questions. The best training consists of a mixture of methods, as people learn best in different ways: a combination of lectures, exercises and opportunities for questions works well. If the training is any longer than an hour, build in regular breaks – approximately one every hour and a quarter is a good rule of thumb. It is often hard to justify providing refreshments at meetings in public authorities these days. If they cannot be provided advise delegates to bring a coffee with them, and allow enough time at breaks for people to purchase refreshments from outlets and return. Groups of around 20 work well. Too few and the training is not cost-effective and the benefits that can be gained from interaction are lost. Too many and it becomes more difficult for the trainer to engage everyone successfully.

Some FOI officers may feel confident in their subject matter and able to deliver the training themselves. This can be cost-effective and has the advantage of helping those staff to build a relationship with delegates, which may prove useful when they need to discuss particular requests with them in the future. However, it may not be practical – with limited resources, the FOI officer may not have time to deliver all the training required. Many people do not like public speaking, and this may be another (entirely reasonable) reason for FOI officers preferring not to train colleagues. Whatever the rationale, many organisations choose to bring in an external trainer. If the right trainer is selected, the training can be highly effective.

The gist – using a training provider to deliver in-house training
Before the training:

● Ensure you have a budget.
● Consider whether in-house training is the best way to deliver the messages that you want to convey.
● Specify your need in broad terms – who the training is for; how long it will be; what your objectives are.
● Identify a trainer (or more than one if necessary to satisfy procurement rules or to ensure the cost is competitive) and ask them to quote.
● Identify a venue – finding a room is often the biggest challenge. Make sure it is suitable – big enough to hold the envisaged audience, but not so big that the trainer has to spend the day shouting!
● Refine the specification with the trainer – trainers usually have lots of experience of what works and what doesn't, so listen to their advice. Agree with them the size of each group, how long each session should be, and the content of the course.
● Ensure that you brief the trainer on any messages you want them to give – one of the advantages of in-house training is that it can be customised to suit your needs. Provide the trainer with any local procedures you want them to refer to and details of anyone whom you want colleagues to contact for advice after the training.
● Agree what equipment will be provided – most trainers bring their own laptop but expect clients to provide projectors or screens to display any slides; it is often helpful to provide a flipchart and pens to assist with exercises.
● It is common practice for trainers to supply materials digitally in advance so clients can print them as required – make sure you agree with the trainer a deadline for them to provide the materials, and arrange for them to be printed or circulated to delegates before the training.
● Agree with the trainer how the training will be evaluated – most training companies have their own feedback form (physical or online). If you prefer to use your own, let the trainer know in advance and agree what access they will have to the results.
● Let the trainer know where they need to report to on arrival, and who to ask for.

On the day:

● Ensure someone is available to meet the trainer on arrival, explain housekeeping arrangements (e.g. fire evacuation procedures, toilet facilities, etc.) and deal with any problems that arise on the day.
● Provide a jug of water or easy access to a water cooler – most trainers are house-trained, polite and undemanding. But when training they talk for much of the day so ensuring they are well watered is essential.
● Provide a sign-in sheet so you have a record to show which colleagues have attended. Explain the process to the trainer and if relevant ask them to ensure that everyone signs in.

- Avoid burdening the trainer with unnecessary admin – you want the trainer to focus on delivering the best training possible.

After the event:

- Evaluate the training – if you've agreed to share feedback with the trainer, ensure this happens, and let them know what worked and what didn't.
- Pay your trainer on time – training providers normally invoice after the training. Let them know in advance if you need them to quote a purchase order number.
- Update training records.

Training providers
Here is a list of training providers in the UK. Inclusion in this list does not imply any recommendation.

These organisations supply e-learning products on the FOIA:

- Delta-net International (enquiries@delta-net.co.uk; www.delta-net.com)
- ICO – Tick Tock training video (free) (www.ico.org.uk)
- Kineo (www.kineo.com)
- TrainingCourse.com.

These are providers of external and in-house training on the FOIA:

- Act Now Training (info@actnow.org.uk; www.actnow.org.uk)
- Amberhawk (www.amberhawk.com)
- FOIMan Training (in-house training only) (paul@foiman.com; www.foiman.com)
- PDP Training (www.pdptraining.com)
- Understanding ModernGov (Enquiries@moderngov.com; www.moderngov.com).

Uncooperative colleagues

Commonly, the most challenging part of an FOI officer's job is not applying exemptions correctly, nor dealing with applicants. The most difficult aspect of the work is dealing with colleagues who refuse to co-operate, or may even be actively hostile to the aims of the FOI officer.

Such resistance can take many forms. Perhaps these colleagues are struggling with their job, and regularly fail to meet deadlines because of pressure of work. They may have problems with the FOIA in principle, and rarely spare an opportunity to tell the FOI officer about them. They might resent being told that they have to disclose information against their will. They could be a senior officer or elected official who struggles with the concept of loss of control over information. Finally, they may have something to hide, and the FOIA is, by its very nature, a threat to secrets.

A Whitehall civil servant wrote: 'my colleagues . . . curse FOI, they grumble about having to deal with it, and think it's a waste of time and effort. Why are people asking for this? What on earth can they possibly want it for? All they're going to do is use it to cause trouble for us, to make us look bad.'[29]

Research looking at the experience of FOI officers in UK universities uncovered similar views. When asked about the attitude of senior management to the FOIA, 38% described it as 'begrudging compliance', which was at least better than the 24% with 'resistant' senior colleagues. It is perhaps no surprise that when asked about the three most difficult aspects of handling FOI requests, 92% of respondents cited dealing with colleagues among those three. Only 42% included dealing with applicants in this list.[30]

Among the practical skills that FOI officers therefore need to adopt is the ability to negotiate difficult relationships with colleagues. There are plenty of books and courses which aim to support individuals in dealing with these situations. Typically they suggest the following approaches:

- *Plan ahead* – think about what room for manoeuvre there may be: for example, consider what objections colleagues might have to disclosure of certain information, and what suggestions might therefore be made, such as what exemptions might be relevant.
- *Listen* – don't interrupt and make it clear that you are considering your colleagues' concerns.
- *Be assertive* – be clear about differences in opinion: perhaps it just isn't possible to apply an exemption legitimately in the circumstances; don't be afraid to challenge extreme or unreasonable statements, e.g. 'If we disclose this, no one will ever work with us ever again!'.
- *Suggest solutions* – consider whether a compromise can be found: it might not be possible to withhold everything, but maybe there is one particular paragraph that causes most concern, which it would be possible to justify withholding.
- *Don't be rushed* – if necessary, take more time to think about a situation or seek advice.
- *Keep calm* – if the FOI officer appears to struggle or panic, it is harder to convince colleagues that they know what they are doing. Be careful about body language – what signals are being given off?[31]

One way to counter negativity is for the FOI officer to demonstrate their competence. The more they know about their subject area, when they have an answer for everything, the more their colleagues will come to trust and accept their word. Knowledge of the latest guidance and decisions is the FOI officer's sword and shield.

If necessary, refer matters upward. If there is an FOI champion at the top of the organisation, involve them in difficult discussions. Line managers should also be there to support FOI officers. Ultimately, FOI officers are not going to win every battle. Sometimes a strategic retreat is called for. If the authority, in the person of the decision maker, takes the view that information should be withheld, the FOI officer may need to abide by that. They should accept it professionally (and wait to see if they will be proved right following an appeal).

Finally, no employee deserves to be bullied or intimidated. If FOI officers feel they are being treated in this way, they should seek assistance from their line manager, human resources department or other source of help in (or if necessary outside) their organisation. Many public sector employers give employees access to an employee assistance programme, providing independent confidential advice on workplace welfare, counselling and other services.

Summing up

- Senior level commitment to FOI is essential for implementing policies and procedures within an organisation to comply with FOI legislation successfully.
- It is a good idea to appoint a senior level FOI champion.
- FOI officers should report regularly on FOI to these champions.
- Monitoring and reporting on FOI performance demonstrates the commitment of senior officials and the authority.
- Holding officials to account for FOI performance can help to improve it.
- FOI officers can use FOI request volumes and performance to make the case for additional resources.
- UK public authorities are now expected to publish statistics on FOI compliance.
- Policies and procedures provide an important framework and document the authority's approach to FOI.
- Warn contractors and those bidding for work about the implications of FOI, and contracts should include obligations to assist the authority in answering relevant requests.
- Build FOI into procedures and IT systems through transparency by design.
- There are two main ways to organise FOI within an authority – centralised and devolved.
- FOI officers rely on an eco-system of support across their authority usually including contact points (or FOI liaison officers) in different teams.
- FOI liaison officers' responsibilities vary depending on the way the authority organises FOI administration.

- The role of an employee in the administration of FOI should dictate the level of awareness raising and training to which they are subject.
- Dealing with uncooperative colleagues is the hardest part of an FOI officer's job; knowing how to handle disputes is an essential skill for practitioners.

Chapter 12

Managing FOI requests

Introduction

Compliance with FOI laws is more than an exercise in legal analysis. More than anything else it is a logistical challenge, which requires organisational and attitudinal change. As discussed in Chapter 10, public authorities need an FOI officer or team to oversee the day-to-day administration of FOI. They need to be supported while they put in place an infrastructure of policies, procedures and training, as explored in Chapter 11. With all of this in place, an authority is ready to receive and process a request for information.

This in itself is not as straightforward as it might at first appear. The request has to be received, and not blocked by spam filters. The person who receives it has to know what it is, what to do with it, log its receipt, calculate a time limit by which it must be answered, and identify in which department there is likely to be someone able to answer it. That person must understand the question asked and identify, locate and extract the information requested. This has to be done while ensuring that the services they are primarily responsible for delivering are not disrupted.

Potential consequences of disclosing the information sought in an FOI request have to be considered. Anyone who might be affected by the disclosure should normally be consulted. Where appropriate, the relevant legal justification for refusal of some or all of the information has to be identified. If the information takes the form of a copy of a document, and only some of its content can be disclosed, parts of it will need to be blanked out. A response needs to be drafted specifying which information is being refused and explaining why; this might need the approval of someone with the appropriate authority. The approved response then has to be sent to the correct address, and a record kept of what was sent and when. All of this assumes that the information can be found, is located in one discrete unit of the authority, and that it is clear what can and cannot be disclosed.

If FOI deadlines are to be met, FOI officers have to ensure that a standard workflow is established taking each request from receipt to response, that they can negotiate objections and resistance, and that lessons are learnt when these various procedures do not go to plan. Figure 12.1 illustrates the process of handling an FOI request from receipt to response.

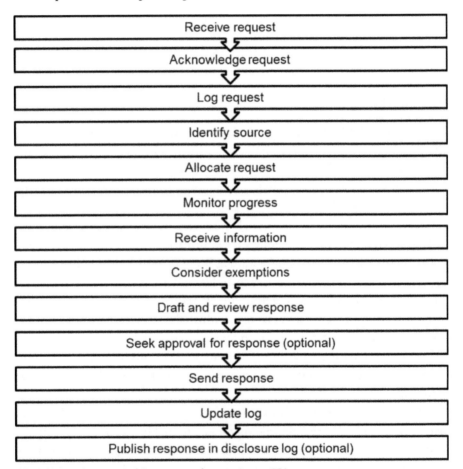

Figure 12.1 *Summary of the process of managing an FOI request*

Receiving requests

Requests have to be submitted to an authority, and authorities should facilitate the public submitting them as much as possible, especially if they want applicants to make their requests in a particular way. The s. 45 code of practice states that public authorities 'should, as a matter of best practice, publish a postal address and email address (or appropriate online alternative) to which applicants can send requests for information or for assistance'.[1]

Some authorities have sought to reduce the numbers of requests submitted by insisting on the use of an online form rather than publishing an e-mail address. This makes it more difficult for those who wish to submit the same request to multiple authorities ('round robin' requests), and for external request submission sites such as WhatDoTheyKnow.com. It can be argued that placing barriers in the way of those seeking to make requests does not fit with the spirit of the legislation. There is also a risk that failing to publish an e-mail address forces applicants and external sites to search out or guess alternative e-mail addresses. This makes it harder to identify and log requests, and could lead to increased disruption to other services.

If FOI officers want requests to be received at a central point, it is best to provide multiple means for those requests to be submitted. If a form is provided, ensure that it asks only for the information required in order to process the request. Asking for more personal information than is necessary breaches data protection laws (notably principle (c) – the minimisation principle - set out in article 5 of the GDPR).

Even where authorities provide instructions on how to make a request, any request received by colleagues throughout the authority – whether by e-mail, text, letter, on a form or even through social media – may be valid. It is essential that all staff are trained to recognise a potential FOI request and know what to do with it.

Acknowledging requests

When a request is received, it is good practice to acknowledge receipt. A suggested text for such an acknowledgement can be found in Appendix 2. This simple expedient reassures the applicant that their request is receiving attention and is an opportunity to draw their attention to a privacy notice explaining how their data will be used (see 'The gist – GDPR, FOIA and being transparent').

The gist – the GDPR, FOIA and being transparent
Managing FOI requests involves handling personal information, and as such is subject to the rules set out in the GDPR. The first principle outlined in the GDPR requires data controllers to be transparent, and elsewhere in the regulation individuals are given a right to be told how their information will be used. Article 13 specifies that certain

information must be provided to individuals at the point that their information is collected.

Public authorities collect information about applicants when they make a request, and process that information for various reasons throughout the course of managing it. The obvious reason for processing this information is to fulfill the obligations in the FOIA by ensuring that the request is answered. However, authorities very often process information about applicants for reasons other than for the purpose of answering the request. They might categorise applicants as journalists, campaigners or private individuals, or discuss the request with colleagues elsewhere if they suspect it has been sent to multiple authorities (i.e. that it is a round robin request). The principle of transparency in the GDPR demands that applicants be informed about these activities if they are going on.

This is the minimum information that an authority is expected to provide:

- contact details for the authority and its data protection officer
- details of what the information will be used for
- a statement setting out the lawful basis for processing the data (the legal obligation to answer the request will be one; but alternative bases will be needed for supplementary activities such as those described above)
- details of who information may be shared with
- details of how long information will be retained
- a reminder of the applicant's rights.

This information can primarily be supplied via the authority's website, but FOI officers should consider how to draw it to the attention of applicants when they make a request. An obvious way of doing this is to include a short statement in any acknowledgement sent out, with an explanation (including a link) of how to access the relevant website page for further details. An example of an acknowledgement including this kind of statement is provided in Appendix 2. A suggested privacy notice for information request handling, based on the UK Information Commissioner's privacy notice, is provided in Appendix 3.

Systems for managing requests

Each request must be logged, which requires a system to be in place. There are specialist systems, but many authorities use spreadsheets or Access databases. Specialist systems such as iCasework typically go beyond simply providing a log of requests received by allowing a workflow to be automated. An FOI officer can allocate a request to staff in a particular team, who then draft a response and upload documents before a manager or the FOI officer is alerted that the response is ready for approval.

The 2017 council survey asked about systems used to monitor FOI requests:

What system(s) do you use to log and monitor FOI requests? e.g. spreadsheet, Access database, specialist software (please identify the brand/supplier if so).

Analysis of responses revealed that authorities using specialist software to manage requests did not perform significantly better than those that did not in meeting the 20 working day deadline for answering FOI requests. If anything, authorities that used a simple spreadsheet to log and monitor FOI requests were more likely to be among the better performing local authorities (those that achieved compliance with this deadline in more than 90% of cases). An FOI officer at one of these authorities explained: '[A] spreadsheet meets our needs and always has done – I employ a keep-it-simple philosophy.'[2]

However, improvements to performance in dealing with FOI requests might not be the only reason for adopting a specialist system. Such systems may lessen the FOI officer's workload by automating more activities, and can also facilitate reporting of statistics. Very often the system may support other activities such as the management of other correspondence, comments and complaints the authority receives.

As might be expected, it is more common for larger authorities to adopt specialist systems. They are more likely to have the financial wherewithal to procure such systems, and the volume of requests may also dictate the need for more sophisticated management techniques. Smaller authorities are more inclined to adapt available office software or 'piggy-back' on existing technology such as customer relationship management systems.

Authorities often use an e-mail client (typically Microsoft Outlook) and may use other technology to store correspondence and case notes, or to search for information. Some specialist software integrates all the various systems used. See 'The gist: systems used to log FOI requests' for a list of systems used.

The gist: systems used to log FOI requests
Many authorities use a spreadsheet to log FOI requests; these can be surprisingly sophisticated in their functionality. JISC Infonet (www.jisc.ac.uk/reports/information-legislation-and-management-survey-2016) provides a free logging tool based on an Excel spreadsheet, which calculates due dates and facilitates various reports. Though aimed at higher education institutions, it could be easily adapted for use by other authorities.

The 2017 council survey found that local authorities commonly use Access databases and SharePoint tables to log FOI requests. For example, a respondent from a London borough explained that it used a SharePoint Team Site to store copies of requests and replies, and a specialist system to log requests on receipt. One council used a Lotus Notes application.

A number of specialist systems are used in the public sector. The most well known is probably iCasework, used by central government departments in the UK and the Isle of Man, and by about 10% of the English local authorities that responded to the 2017 council survey. A full list of the specialist systems councils use is provided below, together with URLs for the suppliers' websites (note that inclusion in this list does not amount to an endorsement of any particular product).

In the NHS, a care quality system called DATIX (https://www.datix.co.uk/en/) is in common use for logging clinical care incidents. The suppliers have developed a module to track FOI requests and many NHS bodies use it. eCase (ecase.co.uk) and CycFreedom (gsaltd.com) are solutions commonly used by police forces.

At one stage, the company behind WhatDoTheyKnow.com, mySociety, offered a variation on the WhatDoTheyKnow technology (WhatDoTheyKnow for Councils) to local authorities as a means to manage and publish requests. Brighton and Hove Borough Council adopted the system for a while. However, this is no longer offered as 'the assumption of immediate publication in particular placed us in position as both poacher and gamekeeper, creating a conflict of interest we weren't comfortable with'.[3] Since then, mySociety has worked with the London Borough of Hackney to explore other ways that they can help with the management of the FOI lifecycle.[4]

These are the specialist systems the local authorities that responded to the 2017 council survey use:

- AXLR8 customer relationship management (www.axlr8.net)
- Firmstep customer experience platform (www.firmstep.com)
- House-on-the-Hill's FOI, Case & Complaints Software (http://houseonthehill.com/supportdesk/solutions/foi-request-management/)
- iCasework (https://www.icasework.com)
- Iken case management software (https://www.iken.co.uk)
- Infreemation (from Digital Interactive) (www.digital-interactive.com/products/infreemation)
- Microsoft Dynamics customer relationship management (https://dynamics.microsoft.com/en-gb/)
- Objective ECM (enterprise content management) software with a case management module (www.objective.co.uk/products/objective-ecm)
- Pentana Performance, previously Covalent (from Ideagen) (https://www.ideagen.com/products/pentana-performance/)
- Respond, sometimes referred to as Respond Centerpoint (from Aptean) (www.aptean.com/uk/respond)
- SERVICEmail customer relationship management system (Blue Flag Technologies) (www.blueflag.co.uk)
- Verint, previously known as LAGAN case management software (www.verint.com)
- Vuelio communications management software (www.vuelio.com/uk/).

What information should be recorded?

The system used to log and monitor FOI requests needs to record enough information to allow FOI officers to track the progress of requests, and to report on them afterwards. Typically, this includes as a minimum:

- a case reference number
- the name of the applicant
- the organisation (if relevant)
- the applicant's address (e-mail and/or postal address)
- a note of the type of request (FOI, EIR or, often, subject access request)
- a summary of the request and its subject matter
- the date received
- the date due (sometimes automatically calculated based on the date of receipt)
- the date the response is sent.

FOI officers may decide to record more details, for example it is common to record who a request has been allocated to (or where the information is to be sourced from). Details of any clarification sought, and dates of relevant correspondence may be logged. Some record type of applicant, choosing from categories such as journalist/media, commercial, member of public, campaigner, charity, other public body, and so on. Whether information was disclosed in full, in part or not at all, and which exemptions or other provisions were cited, may also be recorded.

FOI officers should bear in mind their obligations under the GDPR to be transparent (see 'The gist – the GDPR, FOIA and being transparent'), to minimise the amount of data recorded about the applicant, and only record what is necessary. If recording type of applicant, for example, they should consider why this data is necessary and document their reason for including it in FOI procedures.

As well as simply facilitating the logging of requests, systems may be designed to:

- send out automated reminders for colleagues tasked with providing information or responding to requests, typically sent at 10, 15 and 20 working days
- have reporting functionality, enabling ready reporting of compliance
- have workflow functionality, facilitating the progress of the request through

the authority from receipt and logging, through collation, approval and
eventually to response

- manage documents, enabling requests, responses and often the information
  itself to be stored within the system
- provide redaction support, enabling documents to be redacted as necessary
  within the system
- incorporate disclosure log support, enabling responses to be published
  directly from the system.

Which requests should be logged?

The definition of a valid FOI request in the UK is set out at s. 8 of the
legislation, as discussed in Chapter 2:

> (1) In this Act any reference to a 'request for information' is a reference to such a
> request which—
>   (a) is in writing,
>   (b) states the name of the applicant and an address for correspondence, and
>   (c) describes the information requested.

The reason for making this definition so loose is that it does not require
applicants to have any specialist knowledge of the FOIA to make a request and
benefit from the rights it gives them, but this presents a difficulty for FOI
officers. In theory, at least, every written (and in the case of EIR requests, oral)
enquiry is a valid request. Every question about opening hours, request for a
leaflet, press enquiry to the press office, and so on. As Hazell, Worthy and
Glover described the situation in relation to central government departments:
'The wide base of the mountain is all FOI (or non-routine) requests. This is
supported by an even broader base of subterranean "routine" departmental
correspondence which does not form part of FOI monitoring statistics.'[5]

It would be impractical to log every enquiry that meets the technical definition
of an FOI request. FOI officers therefore need to select which of these enquiries
to treat as FOI requests (which should be logged, monitored and reported on),
and which to treat as 'business as usual' or routine enquiries.

The 2017 council survey asked whether councils had criteria to help them
decide what to handle as an FOI request. Very few had any criteria in place for
this. Typically they used 'common sense' [response 2] and 'best judgement'
[response 3] to decide. Guidance published by the MoD jointly with the ICO in
2008 suggested that requests should be distinguished as follows:

- Treat requests that can be answered without question, e.g. for recruitment brochures, leaflets or press releases, and requests for information that is not recorded, e.g. 'please explain your policy on . . .' as 'business as usual'.
- If the request needs to be 'actively considered' treat it as an FOI request.
- If it is likely that the information will not be disclosed treat it as an FOI request.[6]

Central government has been publishing quarterly and annual statistics on FOI requests since 2005, which requires that a standardised approach to logging requests be adopted. The annual reports explain the criteria that government departments are expected to apply. For monitoring purposes, an information request is defined as one:

1. Which meets the criteria in section 8 of the Freedom of Information Act and if the request falls under the Environmental Information Regulations it includes requests made in any form or context, including oral requests; and

2. Which is a request for information that is not already reasonably accessible to the applicant by other means; and

(i)   Which results in the release of one or more documents (in any media) or inclusion of extracts of documents in the information released; or

(ii) Results in information being withheld under an exemption or exception from the right of access (either the Freedom of Information Act or the Environmental Information Regulations); or

(iii) The request is not processed because the department estimates the cost of complying would exceed the appropriate limit in accordance with section 12 of the Freedom of Information Act; or

(iv) The request is not processed because the department is relying on the provisions of section 14 of the Freedom of Information Act; or

(v)   Where a search is made for information sought in the request and it is found that none is held.[7]

The only circumstance not covered here, but in which it would generally be desirable to log a request under the FOIA, is where the applicant cites the FOIA or the EIR in their request. More entertainingly, one FOI officer in central government suggested to researchers that requests should be logged as FOI requests where 'the official who received the request [was] gritting their teeth'.[8]

In the early days of the FOIA, arguments about whether requests should be processed under FOI procedures were commonplace. This may have become less of an issue, but it is still worth documenting criteria so that requests can be logged and monitored consistently (an increasingly important issue if public authorities are to be expected to publish their performance statistics). Guidance can also be used to resolve the occasional argument about what should be treated as FOI and what shouldn't. This can happen on both sides. Colleagues may be reluctant to treat enquiries as FOI requests if systems and procedures for handling them are particularly onerous. Journalists in particular often feel aggrieved at their enquiries being treated as FOI requests, as they fear it is a way for their enquiry to be 'kicked into the long grass'. FOI officers must know, though, that however an enquiry is badged, as long as recorded information is sought, it meets the definition of being an FOI request in the FOIA, and must be handled in accordance with the FOIA's requirements at a bare minimum. Press enquiries are dealt with in more detail in Chapter 13.

In other jurisdictions, there may be stricter definitions of a valid request, helping staff involved to avoid having to deal with the difficulties described above. In the Isle of Man, for example, applicants are required to fill in a form for their request to be valid.

Should the identities of applicants be circulated?

One perennial argument among FOI officers is whether to disclose the identities of applicants to colleagues within the authority. Many take the view that it is good practice for the FOI officer or team to remove the name and contact details of an applicant before forwarding the request to colleagues, pointing to the oft-quoted principle that the FOIA should be 'applicant blind'. One former FOI officer commented: 'It is so much of a distraction that I fundamentally disapprove of the idea of letting your colleagues know who the requester is.'[9]

There are, though, equally strong feelings on the other side. FOI officers who adopt such policies often face resistance from colleagues who might argue that they need to know the identities of applicants, especially if they are to know when a pattern of requests is becoming vexatious, for example, or when to aggregate the costs of requests. When facing the wrath of a senior officer demanding to know who has made a request, it can be hard to explain why they can't be told. (Though the fact that the senior officer is so desperate to know might raise a question mark over how impartial they are likely to be!).

Aside from the 'applicant-blind' argument, there is a firm legal basis for restricting circulation of applicant identity, at the very least. The identity of most applicants is personal information and must be processed in line with data protection laws (though not where a request is made in a company's rather than an individual's name). This doesn't mean that the applicant's name can *never* be disclosed to colleagues but that a 'need to know' policy should be in place.

The 2017 council survey asked English councils whether requesters' names were 'routinely removed from requests before they are circulated more widely within the authority'. Perhaps surprisingly, two-thirds of respondents stated that names of applicants are disclosed to colleagues. At first sight, this might be concerning, but most of these authorities were operating a 'devolved' approach to FOIA management. Colleagues in other teams needed to know who the applicant was, as they responded directly to them.

FOI officers should give serious thought to this, however. Where a centralised process is used to manage FOI requests, it is normally very difficult to argue that wider circulation of the applicant's identity is justified, except in very specific circumstances. One argument for adopting a more centralised approach might well be that it facilitates the better protection of applicants' identities. Whatever approach is taken, it would be sensible to document the chosen policy, including the circumstances in which identities will be shared more widely within the authority.

Allocating requests

The FOI officer or team should allocate the request to a team, so they can locate the information and return it to them (centralised approach) or continue to process it (devolved approach). The FOI officer generally identifies the appropriate team through their knowledge of the organisation.

They may be helped in this by FOI liaison officers (see Chapter 11) in other teams, who should be able to advise whether their team is likely to hold the information, or indeed whether it is held at all. If a request covers the whole authority, or several teams across it, the FOI officer or team commonly retains control of the request even when a devolved approach is more generally followed. It can be helpful to maintain a list of commonly requested subject areas and the likely sources of that information, especially if staff turnover within the FOI team is high.

FOI triage

Once a team is tasked with an FOI request, the staff member who acts as the FOI liaison officer or equivalent should assess the request. There are some key questions that need to be answered as soon as possible:

- *Is the request so routine that it can be dealt with straight away?* If so, it is advisable to deal with it immediately so that resources can be focused on more difficult enquiries.
- *Is the request clear enough to be able to identify the information requested?* If not, the applicant will need to be contacted for clarification (see Chapter 13).
- *Is the information held?* The answer to this question won't always be straightforward, but if possible it should be determined quickly, since all other work depends on knowing this fact. In addition, it rarely makes sense to an applicant when an authority responds after a long delay to say that information is not held (even though sometimes it may legitimately take a long time to establish this). If the information isn't held by the team concerned, but it is known that it is held by another team, the FOI officer or team clearly needs to be informed of this as early as possible. If it is suspected that the information is held by another authority, whoever is responding to the request should advise the applicant of this (or consider transferring the request, as appropriate).
- *How much will it cost to answer the request?* If it is estimated that it will cost more than £450 (or £600 for central government) to reply to the request, the request can be refused (or charged for), as discussed in Chapter 2. If the liaison officer believes that answering the request will exceed the cost limit, they should estimate the cost as soon as possible. Even if the estimate is for less than the cost limit, where it is necessary to collate information from several teams to answer a request, it may be that the combined estimates would exceed the cost limit. Therefore FOI liaison officers should contact FOI officers for advice as soon as possible if they have any concerns over the time required to comply with a request.
- *Are there any third parties (other organisations or individuals) who need to be consulted about the information?* If any of the affected information was provided by a third party, or its disclosure is likely to affect them, it is good practice to consult them. The sooner they can be contacted the better, to allow them enough opportunity to study the request, and for their views to be considered before sending a response.
- *Does any information need to be withheld for any reason?* If it is likely that an exemption should be considered, this ought to be flagged at an early stage, and advice sought as relevant. Consideration and application of exemptions is one of the most time-consuming aspects of dealing with FOI requests. Being slow to realise that exemptions need to be considered is a common reason for responding late to FOI requests.

Searching for information

Those tasked with providing information should conduct a search to find it, which may be easier said than done. Information is rarely available at the touch of a button, as some applicants appear to expect. Searches usually consist of a combination of knowledge, use of finding aids, and intuition. Good records management can certainly help, but as one FOI officer commented:

> I think what we found in terms of FOI is that the ability to retain information is based on a person and not a system. It is the person who knows what keyword it is. It is the person that knows what the subject area is. It is the person that interprets a request. It's the person that says 'this department is the one that you need to go to because they had dealings over this'. So a lot of the knowledge is with the person.[10]

This was echoed in the responses English local authorities gave to the 2017 council survey. As might be recalled from Chapter 10, one FOI officer at a high-performing council observed that one reason for their success was the length of time he and a colleague had worked there. Therefore they had a thorough knowledge of where information was likely to be located.

A problem that FOI officers, FOI liaison officers and others engaged in searching for information in response to an FOI request are likely to encounter is knowing how far to go. In many cases it is obvious what information is relevant and exactly where it can be retrieved from. However, often FOI officers or liaison officers don't know for sure where information might be found. If someone asks for correspondence on a particular subject, let's say, how do they know that relevant correspondence won't be found in every team within the authority? If the authority is very large and complex, this could become an impossibly daunting task.

This is not an ideal situation for the applicant either. If it is an impossibly daunting task to answer their FOI request, the authority is likely to estimate that it would cost more than the appropriate limit to locate and retrieve the information required, and refuse their request.

Authorities are not required to carry out such exhaustive searches. As the s. 45 code suggests, following decisions by the Commissioner and tribunals (see 'The gist: Doctor Who and the search of infinity' on page 191):

> …searches should be conducted in a reasonable and intelligent way based on an understanding of how the public authority manages its records. Public authorities should concentrate their efforts on areas most likely to hold the requested

information. If a reasonable search in the areas most likely to hold the requested information does not reveal the information sought, the public authority may consider that on the balance of probabilities the information is not held.[11]

Those searching for information should consider whether it is likely to be held outside the obvious places, for example:

- in back-ups containing deleted e-mails[12]
- in discussions using private e-mail accounts, WhatsApp or other social media applications[13]
- on employees' personal devices (e.g. mobile phones, tablets, laptops)[14]
- in cloud storage[15]
- in off-site record stores.[16]

Whether or not information is held depends on whether it has been recorded for the purposes of the public authority's business. Information held on behalf of others need not be provided, including employees' personal correspondence held on authority servers, and party political correspondence or records and constituency or ward correspondence that elected officials have stored on an authority's systems. A more detailed discussion of when information is held for the purposes of answering FOI requests can be found in Chapter 2.

Searching for information includes all the activities described in the fees regulations:

- identifying whether the information is held
- locating the information
- retrieving the information
- extracting the information.[17]

Very often it is necessary to involve several colleagues in a search for information. In order to ensure that searches are carried out consistently, the person co-ordinating the search – the FOI officer, an FOI liaison officer or another individual – should set out clear instructions stating:

- which records or systems need to be searched
- which search terms to use (specific terms to be searched for in an e-mail account, say) or where else to seek information (e.g. to check a physical file or notebook for references to a particular subject or event)

- a deadline for returning any located information with details of how to provide it.

Once the information has been collated through these activities, consideration can be given as to whether it can be disclosed.

The gist: Doctor Who and the search of infinity

Information Commissioner Decision Notice FS50366306: Cardiff Council, 30 August 2011

Mr Hastings wanted to see correspondence between the BBC and Cardiff City Council in relation to the making of the BBC television series *Doctor Who*. The council refused citing s. 12, arguing that as they could not rule out the possibility that any member of staff across the council had received such correspondence, they would have to ask large numbers of staff to search their records. They variously estimated that up to 15,000, 6,000, 600 or 300 staff would need to do this for anything from a minute up to 10 minutes each.

The Information Commissioner was unimpressed by the inconsistency of Cardiff City Council's argument and pointed to the fact that the council had conceded that it was most likely that any relevant information would be held in the Highways and Communications departments. The Commissioner argued that most staff in the other departments would know more or less instantly whether they held relevant information and concluded that it would be feasible for the request to be answered within the cost limit.

The Commissioner's decision was upheld by the FTT.[18]

Consulting third parties

The s. 45 code of practice recommends that third parties affected by FOI requests should be consulted, and there are good reasons for doing so.

If individuals' personal information is affected, the fairness and transparency principle in the GDPR normally demands that they are informed before any disclosure is made. Where possible this should be done without identifying the applicant. When this is not possible, thought should be given as to how to balance the rights of individuals (for example by checking that the applicant is aware that the subject will be told of their request). If the affected individuals have already been told that their personal information will be disclosed it may not be necessary to contact them when a request is received. For example, if employees have previously been informed that certain information about them will be made available on request, or a notice included in a public consultation document states that the names of respondents and their views will be published.

Third parties of all kinds, whether individuals, companies or other organisations, often know the information and the implications of its disclosure better than the public authority. Their opinion of any proposal to disclose information may assist an FOI officer or liaison officer to better argue the case for withholding information. Alternatively, it may help them decide that disclosure would have limited adverse effect.

Ultimately, though, it is for the public authority to decide whether to disclose information. If a third party expresses concern, the FOI officer or liaison officer should decide whether that concern is justified, consulting colleagues as necessary. If a third party fails to respond to enquiries, it is the authority's duty to reach a decision within normal timescales, unless the consultation aims to establish the public interest in maintaining an exemption. Waiting for a response to a consultation is not in itself a legitimate reason for delaying a response. That said, it is possible to envisage circumstances in which a public authority might decide that the risk of litigation or other harm resulting from disclosure in the absence of a third party's views outweighs the risk of breaching the FOIA's requirements.

'Round robins'

One kind of consultation sometimes attracts the concern of applicants: when public authorities discuss FOI requests among themselves. This tends to happen most when a 'round robin' request has been received. It may take the form of:

- FOI officers (or others) asking colleagues at other authorities for their views on how to handle a request
- sector leadership bodies circulating advice about how to deal with a particular 'round robin' request, for example, the Cabinet Office or central government clearing house advising government departments, Universities UK advising higher education institutions or the National Police Chiefs Council advising police forces.

In the past these sort of activities have been conducted routinely without much thought. There may be good reasons for public authorities to collaborate in these ways. At the local level it might not be immediately apparent that any harm could result from disclosure, but staff of the national body can see that the applicant or another person might be able to piece together responses from across the country to ascertain sensitive information (through what is known as a 'jigsaw effect'). In such cases, it is desirable for the national body to flag concerns with other authorities and make recommendations. As some authorities – such as parish councils or schools – have very limited resources, they may rely on picking the brains of better informed colleagues from outside their organisation to apply the law correctly.

FOI officers and others need to be careful when discussing requests with people in other organisations. Discussing requests from individuals can constitute processing their personal information. The Information Commissioner has criticised the Cabinet Office in the past for circulating names of applicants together with details of their requests across central government.[19] This was particularly because of the lack of transparency over what was happening, but bearing in mind the GDPR's renewed emphasis on there being a lawful basis for processing personal information, FOI officers should consider carefully whether such discussions and sharing of information about requests and requesters can be justified. At the very least, they should warn applicants that their requests may be discussed with other authorities in their privacy notices.

FOI officers may also consider issuing guidance to colleagues on discussing requests in online forums. They should be aware that some such forums are public, so applicants may learn of any discussion of their request. It is important that colleagues prioritise the advice of their FOI officer over that of colleagues in other authorities who may not be as well informed about the FOIA's requirements.

Keeping on track

Busy colleagues may not automatically be inclined to prioritise FOI requests over their other work. It is good practice to remind those tasked with answering a request that it still awaits response. Many specialist FOI systems provide for regular e-mail reminders or other prompts to be sent to specified members of staff, typically sent at 10, 15 and 20 working days after the initial request was received. An FOI officer from a surveyed local authority commented, 'The auto reminders kept FOI at the front of officers' minds.'[20]

Since automated reminders can soon become commonplace and easier to ignore, it can be helpful to adopt a more human approach when nudging colleagues about outstanding requests. FOI officers should not be afraid to pick up the phone to ask their colleagues how things are going, or even to drop by to see if they need help. One of the local authorities which had particular success in meeting FOIA deadlines suggested that this approach had been a key factor: 'The FOI team . . . flag requests to officers with a return date 1 week before the absolute deadline and then chase until the request is complied with.'[21]

With more complex requests, it may be a good idea to schedule regular progress meetings to identify and address emerging issues. If colleagues do not show initiative, it falls to the FOI officer to ensure that requests are kept from the bottom of the in-tray. 'We are happy to engage with colleagues to discuss/discourage application of exemptions and conduct public interest tests.'[22]

If teams regularly fail to meet deadlines, it may be necessary to involve senior management to encourage better performance, as discussed in Chapter 11.

Where a centralised approach is adopted, it is sensible to build in time to allow for the FOI officer or team to do their job once information is returned. One FOI officer recommended: 'Require your service teams to return all responses within ten working days – this gives some leeway to improve where responses are complex, insufficient or incomplete.'[23]

Providing advice

Even where a devolved approach to FOIA management is taken, FOI officers are often called on to provide advice about handling requests. It is therefore necessary for them to have and maintain expertise in the aspects of the FOIA that many of their colleagues may struggle with. In particular, FOI officers need to be prepared to assist colleagues with questions on:

- application and drafting of exemptions
- application and estimation of the cost limit
- whether a request is likely to be vexatious
- whether information is 'held'
- other technical issues relating to the FOIA and related legislation.

Preparing material

Once all relevant information has been provided to staff responsible for collating it, they should prepare it carefully. Many searches result in a large volume of documents. This is one area of the FOI handling process in which archivists, records managers and other information professionals should have particular aptitude. This is a possible approach to preparing materials:

- Decide on the order in which documents will be presented and sort them into this order – chronological, reverse-chronological or whatever is appropriate in the circumstances.
- Number documents and create a schedule listing them.

- Create a copy of the schedule and documents (either digitally or physically) and retain it with a copy of the response.

If the information consists of e-mail correspondence, there will be particular issues such as duplication of e-mails within chains. The guidance provided by the Scottish Information Commissioner to their staff suggests how to manage this:

- Save e-mails as HTML documents.
- Open HTML documents and insert page breaks at the end of each e-mail in the chain, leaving one e-mail per page.
- Delete duplicate pages.
- Take care to keep e-mails together when necessary (e.g. where a reply refers directly to something said in the e-mail it is responding to, such as 'in point 6 of your e-mail below').[24]

It can be helpful to watermark or stamp documents that are being disclosed to demonstrate that they have been released under FOI. Should the information be published or lost by the applicant or anyone else, it will be clear that the information has been disclosed deliberately, rather than the subject of a data security breach by the authority.

Redaction and hidden data

Where it is intended to provide copies of documents to applicants, and it is decided that some of the information is exempt from disclosure, the documents will need to be redacted. The following principles, which are based on guidance from TNA, should be adopted:

- *Use a copy* – carry out redaction on a copy of the original document.
- *Redact or summarise* – only use redaction if words, sentences or paragraphs within a document need to be withheld; if redaction would result in whole pages of black ink, it is better to summarise the information that can be disclosed.
- *Knowledge* – someone who understands the information and can identify the information that is exempt should conduct redaction.
- *Minimise redaction* – only redact the information that is exempt – if only two words in a sentence are exempt, don't redact the whole sentence.
- *Beware Sherlocks* – analysis of the size and shape of redactions might allow redacted text to be deduced; similarly, think about whether information

elsewhere in the document, or the context in which a redacted phrase appears, might lead an intelligent reader to guess what has been concealed.

● *Avoid reversals* – be careful to ensure that redactions cannot be reversed; check that digital files have been redacted and saved in a format that cannot be reversed, and ensure that redactions to physical documents cannot be seen through if held up to the light.

● *Keep records* – retain copies of redacted and unredacted versions of documents.[25]

There are various methods for carrying out redaction. Black marker pens are commonly used, but are not advisable for a number of reasons:

● Unless photocopied several times, it is usually possible to read redacted text by holding the document up to the light.
● The ink tends to bleed through the paper, perhaps obscuring information that should be visible.
● It can look scruffy.

Alternative physical methods include use of correction fluid or tape, or sticking post-it notes over the area to be redacted, before photocopying. The most commonly used digital redaction tool is Adobe Acrobat Professional, which is probably the best option as long as the person carrying out the redaction is careful to apply the redactions made and save the document under a new file name.

Where datasets are being disclosed, it is important to ensure that there are no hidden fields or tables. At least two London boroughs (Islington and Kensington and Chelsea) have received monetary penalties from the Information Commissioner for accidentally disclosing personal information hidden in a pivot table within a spreadsheet disclosed in response to an FOI request (see 'The FOI officer's development' in Chapter 10). One way to limit this risk is to save spreadsheets as .csv files; not only is this an 'open' format (see Chapter 9), but it strips out hidden pivot tables.[26]

Approving responses

Who has the final say over what is disclosed? It is legitimate for FOI officers or liaison officers to accept this responsibility, but an authority may choose to ask senior officers to make decisions about FOIA disclosures or the application of exemptions.

Given the junior position of many FOI officers within their authorities, they may (quite reasonably) be reluctant to take responsibility for making the final decision on whether information can be disclosed. They are unlikely to be in the best position to do so, as however expert they may be on matters relating to the FOIA, they may not be familiar with the subject matter concerned. Finally, it could be argued that if they are too involved in the final decision, their ability to provide transparently impartial advice might be comprised, should the request later be subject to internal review.

The contrary argument has much in common with the argument for adopting a centralised approach to FOI management. If responses are approved centrally by the officer or team with lead responsibility for FOI compliance, it is easier to ensure that they go out on time. Conversely, if managers in teams across the authority are given the final say, responses could be delayed, since dealing with FOI matters is not their priority.

The latter appears to be borne out by the answers from English local authorities to the 2017 council survey. Respondents from 60 councils answered a question about who approved responses to FOI requests. Just over half of them (31) indicated that FOI responses were approved by senior managers within the team that provided the information. However, when the responses are broken down by performance, the results are startling: the FOI officer or team approved responses in 20 out of the 31 councils that met FOIA deadlines more than 90% of the time in 2016, and heads of service or similar approved responses in 10 out of 11 of the councils that struggled to meet FOIA deadlines in 2016 (less than 80% of the time).

It seems that empowering central FOI officers or teams to make the final decisions about disclosures (suitably supported) is a productive way to improve performance against FOIA deadlines.

The involvement of press offices is discussed in Chapter 13. Press officers should not normally approve responses, but authorities commonly share draft responses with them before they are sent out.

Sending responses

Once the response has been drafted, enclosed material prepared, and approval provided as necessary, it can be sent out. The system used to log requests should be updated to record the date on which the request was fulfilled. If the authority maintains a disclosure log, this should also be updated.

Keeping records

A copy of the response and all disclosed material should be retained securely, whether in digital or physical form, including redacted and unredacted copies of documents where relevant. The FOI officer or FOI liaison officer should retain correspondence and notes on the processing of the request, depending on who co-ordinated the processing of the request.

The authority's retention schedule should include guidance on how long these records should be kept. Records are needed for as long as an authority is likely to need to defend its position. If no complaint is received, or once a complaint has been resolved, it is not normally necessary to retain records for very long, so it may be appropriate to adopt a relatively short retention period of a year or two from the closure of the case for records of requests (see for example, the ICO's retention schedule).[27] Authorities may keep anonymised records of requests for longer if they are useful for reference purposes.

FOI officers and their colleagues should remember that 'meta-requests' – where an applicant asks to see records of how their request was handled – are valid under the FOIA. Journalists have found out how their requests were handled using this approach,[28] with one discovering that officials at the Department of Transport had made rude comments about him in e-mail exchanges.[29] Officials should remember to express themselves professionally at all times (or at least be polite about applicants) when communicating about FOI requests.

Summing up
- Provide a single central point of receipt for requests, but make it easy for applicants to submit requests in whichever common format they wish.
- Ensure that colleagues know what to do if they receive a request direct.
- Specialist systems can be used to log requests, but a simple spreadsheet can be just as effective.
- Provide clear guidance on when to handle and log correspondence as FOI requests, and when to treat it as 'business as usual'.
- Ensure that applicants' personal information is handled in line with data protection laws and their other rights.
- Note that knowledge and persistence are more important in achieving compliance than technology.
- Give clear instructions to those carrying out searches for information.
- Conduct searches in an intelligent and reasonable way, based on an understanding of the way in which the authority operates.
- Keep records of how searches are conducted and who has been asked to do them.
- Regular reminders help keep request handling on track.

- Develop procedures for preparing and redacting documents.
- Take particular care to check that personal information is not hidden within datasets.
- Decide who will approve responses.
- An empowered and supported FOI officer or team, able to make their own decisions on disclosure, can make a big difference in meeting deadlines.
- Keep records of responses and material disclosed.

Chapter 13

Communicating with applicants

Introduction

One of the problems with regulating any activity is that it can become an exercise in compliance. Organisations adopt a 'tick box mentality', which can get in the way of what the legislation is trying to achieve. FOI is no different.

FOI laws are essentially about customer relations. Remember that one of the aims of the FOIA was 'to increase trust in public authorities'. It has been said that this was an unrealistic target for legislation, but perhaps it isn't for individual public authorities, and in particular for individual FOI officers. Laws don't increase trust – people do. Providing FOI is a public service, and FOI officers should aim to deliver it well and positively.

Some public officials balk at the phrase 'customer service'. Whatever they are called – customers, members of the public, citizens – if they make an FOI request, they are asking our authority to deliver a service. This is no different from any other service that a public authority might provide, whether it relates to housing, education, health care, record offices or libraries. Whatever the law may say about providing these services, they are much more likely to work well and be appreciated by those they are being provided to if public authorities consider the needs of those they are interacting with. In other words, if they aim to provide a good service to their customers.

The way that FOI officers and their colleagues communicate with the public is therefore important. In some situations, the manner in which a public authority engages with applicants may be of more significance than whether the information requested is ultimately provided.

Think of the points at which contact is made with the public as an opportunity; it could be to try to shut down an issue, to use clever language to avoid having to disclose something, or to make clear to someone that exercising their rights is considered a waste of the authority's time and resources. This is unlikely to leave the applicant with a positive opinion of the organisation or its employees. On the other hand, an FOI officer can use their contact with the public to demonstrate their professionalism, to show off the authority at its best, to win over a critic. The way staff in a public authority communicate with applicants and other correspondents affects how it is seen by the outside world.

First contact

Most people's first experience of an authority's FOI service will be via a visit to its website. FOI pages should be prominent, and ideally accessible throughout the website. For example, the website of TNA has a 'Freedom of Information' link in a list of hyperlinks related to legal requirements at the bottom of its standard page template (see Figure 13.1).[1] It should be easy to locate FOI pages using any search tool provided on the site.

The National Archives Kew, Richmond, Surrey, TW9 4DU Tel: +44 (0) 20 8876 3444	Find out more	Websites
	Contact us	Blog
	Press room	Podcasts and videos
	Jobs and careers	Bookshop
	Friends of The National Archives	Image library
		UK Government Web Archive
		Legislation.gov.uk
		The Gazette
Standard opening times	**Site help**	**Legal**
Monday Closed	Help	Terms of use
Tuesday 09:00 – 19:00	Website A-Z index	Privacy policy
Wednesday 09:00 – 17:00	Accessibility	Cookies
Thursday 09:00 – 19:00		Freedom of Information
Friday 09:00 – 17:00		Transparency
Saturday 09:00 – 17:00		Our fees
Sunday Closed		
Full opening times		

Figure 13.1 *Example of how website navigation can be designed to ensure that an FOI web page is easy to locate* [2]

The FOI pages themselves should include the publication scheme guide, possibly a disclosure log (see Chapter 8) and guidance for potential applicants. As discussed in Chapter 12, the s. 45 code of practice encourages authorities to publish contact details to enable individuals to make requests. Some authorities encourage potential applicants to first check their publication scheme and (if relevant) disclosure log before submitting a request. This is good practice and may have the result of preventing unnecessary requests from being made, as well as helping the individual to find what they are looking for more quickly. It is essential to ensure that publication schemes and disclosure logs are easy to navigate, or the benefits of this approach will be lost for both applicants and authority.

Providing assistance to potential applicants

Section 16 of the FOIA and reg. 9 of the EIR require that advice and assistance be provided to applicants and state that by following the guidance set out in the relevant codes of practice, a public authority will meet this requirement.

The public may be unaware of their rights, and it may be appropriate to draw a potential applicant's attention to them in some cases. For example, a member of the public might ask a public authority employee about a particular subject over the telephone or in person, and the employee is unable to answer the question on the spot. Rather than simply replying that they don't know the answer to the question, they would advise the individual to put their query in writing so it can be handled as an FOI request.

The s. 45 code of practice suggests that public employees should give assistance to potential applicants who cannot put their request in writing. Authorities should bear in mind the Equality Act's requirement to make reasonable adjustments to ensure that someone with a disability is not unfairly disadvantaged. Assistance could include directing the applicant to another person or agency who can assist them in making a request (e.g. Citizens Advice), or offering to take a note over the telephone and sending the note to the applicant to confirm their request.[3]

Clarifying requests

Advice and assistance is required when someone submits a request which is too broad or needs to be clarified. The old 2004 s. 45 code of practice suggested ways that an FOI officer might assist applicants (though notably this is omitted from the 2018 revision), such as providing:

- an outline of the different kinds of information that might be relevant
- access to catalogues or indexes of records that might be relevant
- a general response setting out options for further information that could be provided.[4]

An important point to bear in mind is that applicants usually have very little knowledge of how authorities retain information. Therefore, it is unreasonable to expect applicants to quote reference numbers or use the specific terminology used by an authority to describe information.

Remember that engaging with applicants can be helpful to the public authority. Often when a request is submitted that might be described as a 'fishing trip' – one which captures a broad range of information – it has been made because the applicant doesn't understand the way that information is retained. A phone call or e-mail to the applicant explaining what is held can result in them agreeing to reduce the scope of their request. Simply asking 'what is it that you're trying to get at?' can help the FOI officer to suggest alternative approaches that will be more productive for the applicant, and simultaneously reduce the burden of work for the authority.

FOI officers and their colleagues should be careful not to give the impression to an applicant that they must explain why a request has been made, but if they make clear they want to understand the applicant's request and ensure they receive a useful response, it is perfectly reasonable to ask questions about their aims. If an applicant is unwilling to explain the purpose of their request, their wishes should be respected.

The code of practice issued by DEFRA in support of the EIR demonstrates some differences between the EIR and the FOIA. Notably, the EIR require that applicants provide clarification about their request within 20 working days of being asked to do so. There is no statutory deadline in the FOIA; technically, once the applicant clarifies the details of an FOI request, it is effectively a new request. The 20 working days can start from when clarification is provided (although FOI officers in practice may use their discretion if the clarification is on a minor point).

Advice will also need to be provided in circumstances where it is estimated that the cost of compliance will exceed the appropriate limit. Indeed, not providing such advice may lead to an authority being ordered to disclose the information.[5] More guidance on this topic can be found in Chapter 2.

When might clarification be necessary?

Section 1(3) removes the duty to provide information from authorities in circumstances where they require further information to identify and locate it, and have informed the applicant of this. There are various reasons why an FOI officer might need to ask for further information, for example the request is unclear, there is more than one way to interpret it, or the request is worded in too general or unclear a manner to be able to identify what information is sought.

Whatever the reason, it is important that FOI officers and their colleagues do not make assumptions about what an applicant is looking for. For example, if someone asks for all complaints received in the last year, it is often necessary to go back to the applicant and provide them with options:

- Are you wanting the figures for the calendar year or the financial year?
- Are you interested in complaints made by the public or grievances lodged by employees?
- We keep a log of complaints, but only of those that are formally investigated. There may be other information in e-mail accounts. Will the provision of the log meet your needs?

Effectively, if there is any doubt or room for misinterpretation, clarification shoud be sought. Making the decision for the applicant may result in them being disappointed in the outcome, and perhaps then asking for the information that has been discounted. Then the authority's employees will end up having to carry out more work than would otherwise have been the case.

Means of communication

Responses to requests have to be in writing, but it is not necessary for every communication with the applicant to be written. Often those making requests respond better to a telephone call than an e-mail. FOI officers are more likely to come across as a human being trying to help over the telephone than via e-mail or letter. No matter how carefully correspondence is written, it can appear officious or be misunderstood. When people hear someone on the telephone, they can pick up on signals in the tone of the caller's voice that encourage trust. FOI officers should be ready to pick up the phone where clarification is required. Often it can save a lot of time over exchanging a series of e-mails.

The shortcoming of telephone calls is that unless they are recorded it is not possible to prove what has been agreed during the conversation. However, this limitation can be addressed simply by the FOI officer noting the outcome of a telephone conversation (e.g. the applicant agreeing to vary their request) in an e-mail, sending it to the applicant afterwards, and asking them to confirm they are happy with the summary of the conversation.

There is nothing wrong with seeking clarification by e-mail or letter in principle, but FOI officers should consider what is the most productive way to clarify an unclear request.

The gist: the myth of the applicant- and purpose-blind principle
K v IC, EA/2014/0024, 2 June 2014, para. 19
There is a widely accepted principle in FOI that requests should be processed in an applicant- and purpose-blind manner.

Broadly speaking, these are good principles to be guided by. In most circumstances, applicants should be entitled to receive information no matter who they are, or why they want it. However, the FTT pointed out in *K v IC* that these principles should not always be followed, and to say otherwise is a 'misleading oversimplification'. In particular, the FTT listed the following circumstances in which these principles are not relevant:

- when the motives of a campaign group are relevant in considering the public interest in disclosure
- when deciding whether to aggregate costs under s. 12
- when deciding whether a request is vexatious
- when it may be appropriate to consider what the applicant's purpose is when providing advice and assistance
- when the ability of an individual to access the information is relevant when considering whether s. 21 (information otherwise accessible) applies
- when the identity of someone who asks for personal information dictates whether s. 40(1) or s. 40(2) are likely to apply.

In particular, in this case, the argument was made that the applicant's request was not valid because it depended on the context of their relationship with their local authority and knowledge of previous correspondence that had led to the request. The FTT was not impressed by this argument. The principle of applicant- and purpose-blind processing of FOI requests is just a rule of thumb, and should not be applied in a blanket manner, particularly if it is likely to disadvantage the applicant.

What do they know and request portals

In the UK, a popular means for FOI requests to be submitted is via the website WhatDoTheyKnow.com, established by the not-for-profit social enterprise mySociety, which seeks to use technology to empower individuals.[6]

The WhatDoTheyKnow site allows people to submit FOI requests. Any responses or correspondence relating to the request are automatically published online. FOI officers may want to warn colleagues that any responses they send to requests made via the site will be published, including their name and contact details if included in the response.

In the past, some authorities in the UK have refused to respond to requests made via this website, citing a number of reasons. The Information Commissioner explicitly states that requests made via the site will be valid, as long as the applicant includes a name and describes the information requested.[7]

The software used for WhatDoTheyKnow (Alavateli) has been used to establish similar portals in other countries.[8] MySociety has published evidence suggesting that applicants receive responses more quickly when they use such sites.[9] In Mexico, an internet portal is provided under the FOI law, and applicants are encouraged to submit their requests online.[10]

The gist: is a request made via social media valid?
The ICO's view is that requests are valid as long as they meet the definition of a 'request for information' set out in s. 8 of the FOIA (see Chapter 2), even those submitted via Facebook, Twitter or other social media, or via websites that facilitate the making of requests (such as the WhatDoTheyKnow.com website).

Twitter in particular poses difficulties in this context. Owing to the relatively short length of tweets (even since the maximum length was extended), it may be difficult to fit the name of the applicant and a description of the information into the body of a single tweet. Similarly, it is difficult in most circumstances for a public authority to provide all of the requested information in a tweet. The ICO's answers to these issues can be summarised as follows:

- As long as it is possible to identify the applicant's name – perhaps by looking at their Twitter profile – this suffices to meet the obligation to provide a name.
- An authority can publish information via their website (their disclosure log if they have one), and then the tweeted response just needs to include a link to it.

However, in a case that reached the FTT (*Ghafoor v IC*, EA/2015/0140, 9 November 2015), the panel took the view that public authorities should not have to go looking for the identity of the applicant, so unless all the required attributes were provided within the body of the tweet, it would be unlikely to meet the definition of a valid request. This places a question mark over whether most requests submitted via Twitter are valid. It should be remembered though that the FTT's decisions do not set precedent, and the ICO has not changed its advice as a result of this decision. Indeed, it appears that the Cabinet Office is also satisfied that requests submitted via social media, including Twitter, are valid requests under the FOIA.[11]

FOI officers therefore need to ensure that colleagues who manage social media accounts for their authority are aware of the possibility that requests may be submitted via those routes, and know what to do when a request is received in this way.

'Googling' applicants

Sometimes it can be tempting to use a search engine to find out about an applicant, whether through curiosity or perhaps when there is a policy that requires a certain type of applicant (e.g. journalists) to be flagged. However, a few words of warning.

First, carrying out a search for information about an individual applicant constitutes the processing of their personal information, meaning that data protection laws apply. For example, it would normally be expected that applicants be warned that making a request will result in such a search being carried out, and be necessary to identify a lawful basis for the search from article 6 of the GDPR (see Chapter 6).

Second, even if they aren't informed that a search will be made, the applicant may find out. Many applicants have websites, and just as public authorities collect data about visitors to their sites, they are likely to use software to analyse the popularity of their online presence. Software such as Google Analytics commonly provides reports on the searches that have resulted in someone visiting a particular page, so if an FOI officer searches on the name of an applicant, and clicks on a link to visit the website of the individual, this is logged by the website. If the search is conducted shortly after the request has been submitted, and the applicant can see that it was carried out in the area of the country to which they submitted their request, and perhaps uses the exact form of their name that was provided in their request, they will be able to conclude that a search has been carried out by someone in the public authority as a result of their request.

This is exactly what prompted a PhD student at the University of Sussex to carry out an experiment to establish how often employees of universities carried out searches on FOI applicants. Within 24 hours of sending out a request using a carefully chosen pseudonym, a fake website attracted hits from 30 different individuals at the universities to which the request had been sent. A third of visitors downloaded a fake CV that had been placed on the site, and many visited the pseudonym's Twitter page. The researcher gained a valuable insight into the extent of this activity.[12]

'Googling' an applicant can result in getting caught out by Google.

Around the world: Canadian traffic lights
Academic Alasdair Roberts described the way that Canadian government departments used a traffic light system to classify requests. Request files were 'amber lighted' or 'red lighted' depending on how sensitive the requested information was likely to be, or whether the request was sent by a journalist or politician. Those answering requests even had to complete forms indicating the communications implications of disclosures before a decision was taken to disclose it.

A database called CAIRS (the Coordination of Access to Information Requests System) was used to monitor the progress of sensitive requests, effectively providing the ability to keep track of what particular applicants were asking for across government. As a result there were delays to responses to requests made by journalists and politicians. Professor Roberts warned that routines aimed at managing compliance can prioritise control over transparency and accountability.[13]

Journalists

Journalists can usually contact a public authority's press office or equivalent if they want to get a quick answer to a question. Many find that going through the process of submitting an FOI request is too slow, given the speed that stories often move at.[14] However, as investigative journalist David Hencke explained to Matt Burgess, the ability to make FOI requests has value for journalists, as it allows them to create a 'much more accurate, detailed and hard hitting story that people can't challenge very easily because it is all based on documents'.[15]

Many public authorities have policies requiring FOI requests from journalists to be flagged with their press office. FOI requests made to a range of public authorities (in government, the higher education sector, and local authorities) during the preparation of this book confirmed that this is common practice in the UK.

Most journalists are probably aware (or at least suspect) that press offices are informed when they make an FOI request, but given the requirements of data protection law, it is advisable to be open about such practices. It is also important to ensure that such arrangements do not lead to journalists being disadvantaged over other applicants, as was apparently the case in Canada (see 'Around the world: Canadian traffic lights').

Press officers should not be allowed to alter information being sent out, but they may suggest changes to the wording of responses or provide contextual information to be included. More usually, the point of such arrangements is to ensure that press offices are forewarned of disclosures. There can be benefits for journalists where this happens. Matthew Davis, a journalist who makes a lot of FOI requests in the UK, has found it a positive experience with some authorities, like the Driver and Vehicle Licensing Agency (a government agency): 'I will get a response from the Freedom of Information team and a prepared response from the press office as well, and not a nasty response from the press office, but a sort of an explanation from the press office and an invitation to ring them up to discuss it further.'[16]

The fact that journalists usually ask for information in order to keep the public informed may strengthen their legitimate interest in accessing personal information, since the interests of the journalist and the public coincide.[17] The fact that a journalist is asking for information may strengthen the case for disclosing it in some cases.

Responses

The most important communication that a public authority has during the course of dealing with an FOI request is its response. Applicants are most satisfied when information is disclosed, but even when providing the information sought, FOI officers or their colleagues should think carefully about the content of their responses and the tone they use.

The response is perhaps even more important when information is being withheld, since it helps applicants understand why they can't have the information they have asked for. In these circumstances the law – s. 17 of the FOIA or reg. 14 of the EIR – specifies what must be included.

There are clear benefits to be gained for both applicants and authorities from the provision of a good response to an FOI request. Applicants are better informed, whether through receiving the information they requested or through a better understanding of why they can't have it. The benefit for the authority is that well-drafted responses to FOI requests can improve relations with applicants and the wider community. They can make the difference between enquiries being concluded swiftly, and months or even years of costly dispute.

The following paragraphs outline what should be included in responses to FOI requests. Some suggested response templates are provided in Appendix 2.

Releasing the information

If there are no concerns with disclosing information, a response still needs to be issued even though the FOIA does not specify its content. The very first section of the Act outlines the basic duty: to confirm that the information is held, and in that eventuality to communicate it to the applicant.[18] If the applicant has stated that they want the information to be provided in a particular format, this request must be met, as long as it is reasonably practicable to do so.[19]

Much of what is specified at s. 17 of the FOIA for refusal notices applies equally to affirmative responses. The s. 45 code of practice suggests that the following elements should be included in any response:

- A statement that the request has been dealt with under the Act;
- Confirmation that the requested information is held or not held . . . or a statement neither confirming or denying whether the information is held;
- The process, contact details and timescales for the public authority's internal review appeals process;
- Information about the applicant's further right of appeal to the Information Commissioner and contact details for the Information Commissioner's Office.
- If some or all of the information cannot be disclosed, details setting out why this is the case, including the sections (with subsections) the public authority is

relying on if relevant. When explaining the application of named exemptions, however, public authorities are not expected to provide any information which is itself exempt.[20]

As discussed in Chapter 9, disclosure under the FOIA or the EIR doesn't necessarily mean that the applicant is entitled to do what they wish with the disclosed information. The copyright in information that originated with third parties generally remains with them; public authorities retain copyright in information that they created. The response should set out whether re-use is permitted under the Open Government Licence or other terms, and that permission to re-use third-party data should be obtained from the relevant third parties. If a licence is not being granted at this stage, instructions (or a link to such instructions) should be provided on how re-use can be applied for.

There is no restriction on what further information can be included. It is often desirable to provide some context for the information that is being disclosed (the sort of information that a press office might supply if the disclosure is to be made to a journalist). It is up to the public authority to decide the extent to which it wishes to do this. Bear in mind, as always, that being helpful now can lead to less work in the long run.

Fully or partially refusing requests

Section 17 of the FOIA spells out what a refusal notice must include in several circumstances. If the authority is neither confirming nor denying whether it holds information or if it is refusing to provide information because of an exemption, it must:

- state that this is the case
- specify which exemption applies
- explain why it applies.

The Information Commissioner's guidance states: 'The explanation in the refusal notice should be detailed enough to give the requester a real understanding of why the public authority has chosen not to comply with the request'.[21]

If the exemption is qualified, the reason for claiming that the public interest in maintaining the exemption outweighs the argument for disclosing the information must be provided. This is also the case if neither confirming nor denying whether information is held.

When setting out these arguments care should be taken to ensure they are relevant to the specific exemption claimed. If more than one exemption is applied, the arguments should be set out separately for each one. There has been a lot of debate as to whether public interest arguments can be 'aggregated' – all the arguments for all the exemptions listed together. The consensus appears to be that however they are set out, it should be clear which arguments are relevant to which exemption. Certainly this is going to make it easier for the applicant to understand.

If the public authority needs longer to consider the public interest, its refusal notice must still be issued within 20 working days, stating when it expects to reach a decision on the public interest (the s. 45 code suggests that, where possible, this should be no longer than a further 20 working days later).[22]

Requests can be refused for other reasons than the application of exemptions. A s. 12 refusal needs to state that the request is being refused as the authority has estimated that compliance would exceed the appropriate (or cost) limit. It doesn't actually require that the total estimated cost be set out, or indeed how this conclusion was reached, but to comply with s. 16 there should at least be an explanation of whether and how the request can be brought within the cost limit.[23] As it is necessary to retain a record of how the estimate was arrived at, it is hard to think of a good reason not to provide at least a brief outline of the reasoning in the response. Applicants are much more likely to accept the refusal if they can see that the authority isn't just plucking figures out of the air.

Vexatious requests are difficult by their nature. A misplaced word here, an ambiguous sentence there, and an already difficult situation can be further inflamed. If the decision has been taken to refuse a request as vexatious, a refusal notice still needs to be issued. The Information Commissioner recognises that the circumstances may dictate how much detail it is appropriate to go into when explaining why this route is being taken.[24] The first time a response is sent out, the applicant should be told that further requests of this nature (exactly which requests will depend on why the request has been deemed vexatious) will not be answered. In this case, any further vexatious requests will not have to be responded to, though it will still be important to keep a record of their arrival.

Finally, all refusal notices must contain details of the authority's internal review procedures, and explain how to contact the Information Commissioner if applicants wish to appeal the decision.

Regulation 14 governs refusal notices in the EIR. The only significant difference is an additional duty in relation to the exception at 12(4)(d) covering 'unfinished documents'. Where information has been refused on these grounds, an estimate must be provided as to when the material is likely to be completed, and if the information is being produced by another authority, they must be identified.

Use plain English

Aside from incorporating the elements listed above, it is important to consider the manner of the response. Often the difference between a 'good' and a 'bad' response is less to do with what's included or not included, and more to do with the way that the information is imparted. Anyone who has made an FOI request themselves will be familiar with responses that are technically correct, in the sense that they tick all the boxes above, but are less than helpful.

The ICO's guidance states that: 'It is . . . good practice to use plain English and avoid the use of jargon or abbreviations whenever possible.'[25] This should be inarguable, yet many responses fail to meet this standard. Yes, the FOIA is a legal instrument, but it is not essential to talk in legalese. Applicants don't need a detailed explanation of the Act. It is best to avoid quoting huge extracts from legislation or case law – it is generally unhelpful. Although there is nothing technically wrong with the following language, from a response by a police force, it is arguably unnecessary and overly formal: 'When a request for information is made under the Freedom of Information Act 2000 (the Act), a public authority must inform you, when permitted, whether the information requested is held.'

Applicants know their rights (or they wouldn't have made a request), and don't need an explanation of the authority's duties. They just want the response to get to the point. Similarly, why use phrases like 'I would contend' when it seems very unlikely that the author ever uses them in normal communications.

There is a perception that because this is a legal requirement, it is necessary to write in a cold, formal manner. It really isn't, and the result is to alienate applicants, and make them more likely to complain. Focus on explanation not legislation.

Avoid 'weasel words'

Remember that the aim of the process is to help the public, not to obstruct them. Their request may not have described information in the exact terms used by the authority but it is not reasonable to expect this from an applicant. While the FOI officer is not expected to second-guess what an applicant wants, if it is obvious that they intend to ask for something but have not used the right terminology, it is usually appropriate to provide advice to them. Hiding behind 'weasel words' or an overly literal interpretation of a request damages trust more than any disclosure of embarrassing comments.

There are times when an authority is technically within its rights to refuse a request but it is hard to see what is gained by it. The exemption for information that is otherwise accessible to the applicant is designed to encourage public authorities to publish as much as possible, and to help them manage their FOIA obligations. However, it doesn't have to be applied if it would be easier to answer the question directly. An FOI officer in one council [response 59] responded to an FOI request asking for the number of FOI requests received in 2016 as follows:

Information in relation to performance can be found on the Council's website:

- Select 'Your Council' option from the available menu
- Select 'Meeting Agenda & Minutes'
- Select 'Audit & Assurance Committee'
- Select 'Meetings 12th September 2017'
- Select Item No.9 Additional documents = Appendix 1 A&A 12/109 SIRO Annual Report 2016/17. Page 8.

This is technically correct, but it would have been easier for them, and for the applicant, simply to provide the requested figure.

Provide what has been asked for

It is important to ensure that the applicant is either given what they have asked for, or provided with a valid explanation as to why this is not possible. This is important. If an applicant – whether a journalist, academic or private individual – is conducting research they often rely on collecting comparable data from a number of authorities. If a response includes data other than that described, it may not seem important to the individual drafting the response, but it can make the information provided redundant for the purposes of the applicant. It may simply lead to another request, but even if it doesn't, it could impede the publication of a public interest story.

For example, FOI requests sent to fire and rescue services across the UK revealed that up to 60 fires a week are being caused by faulty appliances such as tumble dryers and fridge freezers.[26] This story was reported in the aftermath of the Grenfell Tower fire, which started when a fridge freezer caught fire. In another example, requests to NHS clinical commissioning groups found that GPs were being offered financial incentives to cut hospital referrals.[27] Whatever the rights and wrongs of these situations, such FOI requests help to inform public debate on important issues, and FOI officers should not be seen as obstructing this kind of public interest activity.

If the problem is that an individual is asking for data in a different form from which it is normally collated, contact the applicant and ask if they are willing to accept the data in the form that the authority has already prepared. In many cases, they are willing to do so, but if an authority wants to depart from what an applicant has asked for, it is necessary to seek their agreement.

Structure responses well

The ICO recommends: 'If the reasons for the decision are particularly complex or several exemptions were applied it may be advisable to split the notice into shorter subsections to make it easier for the requester to follow.'[28]

Set out responses sensibly and clearly to make them as comprehensible as possible for the applicant. Especially when refusing a request, s. 17 and the form of the exemptions used provide us with a ready-made structure.

If a prejudice-based, qualified exemption is used, the following questions must be answered in the response to meet the requirements of s. 17:

- is it possible to confirm or deny whether the information is held?
- which section number and exemption is being applied?
- what is the particular harm (prejudice) that is envisaged and why?
- how likely is this harm (would or would be likely)?
- what arguments have we considered in relation to the public interest for each exemption applied?
- what conclusion have we reached about the public interest in each case?
- how can an internal review be requested?
- how can an appeal be made to the ICO?

In some cases, particularly where several exemptions are being applied, these points could become complex to follow. Many applicants may not even be interested in the detailed arguments – they just want to know whether the information has been disclosed. One way to deal with this is to remove the stages where the application of the exemption is being explained to a separate annex. The covering e-mail or letter briefly explains which exemptions are being applied and to what, and if the applicant wants to understand more about why the exemption applies and what public interest arguments were considered, they can read the annex. This is a common approach in good FOIA responses.

It is common practice to quote the question(s) asked before answering them. This is sensible, but it is easier for both applicant and those responding to quote one question, set out the answer, quote the next question, followed by the answer, and so on. Many responses include a page of questions submitted by the applicant before providing the answers on subsequent pages. The result is that anyone reading the response has to keep leafing backwards and forwards through the response to work out which question a particular answer is responding to.

Put your name to it

As the FOIA and other FOI laws are about openness, it seems odd to hide the identity of those responding to requests unless there is good reason (which there may be in certain circumstances). Certainly FOI officers, responsible for promoting openness and transparency in their authority, should normally be prepared to put their name to a response. If there are reasons why the individual who drafted the response does not want their name to go out, consider whether another official might be prepared to put their name to it (e.g. their line manager or the FOI officer if a colleague has drafted the response). At the very least the response should provide contact details (telephone number, e-mail address) for the applicant to get in touch should they have any questions.

Advantages of a good response

While much of the above is good practice rather than required, there are clear benefits to be gained from getting the response right. The Information Commissioner's guidance on refusal notices lists some:

- There are likely to be fewer requests for internal review as applicants will better understand the reasons why their request was refused.
- There are also therefore likely to be fewer complaints and appeals made to the Commissioner.
- The Commissioner and tribunals will take the quality of the refusal notice into account when considering complaints.[29]

There is another advantage for the practitioner. Sometimes the process of drafting a response can assist in helping an FOI officer decide whether an exemption applies. If it is difficult to explain in the response, it may well be a sign that there is insufficient justification for withholding the information. Ultimately, the authority may have to justify their response to the Information

Commissioner. If it is tricky to draft a response, it is almost certainly going to be difficult to explain to the regulator.

Summing up
- FOI is a public service, and authorities should aim to provide a good service to the public.
- It should be easy to locate FOI pages on a public authority's website.
- Assist those who may want to make a request.
- Remember that applicants don't know the organisation as well as its employees.
- It is OK to ask applicants why they want information if it helps them to get what they want.
- Don't be afraid to pick up the phone.
- Don't make assumptions about what the applicant will be satisfied with – if in doubt, ask.
- Requests should generally be handled in an applicant- and purpose-blind manner, but this is just a rule of thumb.
- Requests made via social media or online portals are valid.
- 'Googling' applicants constitutes processing their personal information, and they can easily find out that it is happening.
- It is common practice to alert press offices when a journalist makes a request, but authorities should be open about this and ensure that journalists are not disadvantaged over other applicants.
- Ensure that responses – especially refusals – are consistent with legal requirements, but also consider the tone used.
- Explain why information is being refused.
- Use plain English and don't rely on technicalities and overly literal interpretations of requests.
- Provide what has been asked for, not just what suits the authority's employees, unless the applicant agrees to an alternative.
- Structure responses logically basing them on the requirements of the legislation, if necessary putting detailed argument in an attached annex.
- Good responses reduce the possibility of receiving complaints, and the regulator may take the quality of a response into account when considering a complaint.

Chapter 14

Internal reviews and appeals

Introduction

FOI laws would be toothless if sending out a response was the end of the story. The ability of applicants to appeal decisions is a crucial aspect of the FOIA. It is inevitable that at times applicants disagree with the decisions made by public authorities. FOI officers are fallible, and do not always apply the law correctly. Very often the decision is out of their hands and more senior colleagues insist on a request being refused whatever they are advised.

It might seem twee, but complaints help organisations and their employees to learn, and FOI is no different from other areas of work in this respect. Whatever stage a complaint may reach there are lessons to learn from it. FOI officers may even be aided by the outcome of complaints. A critical ruling from the Information Commissioner or a court, while uncomfortable at the time, can assist in reinforcing messages that they have been trying to get across to colleagues for years.

The appeal process under the FOIA consists of several stages:

- an internal review
- an appeal to the Information Commissioner
- an appeal to the FTT (information rights)
- an appeal (on a point of law only) to the Upper Tribunal
- an appeal to the Court of Appeal
- an appeal to the Supreme Court.

A very small proportion of requests are taken even as far as the Information Commissioner. This chapter looks at how best to manage internal reviews and the role of the Information Commissioner before summarising the implications of appeal to the various further stages.

Internal review

The Information Commissioner does not have to consider any complaint made to her office where 'the complainant has not exhausted any complaints procedure which is provided by the public authority in conformity with the code of practice under section 45'.[1] Thus it is in a public authority's interests to adopt its own complaints procedure so they get early warning of any complaints that might end up with the Commissioner, and a second opportunity to prevent that outcome. This stage of the appeal process is known as internal review in a FOIA context, and provides an opportunity for authorities to nip expensive appeal processes in the bud.

In practice, very few applicants request an internal review. Hazell, Worthy and Glover noted this, observing that only 5% of requests to central government departments were subject to internal review.[2] Nothing much had changed by 2017 when approximately 6% of requests were subject to one, though where information was partially or fully withheld, the proportion rose to 17%.[3]

Authorities are expected to follow the guidance in the s. 45 code of practice.[4] This states that it is 'best practice' to have a procedure in place for dealing with disputes, noting the requirement at s. 17(7) to inform applicants of the procedure in refusal notices. The code suggests that applicants be advised that requests for internal review should be lodged within 40 working days, with authorities not obliged to accept complaints submitted beyond this point.

Internal reviews should be a 'fair and thorough review of procedures and decisions taken'. The old 2004 code of practice required that reviews be undertaken by someone senior to the person who took the original decision, 'where this is reasonably practicable'.[5] The 2018 code merely indicates that it is best practice 'wherever possible' for reviews to be conducted by 'someone other than the person who took the original decision'.[6]

As there is no legal requirement to have a complaints procedure, there is no statutory time limit on internal reviews. The code states that an acknowledgement should be sent as soon as a complaint is received, informing the complainant when to expect a response, and that they should be kept informed of any delays. It suggests that reviews should not normally take longer than 20 working days, though 'if an internal review is complex' more time may be required.[7] The Information Commissioner states that internal reviews should be completed within 20 working days, or 40 in 'exceptional circumstances'.[8]

Where the outcome is that information that was previously withheld be disclosed, it should be released with the response explaining the outcome of the review where possible.[9] The 2004 code noted that it might be appropriate to apologise to the applicant if mistakes were made.[10] If the outcome is to uphold the authority's original decision, the applicant should be advised of their right to appeal the decision to the Information Commissioner.[11]

EIR complaints

The EIR are different from the FOIA in that they specify that authorities should have a procedure for handling complaints. Applicants are expected to make 'representations in writing' within 40 working days of receiving a response if they are dissatisfied with the way that their request was handled. The public authority is required to consider the internal review and respond no later than 40 working days after the representations were received, though the Information Commissioner recommends, as with internal reviews under FOIA, that reviews are completed within 20 working days where possible. In practice, complaints under the EIR are handled in much the same way as those made under the FOIA.

Practical considerations

The code and the ICO guidance suggest that someone other than the person who handled the request in the first place should conduct reviews. This is easier said than done for many authorities. If the FOI officer handled the request, someone else has to complete the review. This requires someone else to have sufficient knowledge to do so.

This is an area where a devolved approach to FOI management can be helpful. The Irish code of practice provides an illustration of how this can work. The FOI officer is seen as providing an advisory role only. The requests are originally handled by the 'decision makers', and there are separate 'internal reviewers' across the authority who conduct reviews of the decisions taken by 'decision makers' as required. Both the 'decision makers' and the 'internal reviewers' are trained to enable them to fulfill their respective roles.[12]

This is more difficult where an FOI officer has been directly involved in processing a request, i.e where a centralised arrangement is in place. Very often where this happens, the FOI officer's line manager or the 'FOI champion' (see Chapter 11) may be tasked with considering the review. They should be trained in how to consider internal reviews under the FOIA.

Those conducting the review need to have (or assemble) a pack of materials, typically including:

- copies of the request, response and complaint
- any relevant correspondence or other records documenting the decision-making process, such as responses from third parties consulted
- a copy of the authority's FOI procedures
- extracts of the relevant sections from legislation (e.g. the full text of exemptions applied)
- copies of relevant guidance.

As their thought processes and decisions should be documented, some authorities conduct an internal review in the form of a minuted meeting. The FOI officer might act as clerk to the meeting, while the internal reviewer(s) deliberate (some authorities have a panel of officials to consider internal reviews). It is particularly important that thorough records of the process are kept, as it is more likely that requests reaching internal review stage will go on to be appealed to the Information Commissioner. See the end of Chapter 12 for guidance on retaining records.

Questions to consider

Those conducting internal reviews should consider the following questions as relevant to the specific case:

- Has the request been understood?
- Has the right legislation been applied (FOI or EIR)?
- Has the right exemption been cited?
- Has the exemption been correctly applied?
- Has prejudice been demonstrated?
- What public interest arguments were considered?
- Are cost estimates reasonable?
- How thorough was the search?
- How helpful has the authority been?

Responding to the complainant

Responses to the complaint should set out:

- the procedure followed
- what the reviewer(s) considered
- the outcome of the review
- what action will result (e.g. the information will be provided within ten working days)
- how to appeal the decision to the Information Commissioner.

If it is decided to disclose information it is normal practice to provide it at the same time as the decision where possible. However, if the information requires a lot of preparation, such as extensive redactions, the review response may be sent out as soon as the decision is reached with a timescale for providing the information.

The Information Commissioner

The Information Commissioner's function is set out at s. 47 of the FOIA: to promote good practice and the observance of the Act and its codes, to publish guidance and to provide advice. They can issue a practice recommendation to a public authority under s. 48 if it is not following one of the codes of practice. In addition, the Commissioner is required under s. 49 to lay an annual report before each House of Parliament and may report to Parliament at other times (such as when a minister uses their veto to overrule a decision of the Commissioner).

They have a role in enforcing the Act (and the EIR, since they are enforced according to the same rules). They are obliged to consider complaints from applicants unless an authority's complaints process has not been exhausted (as described at the start of this chapter), the complaint is considered frivolous or vexatious, or it is withdrawn.

They have the power to issue the following notices to enforce the FOIA and the EIR:

- decision notices (s. 50(3)(b)), which may require an authority to disclose information if the Commissioner disagrees with their original decision
- information notices (s. 51), which require an authority to hand over information relevant to an inquiry
- enforcement notices (s. 52), which require an authority to take steps to comply with specified requirements of the FOIA or the EIR.

Complaints to the ICO

Less than 1% of requests made to central government end up being appealed to the Information Commissioner.[13] Hazell, Worthy and Glover describe the process of receipt of a complaint by the ICO. First a complaint is received by a central case reception unit, where it is 'logged and screened to see if it can be progressed'. Those that are ineligible (perhaps because a complaint was not first made to the authority or was frivolous) are weeded out. A 'triage' splits requests between:

● straightforward requests, which a complaints officer can deal with
● more complicated requests, which need the attention of a senior complaints officer
● 'priority cases', which are 'time-critical or represent a "path-finder case, the resolution of which could close a number of others, or give direction on a particular topic"'.[14]

This was the process in 2007, and the details are likely to have changed since, but the broad approach described gives a sense of the way that complaints to the ICO are handled on arrival.

Statistics published by the ICO show that the Commissioner's preference is to resolve these complaints informally. In 2016/17, almost half of the 5433 complaints submitted were rejected because an internal review had not been pursued with the authority (30%) or for other reasons (16%). Of the remaining complaints received, half were resolved informally, and a decision notice was issued in the other half of cases (26% of the total number of complaints submitted).[15]

Following the 'triage', the relevant case officer contacts the public authority, very often the FOI officer, asking them to reconsider the case, taking into account the ICO's published guidance.[16] The following examples illustrate what ICO case officers are likely to ask public authorities:

● In relation to a s. 12 refusal: 'Please clarify whether a sampling exercise has been undertaken in order to determine this estimate.'
● In relation to a prejudice-based exemption: 'Please confirm which threshold of likelihood [name of PA] is relying on in this case, the lower threshold that disclosure "would be likely" to have a prejudicial effect or the higher threshold that disclosure "would" have a prejudicial effect.'
● In relation to the application of the commercial interests exemption at s.

43(2): 'Please ensure that you provide evidence which demonstrates a clear link between disclosure of the information that has actually been requested and any prejudice to commercial interests which may occur.'[17]

The ICO expects the authority to respond within 20 working days, and to provide:

- information about the context of the request
- copies of documents that support the arguments made
- background details about the requested information explaining why there are concerns over disclosure
- any legal advice received about the request (this is not obligatory)
- a view on whether the information could be disclosed in redacted form
- a view on whether it might be possible to resolve the case informally, perhaps by disclosing some or all of the information, or by taking some other action.[18]

Authorities are encouraged to keep communications with the applicant open during this period, and if possible to try to resolve the issue directly with them. Public authorities are allowed to change their position on which exemptions apply, but must explain any change of view on this to the case officer and applicant. The ICO states that delays in providing answers to their case officer's questions may result in an information notice being issued to demand the necessary information, or a decision being taken on the available evidence.[19]

If the matter cannot be resolved informally, either because the authority sticks to its position, or because the applicant insists on a formal decision, it is necessary for a decision notice to be issued. The case officer considers the authority's submission and drafts a decision notice, which a senior officer of the ICO approves. It is sent to the authority's chief executive or equivalent by first class post. FOI officers can ask the case officer to send them a copy by e-mail on the same day.[20]

Other action the Commissioner might take

The most common form of enforcement action that the Commissioner takes is to issue decision notices, but they use other methods – formal and informal – to enforce the FOIA and to encourage compliance.

One persistent complaint to the Information Commissioner is that an authority has failed to respond to a request within the appropriate time period. This might be noted within a decision notice. In 2015 an enforcement notice was used to require the Department of Finance and Personnel Northern Ireland to respond to four requests which were 'significantly overdue'.[21] The ICO has faced criticism for not using enforcement notices enough in the past, even when the public perception was that an authority was flouting the rules. Again, the Commissioner appears to favour more informal routes to address compliance issues. An example of an informal method used to promote improved compliance with deadlines is the ICO's monitoring programme. Authorities are effectively 'named and shamed' and kept under review by the ICO.

These are the criteria for selecting authorities to be monitored for a three-month period:

- Four to eight or more complaints about delays in answering requests by an authority have been received by the ICO within a six-month period.
- Where statistics are available, it is clear that an authority is answering requests within 20 working days less than 90% of the time.
- There are media or other reports suggesting there is a problem with compliance.[22]

If a public authority fails to comply with a notice (decision, information or enforcement), the Commissioner can notify the High Court (or the Court of Session in Scotland), which may then rule as if the authority is in contempt of court (FOIA, s. 54). This could result in a fine, sequestration of property, or (though unlikely) a two-year prison sentence for a chief officer.[23] In addition, *in extremis*, the Commissioner can obtain a warrant to enter premises (s. 55 and Schedule 3). The Commissioner also has the power to prosecute individuals and organisations where a request has been made to an authority, and a person has altered, defaced, blocked, erased, destroyed or concealed any record with the intention of preventing its disclosure (s. 77). This can result in a £5000 fine, but the offence has to be prosecuted within six months of it taking place. The result is that there have been no prosecutions at the time of writing, since contraventions may not even be discovered within six months, although a councillor in Kent was charged with the offence in April 2018.[24]

Around the world: complaints and appeals

In Scotland, the FOI(S)A s. 20 requires that applicants submit a request for review within 40 working days of receiving a response (or the date by which a response should have been provided), and the authority must complete its review within 20 working days (s. 21). Once completed, a complaint may be submitted to the Scottish Information Commissioner (s. 47). Appeal beyond the Scottish Commissioner is to the Court of Session on a point of law only (s. 56).

The Isle of Man's FOI Act provides for their Information Commissioner to consider complaints against public authorities (s. 42). As well as the normal routes by which a complaint might be considered, the Commissioner may propose a form of alternative dispute resolution to resolve a dispute (s. 44). Appeal beyond the Commissioner is to the Manx High Court on a point of law only.

In the States of Jersey in the Channel Islands, 'a person aggrieved by a decision' may appeal to the Information Commissioner within six weeks of an authority deciding on their request (Art. 46). The Commissioner's decision can be appealed to the Royal Court on the 'grounds that in all the circumstances of the case the decision was not reasonable' (Art. 47).

The Maltese FOI law requires complaints to be made to the authority within 30 days, and that authorities respond within 10 working days. Appeals to the Information and Data Protection Commissioner must be submitted within a further 60 days. The Commissioner's rulings can be appealed to the Information and Data Protection Tribunal and thence to the Court of Appeal.[25]

India's Right to Information Act allows applicants to ask for a review by someone senior to the public information officer (the FOI officer). Appeals can be made to the State or Central Information Commission which can, if necessary, impose penalties on the public authority.[26]

In Australia, applicants are not obliged to use an authority's internal review process and can go straight to the Information Commissioner if they prefer. Where internal reviews are requested, they must take place within 30 days.[27]

The USA does not have an information commissioner or equivalent. Applicants are advised to contact FOIA public liaisons within the agency in the first instance. Agencies establish their own 'designated appeal authorities'. If disputes cannot be resolved, applicants can contact the Office of Government Information Services (part of the National Archives and Records Administration) which provides 'mediation services'.[28]

Appeals to the First-Tier Tribunal

All notices issued by the Information Commissioner can be appealed to the FTT (Information Rights) under s. 57 of the FOIA. Appeals must be made within 28 days of the notice being signed.[29] In 2016/17, there were 281 appeals against ICO decisions to the FTT. Of the cases heard by the FTT in 2016/17, over 75% upheld the Commissioner's position, with a further 10% partially doing so.[30]

Cases that reach this stage can become very expensive for public authorities. Although there is no fee to appeal, authorities normally appoint legal representation at this stage, and it is common for it to take two years from original request to the decision of the FTT.[31]

The FTT can:

- review whether the notice was lawful
- review the Commissioner's findings of fact
- allow the appeal
- substitute their own decision notice for the Commissioner's disputed notice.[32]

Appeals can be considered on the papers (a legal term meaning that only written statements and evidence will be considered so the FTT will not physically meet the parties involved), or in a formal hearing (held in a courtroom). In the latter case, it is common for public authorities to call witnesses to hearings, sometimes including FOI officers. Convincing witnesses can make a big difference to the outcome of the case. In one case, the Home Office was successful in persuading the FTT that information about a contract should be withheld at least partially because one of their witnesses, the civil servant responsible for managing the contract, impressed the FTT with his in-depth knowledge of the subject matter. The FTT commented that he 'knows his business' in this regard.[33] Conversely, the FTT is unlikely to be impressed purely by the seniority of an official, and if they put forward alarmist arguments it can be damaging, as can be seen in this critique of a witness put forward by the Cabinet Office: 'In short, the unrealistic and inconsistent positions adopted by the Cabinet Office and by Mr Miller severely damaged the credibility of the Cabinet Office's case, and of Mr Miller's evidence, in regard to the documents remaining in dispute.'[34]

Appeals beyond the FTT

Permission must be sought to seek appeal to the Upper Tribunal. Such appeals are on a point of law only, rather than the wide-ranging reviews of the issues carried out at the FTT. If the authority still wants to pursue an appeal following the Upper Tribunal's ruling, the next stage is the Court of Appeal, and beyond that ultimately to the Supreme Court. Only a handful of cases involving the FOIA and EIR have reached the Supreme Court, notably the case involving Prince Charles's letters to government ministers, which took ten years to resolve.

Summing up
- Complaints are an opportunity to learn.
- Internal reviews are not compulsory under the FOIA (though they are under the EIR).
- Internal reviews provide an opportunity to resolve complaints before they reach the Information Commissioner.
- Someone other than the person who originally dealt with the request should consider internal reviews.

- Complete internal reviews within 20 working days preferably, and no later than 40 working days after receipt of the complaint.
- Applicants can complain to the Information Commissioner once they have exhausted the authority's complaints procedure.
- Half of all complaints to the ICO are ruled to be invalid; a quarter are dealt with informally; and a further quarter result in a formal decision notice being issued.
- If a complaint is received, the ICO's case officers will ask an authority to reconsider its position, and attempt to resolve the complaint informally.
- Decision notices can be appealed to the FTT (Information Rights).
- The Commissioner names and shames authorities to encourage improved performance against FOI deadlines.
- Appeal to the FTT and beyond can be time consuming and expensive.

Appendix 1

Methodology of the 2017 council survey on the administration of FOI requests

A sample of roughly a quarter (70) of all principal local authorities in England was selected, consisting of 7 county councils, 9 metropolitan boroughs, 14 unitary authorities, 8 London boroughs and 32 district councils (a slightly smaller proportion of these were selected given the large number of such councils). They were sent an FOI request consisting of 12 questions:

> Dear FOI officer
> I am conducting research into administration of FOI requests and I would be grateful if you could provide the following information.
> Part 1: The following questions aim to establish how requests are logged and monitored.
> 1. What system(s) do you use to log and monitor FOI requests? e.g. spreadsheet, Access database, specialist software (please identify the brand/supplier if so)
> 2. What criteria do you use to decide whether correspondence should be logged as an FOI request or (for example) handled as 'business as usual'?
> 3. Are requesters' names routinely removed from requests before they are circulated more widely within the authority?
> Part 2: The following questions aim to establish what resources your authority allocates to the support of FOI centrally, and whether requests are answered by a central team or devolved to departments across the authority.
> 4. Do you have an individual member of staff and/or team with lead responsibility for FOI (e.g. FOI Officer or Information Governance team)?
> 5. If so, how many FTE staff are there in this team?
> 6. What other responsibilities do staff in this team have? (e.g. data protection, records management, etc)

7. Are responses to FOI requests normally drafted by the central FOI officer/team, or are they drafted by staff in the department with lead responsibility for the subject matter of the request?

8. Who approves responses before they are sent out?

Part 3: The following questions are designed to establish the timeliness of responses and how this is monitored within the authority.

9. How many FOI requests did your authority receive in 2016? Please include requests under the Environmental Information Regulations (EIR) within this figure if you log these separately.

10. How many of those FOI & EIR requests received in 2016 did your authority answer within 20 working days?

11. Who is FOI performance (e.g. request volumes and timeliness) reported to internally?

12. How often are such reports made?

As a former FOI officer myself, I understand the pressures involved and thank you for your time.

There were responses from 64 authorities. The first full response arrived within an hour of the start of the first working day after the request had been submitted (suggesting perhaps that these questions were not too onerous).

Two questions asked about the number of requests received and number answered within 20 working days in 2016 to see if there was any apparent relationship between particular practices and performance against the 20 working day deadline.

Authorities were then banded by performance: 90%+, 81–89%, 80% or less. This made it possible to carry out initial analysis on responses to the specific questions on:

- use of specialist software
- whether names are removed from requests before circulation
- whether there is an FOI officer or team
- whether a centralised or devolved approach is used
- whether performance is reported on
- whether approval is sought for responses (and from whom)
- whether performance is reported on at least monthly.

A small number of authorities that had achieved a performance rate of at least 90% in responding to requests on time were sent further questions, inviting respondents to explain why they thought they were so successful at meeting the deadline, and what advice they would give to other authorities. The covering e-mail noted that these questions were not intended to be handled as an FOI request.

Appendix 2

FOI response templates

The suggested templates below are inspired by 'standard responses' published by the UK Ministry of Justice (and its predecessor, the Department for Constitutional Affairs) in the early days of the UK's FOI regime and still available in the web archive maintained by TNA (see Chapter 4). They include as necessary copyright and re-use notices advocated by TNA (reproduced here under the Open Government Licence v3.0). FOI officers should customise the templates carefully for their own use, ensuring that they meet their authority's needs.

Acknowledging requests

Dear [*applicant's name*]
Thank you for your request for information of [*date of letter/email from applicant*], received by us on [*date letter/email received from applicant*], requesting information about [*subject*].

Your request is being dealt with under freedom of information requirements and will be answered within 20 working days.

If you have any queries about your request do not hesitate to contact me. Please note the information below about your personal information.

Yours sincerely,

[*your name, address, e-mail address and telephone number*]

Your privacy: we use your personal information such as name and address so that we can comply with our legal obligations to respond to FOI requests. For further details about the use of information about you, please see the information request handling privacy notice on our website at [*url of privacy notice*].

Disclosing information as an attachment

Dear [*applicant's name*]

Thank you for your request for information of [*date received*] where you requested information about [*subject*]. The information you requested is [*attached/enclosed - delete as appropriate*].

Copyright and re-use

[*The notice below applies if you are willing to allow re-use of the disclosed material under the Open Government Licence.*]

The information supplied to you continues to be protected by copyright. Use of copyright and database right material expressly made available under this licence (the 'Information') indicates your acceptance of the terms and conditions below.

The Licensor grants you a worldwide, royalty-free, perpetual, non-exclusive licence to use the Information subject to the conditions below.

This licence does not affect your freedom under fair dealing or fair use or any other copyright or database right exceptions and limitations.

You are free to:

- copy, publish, distribute and transmit the Information
- adapt the Information
- exploit the Information commercially and non-commercially for example, by combining it with other Information, or by including it in your own product or application.

[*Alternative if information from a third party is being disclosed or the authority prefers to be asked for permission to allow re-use.*]

Most of the information that we provide in response to freedom of information requests will be subject to copyright protection. In most cases the copyright will be owned by [*insert name of public sector organisation*]. The copyright in other information may be owned by another person or organisation, and this will be indicated on the information itself.

You are free to use any information supplied for your own non-commercial research or private study purposes. The information may also be used for any other purpose allowed by a limitation or exception in copyright law, such as news reporting. However, any other type of re-use, for example by publishing the information in analogue or digital form, including on the internet, will require the permission of the copyright owner.

For information where the copyright is owned by the [insert name of public sector organisation] details of the conditions on re-use can be found on our website at [*insert link*].

Your privacy

We use your personal information such as name and address so that we can comply with our legal obligations to respond to FOI requests. For further details about the use of information about you, please see the information request handling privacy notice on our website at [*url of privacy notice*].

Complaints

If you are dissatisfied with the handling of your request, you have the right to ask for an internal review. Internal review requests should be submitted within two months of the date of receipt of the response to your original letter and should be addressed to: [*contact name and address*].

If you are not content with the outcome of the internal review, you have the right to apply directly to the Information Commissioner for a decision. The Information Commissioner can be contacted at: Information Commissioner's Office, Wycliffe House, Water Lane, Wilmslow, Cheshire, SK9 5AF.

Yours sincerely,

[*your name, address, e-mail address and telephone number*]

Disclosing information as answers to questions

Dear [*applicant's name*]
Thank you for your request for information of [*date received*] where you requested information about [*subject*]. The information you requested is provided below. I have reproduced each of your questions below with the response to each.

1 [reproduce question 1]
   [provide response]
2 [reproduce question 2]
   [provide response]

3   [reproduce question 3]
    [provide response]
4   [and so on…]

[*Continue with Copyright and Re-use and rest of response set out in 'Disclosing information as an attachment'.*]

Where exemptions apply

[*Include the following paragraph in the main response.*]

Exemptions applied

[*Describe information*] is being withheld as it is our view that it is exempt under [*state section and title of exemption*]. Further details are provided in the attached annex.

[*An annex to the main response should contain the following.*]

Annex: why exemptions apply

Information being withheld: [*describe information*]
Exemption that applies: [*provide section number and title of exemption*]
Reasoning:

- [*if class-based exemption, explain how information falls within class*]
- [*if prejudice-based exemption, explain what harm will be caused by disclosure, and whether you are saying that it would be caused or would be likely to be caused*]
- [*if s. 36 applies, explain that qualified person has considered the prejudice/inhibition and what conclusion they reached*]
- [*if s. 40 applies, explain why disclosure would breach the data protection principles*]
- [*if qualified exemption, list public interest arguments in favour of disclosure and public interest arguments against disclosure, and then explain what conclusion was reached and why*]

[*repeat above for each exemption that applies*]
[*remember that redacted documentation may need to be annotated to indicate which exemption applies to which redacted section*]

Where the cost exceeds the appropriate limit

Dear [*applicant's name*]

Thank you for your request for information of [*date received*] where you requested information about [*subject*].

We estimate that to provide this information would exceed the cost limit of £450/£600 [*delete as appropriate*]. In order to provide this information, it would require [*explain what would be involved*]. This means that it would cost approximately [*provide estimate*] to fulfill your request. For this reason we will not be providing the information.

It would be more likely that your request could be fulfilled if you were able to refine your request. [*If possible, provide advice as to how this might be done.*]

Your privacy

We use your personal information such as name and address so that we can comply with our legal obligations to respond to freedom of information requests. For further details about the use of information about you, please see the information request handling privacy notice on our website at [*url of privacy notice*].

Complaints

If you are dissatisfied with the handling of your request, you have the right to ask for an internal review. Internal review requests should be submitted within two months of the date of receipt of the response to your original letter and should be addressed to: [*contact name and address*].

If you are not content with the outcome of the internal review, you have the right to apply directly to the Information Commissioner for a decision. The Information Commissioner can be contacted at: Information Commissioner's Office, Wycliffe House, Water Lane, Wilmslow, Cheshire, SK9 5AF.

Yours sincerely,

[*Your name, address, e-mail address and telephone number*]

Appendix 3

Privacy notice for FOI requests

The UK Information Commissioner's privacy notice covering the processing of information requests is set out below (ico.org.uk/global/privacy-notice/make-an-information-request/). It provides an example of how to comply with the GDPR's transparency requirements (see The gist – the GDPR, FOIA and being transparent in Chapter 12) when receiving FOI and other information requests. It assumes that some information, such as contact details for the public authority, is provided elsewhere in the authority's privacy notice(s) or on their website. Some optional additions are suggested in [bold] to cover handling of personal information that is not required to meet the legal obligation of answering the request. The ICO privacy notice is reproduced under the Open Government Licence v3.0.

Why we use your data
Our primary purpose for using your data is so that we can process your information request.
[In addition, we use your data for the following secondary reasons:

- recording the types of applicant making requests to us by broad category (private individual, business, media, charity, campaign group)
- if you are a journalist or from a media organisation, our press office will be notified that you have made a request so that they are aware of any potential forthcoming news coverage to which they may need to respond
- we sometimes discuss requests that have been received with other public authorities (e.g. [add examples of organisations in sector]) to obtain advice. Although we never deliberately share the identity of applicants in these

circumstances, if you have submitted the same request to a number of authorities, your identity may be obvious to those who have received the request.]

Legal basis for processing

The legal basis for processing your request is article 6(1)(C) of the GDPR, which relates to processing necessary to comply with a legal obligation to which we are subject. In the case of information requests, the legal obligations are set out in:

- General Data Protection Regulations (2016)
- Data Protection Act (2018)
- Freedom of Information Act (2000)
- Environmental Information Regulations (2004)
- RoPSI Regulations (2015)

If any of the information you provide us in relation to your information request contains special category data, such as health, religious or ethnic information the legal basis we rely on to process it is article 9(2)(g) of the GDPR, which also relates to our public task and the safeguarding of your fundamental rights. And Schedule 1 Part 2(6) of the DPA 2018 which relates to statutory and government purposes. [In relation to the secondary purposes listed above, the legal basis is article 6(1)(e), which relates to processing that is necessary for the performance of a task carried out in the public interest or in the exercise of official authority vested in us. [If you are able to specify statute that supports the conduct of the activity in your sector, list it here – some authorities are obliged by law to promote their activities, for instance.]]

What we do with it

When we receive a request from you, we'll record the details of your request in our request logging database. This normally includes your contact details and any other information you have given us. We'll also store a copy of the information that falls within the scope of your request.

[If you are a journalist or media organisation making a freedom of information or environmental information request, we will let our press office know that a request has been received from you and keep them informed of progress. Note that this will not affect the information that you receive.]

If you are making a request about your personal data, or are acting on behalf of someone making such a request, then we'll ask for information to satisfy us of your identity. If it's relevant, we'll also ask for information to show you have authority to act on someone else's behalf.

We'll use the information supplied to us to process your information request and check on the level of service we provide.

If the request is about information we have received from another organisation we'll routinely consult the organisation(s) concerned to seek their view on disclosure of the material.

[In some cases we may consult other public authorities about your request in order to seek advice. Your identity will not be deliberately shared with these authorities, but may be obvious from the context (for example if you have submitted the same request to multiple authorities).]

We compile and publish statistics showing information such as the number of requests we receive, but not in a form that identifies anyone.

How long we keep your data

For information about how long we hold personal data about information requests, see our retention schedule.

What are your rights?

For more information on your rights, please see our main privacy notice.

Notes

Introduction

1   Falconer, C., Speech to the Campaign for Freedom of Information, London, 1 March 2004. Quoted in Hazell, R., Worthy, B. and Glover, M., *The Impact of the Freedom of Information Act on Central Government in the UK: does FOI work?*, Palgrave Macmillan, 2010, 101.

2   Higgerson, D., 'FOI Friday: the power of FOI, pesky press officers, school place race and mouse droppings', 20 November 2017, davidhiggerson.wordpress.com/2017/11/04/foi-friday-the-power-of-foi-pesky-press-officers-school-place-race-and-mouse-droppings .

Chapter 1

1   Worthy, B., *The Politics of Freedom of Information: how and why governments pass laws that threaten their power*, Manchester University Press, 2017, 4.

2   Ibid., 6.

3   Banisar, D., *Freedom of Information Around the World 2006: a global survey of access to government information laws*, Privacy International, 2006, 141.

4   Worthy, B., *Politics of Freedom of Information*, 2017, op. cit., 139.

5   Ibid., 9.

6   UCL Constitution Unit, *International Focus: Mexico*, n.d., www.ucl.ac.uk/constitution-unit/research/foi/countries/mexico.

7   UCL Constitution Unit, *International Focus: India*, n.d., www.ucl.ac.uk/constitution-unit/research/foi/countries/india.

8   Banisar, D., *National Right to Information Laws, Regulations and Initiatives 2017*, 27 September 2017, https://ssrn.com/abstract=1857498 or

http://dx.doi.org/10.2139/ssrn.1857498.

9   *Disclosure of Official Information: a report on overseas practice*, Civil Service Department, HMSO, 1979.

10 Worthy, B., *Politics of Freedom of Information*, 2017, op. cit., 16–17.

11 Gibbons, P., Freudian Slip: the FOI Act that never was, *Freedom of Information Journal*, **12** (1), 2015, 3–5.

12 Worthy, B., *Politics of Freedom of Information*, 2017, op. cit., 32.

13 Ibid., 33–4.

14 Worthy, B., *Politics of Freedom of Information*, 2017, op. cit., 34.

15 Barratt, P., Introduction and Background to the Law. In Carey, P. and Turle, M. (eds), *Freedom of Information Handbook*, The Law Society, 2006, 2.

16 Worthy, B., *Politics of Freedom of Information*, 2017, op. cit., 52.

17 Ibid., 47

18 Ibid., 63

19 Ibid., 84–5.

20 Ibid., 107.

21 Justice Committee, *Post-legislative Scrutiny of the Freedom of Information Act 2000*, HC 96-I, The Stationery Office, 2012, 8.

22 Ibid., 89.

23 Blair, T., *A Journey*, Hutchinson, 2011.

24 Liaison Committee, *Minutes of Evidence HC 150: evidence from the Prime Minister*, answer to Q 438, 2012, https://publications.parliament.uk/pa/cm201213/cmselect/cmliaisn/150/120306.htm.

25 Worthy, B., *Politics of Freedom of Information*, 2017, op. cit., 130.

26 Constitutional Reform and Governance Act 2010, sch. 7.

27 Office of the Scottish Information Commissioner, *Briefing Note on Proposed Amendments to the Freedom of Information (Amendment) (Scotland) Bill Stage 2*, 1, 2012, www.itspublicknowledge.info/nmsruntime/saveasdialog.aspx?lID=5952&sID=377.

28 Protection of Freedoms Act 2012, s. 102.

29 HC Debate, 5 February 1960, vol. 616, col. 1350.

30 Local Government (Access to Information) Act 1985, Schedule 1.

31 Local Audit and Accountability Act 2014; s. 26 is the latest iteration of this requirement.

32 The Local Authorities (Executive Arrangements) (Meetings and Access to Information) (England) Regulations 2012 [2012 No. 2089].

33 The Openness of Local Government Bodies Regulations 2014 [2014 No. 2095], reg. 8.

34 Ibid., Part 2.

35 Department for Communities and Local Government, *Local Government Transparency Code 2015*, 2015, www.gov.uk/government/publications/local-government-transparency-code-2015.

36 Control of Pollution Act 1974, s. 41.

37 Barratt, P., Introduction and Background to the Law, 2006, op. cit., 16.

38 Environmental Information Regulations 1992, [1992 No. 3240].

39 Barratt, P., Introduction and Background to the Law, 2006, op. cit., 16.

40 Protection of Freedoms Act 2012, s. 102.

41 Re-use of Public Sector Information Regulations 2015, [2015 No. 1415].

42 Open Government Partnership, *About OGP*, www.opengovpartnership.org/about/about-ogp.

43 Cabinet Office, *UK Open Government National Action Plan 2016–18*, 2016, www.gov.uk/government/publications/uk-open-government-national-action-plan-2016-18/uk-open-government-national-action-plan-2016-18.

44 Freedom of Information Law 2011 (Jersey).

45 Freedom of Information Act 2015 (Isle of Man).

46 *R (Evans) & Anor v Attorney General* [2015] UKSC 21.

47 BBC News, *Prince Charles Letters to be Released after Supreme Court Ruling*, 2015, www.bbc.co.uk/news/uk-32066554.

48 House of Lords, *Written Statement HLWS134: freedom of information*, 2015, www.parliament.uk/business/publications/written-questions-answers-statements/written-statement/Lords/2015-07-17/HLWS134/.

49 Independent Commission on Freedom of Information, *Independent Commission on Freedom of Information Report*, The Stationery Office, 2016.

50 Campaign for Freedom of Information, *Stop FOI Restrictions*, 2017, www.cfoi.org.uk/campaigns/stop-foi-restrictions/.

51 House of Commons, *Written Statement HCWS566: open and transparent government*, 2016, www.parliament.uk/business/publications/written-questions-answers-statements/written-statement/Commons/2016-03-01/HCWS566/.

52 Ibid.

53 Independent Commission on Freedom of Information, *Independent Commission on Freedom of Information Report*, 2016, op. cit., 52.

54 Labour Party, *For the Many, Not the Few: the Labour Party manifesto 2017*, 2017, 102, www.labour.org.uk/page/-/Images/manifesto-2017/labour-manifesto-2017.pdf.

55 Greenslade, R., Information Commissioner Wants the FOI Act to be Extended, *Guardian*, 2 September 2016,

www.theguardian.com/media/greenslade/2016/sep/02/information-commissioner-wants-the-foi-act-to-be-extended.

56 House of Commons Public Accounts Committee, *Private Contractors – government must get house in order*, media release, 2014, www.parliament.uk/business/committees/committees-a-z/commons-select/public-accounts-committee/news/public-services-private-contractors-report/.

57 Campaign for Freedom of Information, *Extending FOI to Contractors*, 2017, www.cfoi.org.uk/campaigns/extending-foi-to-contractors/.

58 Extension of Freedom of Information in Scotland, Act Now Training, *Blog Now*, 4 April 2016, actnowtraining.wordpress.com/2016/04/04/extension-of-freedom-of-information-in-scotland/.

Chapter 2

1 Freedom of Information Act 2000 (hereafter referred to as FOIA), s. 88.

2 UCL Constitution Unit, *International Focus: India*, n.d., op. cit.

3 Cabinet Office, *Freedom of Information Code of Practice*, 2018, 12, https://www.gov.uk/government/publications/freedom-of-information-code-of-practice.

4 ICO, *Recognising a Request Made Under the Freedom of Information Act (Section 8)*, Information Commissioner's Office, 2016, ico.org.uk/media/for-organisations/documents/1164/recognising-a-request-made-under-the-foia.pdf.

5 FOIA 2000, s. 10(6).

6 The Freedom of Information (Time for Compliance with Request) Regulations 2010, [2010 No. 2768].

7 The Freedom of Information (Time for Compliance with Request) Regulations 2004, [2004 No. 3364], reg. 3.

8 Ibid., regs. 5 and 6.

9 Ibid., reg. 4.

10 ICO, *Time Limits for Compliance Under the Freedom of Information Act (Section 10)*, Information Commissioner's Office, 2015, 6–7, ico.org.uk/media/for-organisations/documents/1165/time-for-compliance-foia-guidance.pdf.

11 Cabinet Office, *Freedom of Information Code of Practice*, 2018, op. cit., 17.

12 *John v Information Commissioner and Ofsted* [2014] UKUT 444 (AAC), 06 October 2014, para. 37.

13 Ibid., para. 38.

14 ICO, *Time Limits for Compliance Under the Freedom of Information Act (Section 10)*, 2015, op. cit., 6–7.

15 ICO, *Recognising a Request Made Under the Freedom of Information Act (Section 8)*, 2016, op. cit., 12.

16 *IPSA v IC and Ben Leapman*, EA/2012/0242, 29 April 2013.

17 *University of Newcastle upon Tyne v the Information Commissioner and the British Union for the Abolition of Vivisection*, GIA/194/2011, 11 May 2011, para. 28.

18 ICO, *Determining Whether Information Is Held*, Information Commissioner's Office, 2015, ico.org.uk/media/for-organisations/documents/1169/determining_whether_information_is_held_foi_eir.pdf.

19 *Innes v Information Commissioner* [2014] EWCA Civ 1086.

20 Protection of Freedoms Act 2012, s. 102.

21 The Freedom of Information and Data Protection (Appropriate Limit and Fees) Regulations 2004 [2004 No 3244], reg. 6.

22 Ibid., reg. 7.

23 The Freedom of Information (Release of Datasets for Re-use) (Fees) Regulations 2013, [2013 No. 1977], reg. 2.

24 The Freedom of Information and Data Protection (Appropriate Limit and Fees) Regulations 2004 [2004 No. 3244], reg. 3.

25 Ibid.

26 Ibid., reg. 4(3).

27 Ibid., reg. 4(4).

28 Ibid., reg. 5.

29 Scottish Information Commissioner, *Charging a Fee or Refusing to Comply with a Request on Excessive Cost Grounds*, 2016, www.itspublicknowledge.info/Law/FOISA-EIRsGuidance/Fees_and_charging/ChargingFOISA.aspx.

30 UCL Constitution Unit, *International Focus: South Africa*, n.d., www.ucl.ac.uk/constitution-unit/research/foi/countries/southafrica.

31 ICO, *Dealing With Repeat Requests (Section 14(2))*, Information Commissioner's Office, 2015, ico.org.uk/media/for-organisations/documents/1195/dealing-with-repeat-requests.pdf.

32 *R (on the application of Evans) and another (Respondents) v Attorney General (Appellant)* [2015] UKSC 21.

33 House of Commons, *Written Statement HCWS566*, op. cit.

Chapter 3

1 ICO, *The prejudice test*, v.1.1, Information Commissioner's Office, 2013, 8, https://ico.org.uk/media/for-organisations/documents/1214/the_prejudice_test.pdf.

2   Scottish Information Commissioner, *Section 33: commercial interests and the economy – exemption briefing*, vol. 2.05, 2015, 4, www.itspublicknowledge.info/nmsruntime/saveasdialog.aspx?lID=2583&sID=123.

3   Freedom of Information Act 2014 (Ireland), ss. 33 and 36.

4   Mendel, T., *Freedom of Information: a comparative legal survey*, 2nd edn, UNESCO, 2008.

5   Cabinet Office, *Freedom of Information Code of Practice*, 2018, op. cit., 17.

6   Mendel, T., *Freedom of Information: a comparative legal survey*, 2008, op. cit.

7   Decision Notice FS50121803, Information Commissioner's Office, para. 60.

8   Ibid., paras. 61–3.

9   Decision Notice FS50482733, Information Commissioner's Office.

10   Decision Notice FS50521432, Information Commissioner's Office.

11   *Queen Mary University v IC and R. Courtney*, EA/2012/0229, 2013, para. 21.

12   ICO, *Information Intended for Future Publication and Research Information (sections 22 and 22A)*, vol. 1.1, Information Commissioner's Office, 2017, ico.org.uk/media/for-organisations/documents/1172/information-intended-for-future-publication-and-research-information-sections-22-and-22a-foi.pdf.

13   ICO, *Safeguarding National Security (section 24)*, vol. 1.0, Information Commissioner's Office, 2012, ico.org.uk/media/for-organisations/documents/1174/safeguarding_national_security_section_24_foi.pdf.

14   *Chris Cole v IC and Ministry of Defence*, EA/2013/0042 & 0043, 2013.

15   *ICO, Defence (section 26)*, vol. 1.0, Information Commissioner's Office, 2016, ico.org.uk/media/for-organisations/documents/1181/defence-section-26-foia-guidance.pdf.

16   *All Party Parliamentary Group on Extraordinary Rendition v IC & Ministry of Defence* [2011] UKUT 153 (AAC), April 2011, paras. 64–5.

17   *Campaign Against the Arms Trade v IC & Ministry of Defence* (EA/2007/0040), 26 August 2008, paras. 70–1.

18   Ibid., para. 95.

19   *Ministry of Justice v IC and Dr Chris Pounder*, EA/2012/0110, 23 July 2013, para. 119.

20   Decision Notice FS50611149, Information Commissioner's Office, para. 29.

21   Decision Notice FS50216279, Information Commissioner's Office, paras. 72–3.

22   Decision Notice FS50502589, Information Commissioner's Office.

23   Decision Notice FS50474293, Information Commissioner's Office.

24   ICO, *The Economy (section 29)*, Information Commissioner's Office, 16 August 2017, ico.org.uk/media/for-organisations/documents/1177/theeconomy.pdf.

25   Ibid.

26 Decision Notice FS50474293, Information Commissioner's Office.

27 *Ganesh Sittampalam v IC and Crown Prosecution Service*, EA/2014/0001, 9 July 2014, para. 68.

28 *Alan Digby-Cameron v IC and Bedfordshire Police and Hertfordshire Police*, EA/2008/0023 and 0025, 26 January 2009, para. 14.

29 *Voyias v IC and London Borough of Camden*, EA/2011/0007, 22 January 2013.

30 *Alan Digby-Cameron v IC and Bedfordshire Police and Hertfordshire Police*, EA/2008/0023 and 0025, 26 January 2009, para. 14.

31 *Ganesh Sittampalam v IC and Crown Prosecution Service*, EA/2014/0001, 9 July 2014, para. 56.

32 *Brown v IC and Ministry of Justice*, [2016] UKUT 255 (AAC), 25 May 2016.

33 ICO, *Public Audit Functions (section 33)*, Information Commissioner's Office, 18 December 2013, 3 ico.org.uk/media/for-organisations/documents/1210/public-audit-functions-s33-foi-guidance.pdf.

34 Ibid., 6.

35 Ibid.

36 ICO, *Government policy (section 35)*, 2016, 11 ico.org.uk/media/for-organisations/documents/1200/government-policy-foi-section-35-guidance.pdf.

37 Ibid., 25.

38 Ibid., 37.

39 *Guardian Newspapers Ltd and Heather Brooke v Information Commissioner and BBC*, EA/2006/0011 and 0013, 8 January 2007, para. 99.

40 FOIA s. 36(1)(a).

41 *McIntyre v Information Commissioner and the Ministry of Defence*, EA/2007/0068, 4 February 2008.

42 FOIA s. 36(4).

43 *Guardian Newspapers Ltd and Heather Brooke v Information Commissioner and BBC*, EA/2006/0011 and 0013, 8 January 2007, para. 26.

44 Ministry of Justice, *Section 36 – Prejudice to Effective Conduct of Public Affairs: qualified persons appointed under section 36 of the Act*, Ministry of Justice, 2009, http://webarchive.nationalarchives.gov.uk/20100512160448/http:/www.foi.gov.uk/guidance/exguide/sec36/annex-d.htm.

45 *IC v Malnick and ACOBA* (GIA/447/2017), 1 March 2018, para. 56.

46 Ibid., para. 32.

47 *Guardian Newspapers Ltd and Heather Brooke v Information Commissioner and BBC*, EA/2006/0011 and 0013, 8 January 2007, para. 60.

48 Ibid., para. 65.

49   Ministry of Justice, *Section 36 – Prejudice to Effective Conduct of Public Affairs: qualified persons appointed under section 36 of the Act*, 2009, op. cit.

50   Official Information Act 1982 (New Zealand), s. 9(2)(f).

51   Official Information Act 1982 (New Zealand), s. 9(2)(g).

52   Wadham, J. and Griffiths, J., *Blackstone's Guide to The Freedom of Information Act*, 2005, 24.

53   ICO, *Communications with Her Majesty and the Awarding of Honours (section 37)*, Information Commissioner's Office, 12 June 2017, 16-21, ico.org.uk/media/ for-organisations/documents/1194/communications_with_her_majesty_and_ the_awarding_of_honours.pdf.

54   *People for the Ethical Treatment of Animals Europe v IC and the University of Oxford*, EA/2009/0076, 13 April 2010, para. 30.

55   *Hepple v IC and Durham County Council*, EA/2013/0168, para 31.

56   Ibid.

57   *People for the Ethical Treatment of Animals Europe v IC and the University of Oxford*, EA/2009/0076, 13 April 2010, para. 68.

58   Decision Notice FS50098767, Information Commissioner's Office.

59   Decision Notice FER0082136, Information Commissioner's Office.

60   *Ministry of Justice v IC and Joanna Shaw*, EA/2015/0160, 18 March 2016, para. 27.

61   *Bellamy v Information Commissioner & Secretary of State for Trade & Industry*, EA/2005/0023, 8 May 2006.

62   *Mersey Tunnel Users Association v Information Commissioner & Merseytravel* EA/2007/0052, 15 February 2008.

63   *Department for Health v Information Commissioner*, EA/2008/0018, 18 November 2008, paras. 52–3.

64   *Department for Work & Pensions v IC & Zola*, EA/2012/0207,0232 and 0233.

65   ICO, *Prohibitions on disclosure (section 44)*, Information Commissioner's Office, 25 July 2016, ico.org.uk/media/for-organisations/documents/1186/section-44- prohibitions-on-disclosure.pdf.

Chapter 4

1   The Transfer of Functions (Information and Public Records) Order 2015 [2015 No. 1897].

2   Ibid.

3   Department of Public Expenditure and Reform (Ireland), *Code of Practice for Freedom of Information for Public Bodies*, September 2015, para. 2.16, http://foi.gov.ie/download/foi-code-of-practice/?wpdmdl=1247.

4 Council of Ministers (Isle of Man), *Freedom of Information Act 2015 Code of Practice*, November 2015.

5 Office of the Information Commissioner (States of Jersey), *Article 44 Code of Practice: The Freedom of Information (Jersey) Law*, 2011, December 2014, https://oicjersey.org/wp-content/uploads/2015/01/Code-of-Practice-Article-44.pdf.

6 Access to Information Act (Canada), R.S.C., 1985, c. A-1, s. 70(1)(c).

7 Ministry of Justice, *Freedom of Information*, n.d., http://webarchive.nationalarchives.gov.uk/20100403061931/www.justice.gov.uk/guidance/freedom-of-information.htm.

8 Ministry of Justice, *Standard responses*, n.d., http://webarchive.nationalarchives.gov.uk/20100407160107/www.justice.gov.uk/guidance/foi-procedural-responses.htm.

9 Office for Government Commerce, *FOI (Civil Procurement) Policy and Guidance*, vol. 2.0, November 2008, http://webarchive.nationalarchives.gov.uk/20151012132921/https://www.gov.uk/government/uploads/system/uploads/attachment_data/file/62062/ogc-foi-civil-procurement-guidance.pdf.

10 PPN 01/17 *Update to Transparency Principles*, Crown Commercial Service, 16 February 2017, www.gov.uk/government/publications/procurement-policy-note-0117-update-to-transparency-principles.

11 *Who Are We?*, RTI Foundation of India, n.d., www.rtifoundationofindia.com/aboutus.

12 *Who We Are*, Open Democracy Advice Centre, n.d., www.opendemocracy.org.za/index.php/who-we-are.

13 Department of Public Expenditure and Reform (Ireland), *Code of Practice for Freedom of Information for Public Bodies*, 2015, op. cit., para. 2.16.

Chapter 5

1 Cabinet Office, *Freedom of Information Statistics: October to December 2017 and annual tables*, 26 April 2018, https://assets.publishing.service.gov.uk/government/uploads/system/uploads/attachment_data/file/702103/foi-statistics-q4-2017-and-annual-statistical-tables.pdf.

2 UNECE, *Convention on Access to Information, Public Participation in Decision-Making and Access to Justice in Environmental Matters*, United Nations Economic Commission for Europe, 25 June 1998, Art. 1, https://www.unece.org/env/pp/treatytext.html.

3   UNECE, *The Aarhus Convention: an implementation guide*, 2nd edn, United
    Nations Economic Commission for Europe, 2014, 19,
    https://www.unece.org/env/pp/implementation_guide.html.

4   ICO, *The Exemption for Environmental Information (section 39)*, Information
    Commissioner's Office, 2015, 5, https://ico.org.uk/media/for-organizations/
    documents/1043419/exemption-for-environmental-information-section-39.pdf.

5   Ibid., 8.

6   Environmental Information Regulations 2004 [2004 No. 3391] (referred to as EIR
    hereafter), reg. 2(2).

7   EIR reg. 2(2)(b)(i).

8   EIR reg. 2(2)(b)(ii).

9   EIR reg. 3(3).

10 EIR reg. 3(4).

11 EIR reg. 2(2)(d).

12 EIR reg. 2(2)(c).

13 *Fish Legal v Information Commissioner* [2015] UKUT 0052 (AAC)

14 ICO, *Public authorities under the EIR*, Information Commissioner's Office, 29
    February 2016, 7. https://ico.org.uk/media/for-organizations/
    documents/1623665/public-authorities-under-eir.pdf.

15 *Fish Legal v Information Commissioner*

16 Decision Notice FER0621831, Information Commissioner's Office.

17 EIR reg. 2(1).

18 ICO, *What Is Environmental Information? (Regulation 2(1))*, Information
    Commissioner's Office, 2016, ico.org.uk/media/for-organisations/
    documents/1146/eir_what_is_environmental_information.pdf.

19 Ibid.

20 UNECE, *The Aarhus Convention: an implementation guide*, 2014, op. cit., 50.

21 ICO, *What Is Environmental Information (Regulation 2(1))*, 2016, op. cit.

22 Decision Notice FS50519817, Information Commissioner's Office.

23 ICO, *What Is Environmental Information (Regulation 2(1))*, 2016, op. cit.

24 *Ofcom v Information Commissioner*, EA/2006/0078, 4 September 2007, para. 28.

25 Based on *The Department for Energy and Climate Change v Information
    Commissioner & AH*, (Henney) [2015] UKUT 0671 (AAC), paras. 93–5.

26 *Mayor and Burgesses of the London Borough of Haringey v IC*, EA/2016/0170, 27
    January 2017.

27 *Omagh District Council v Information Commissioner*, EA/2010/0163, 20 May 2011,
    para 33.

28 *BEIS v Information Commissioner and Henney* [2017] EWCA Civ 844, para 53.

29 *DfT, DVSA and Porsche Cars GB Limited v Information Commissioner and John Cieslik*, [2018] UKUT 127 (AAC), 12 April 2018.

30 *Black v Information Commissioner*, EA/2011/0064, 8 September 2011.

31 ICO, *What Is Environmental Information (Regulation 2(1))*, 2016, op. cit.

32 *London Borough of Southwark v Information Commissioner, Lend Lease (Elephant and Castle) Limited and Glasspool*, EA/2013/0162, 9 May 2014.

33 *The Department for Energy and Climate Change v Information Commissioner & AH*, (Henney) [2015] UKUT 0671 (AAC).

34 *Ofcom v Information Commissioner*, EA/2006/0078, 4 September 2007.

35 *Watts v Information Commissioner*, EA/2007/0022, 6 July 2007.

36 Amin, L. and Montague, B., *EIRs Without the lawyer*, Centre for Investigative Journalism, 2013, 14.

37 EIR reg. 4.

38 EIR reg. 5.

39 EIR reg. 6.

40 EIR reg. 5(2).

41 EIR reg. 8.

42 EIR reg. 9.

43 EIR reg. 16.

44 EIR Part 5.

45 ICO, *Information Held by a Public Authority for the Purposes of the EIR (Regulation 3(2))*, Information Commissioner's Office, 2013, 3, ico.org.uk/media/for-organizations/documents/1640/information_held_for_the_purposes_of_eir.pdf.

46 EIR reg. 5(2).

47 ICO, *Time Limits for Compliance: Environmental Information Regulations*, Information Commissioner's Office, 25 September 2013, 6, ico.org.uk/media/for-organizations/documents/1622/time-for-compliance-eir-guidance.pdf.

48 Decision Notice FER0355639, Information Commissioner's Office.

49 EIR reg. 7.

50 ICO, *Charging for Environmental Information (Regulation 8)*, Information Commissioner's Office, 2016, 6, ico.org.uk/media/for-organizations/documents/1627/charging-for-environmental-information-reg8.pdf.

51 *East Sussex County Council v Information Commissioner*, C-71/14.

52 *Markinson v Information Commissioner*, EA/2005/0014, 28 March 2006.

53 ICO, *Charging for Environmental Information (Regulation 8)*, 2016, op. cit.

54 EIR reg. 8(8).

55 EIR reg. 12(4)(b).

56 EIR reg. 14.

57 EIR reg. 12(2).

58 Directive 2003/4/EC of the European Parliament and of the Council of 28 January 2003 on public access to environmental information and repealing Council Directive 90/313/EEC, *OJ L*, 41, 14 February 2003, Recital 16.

59 *Dransfield v IC & Devon CC; Craven v IC & DECC* [2015] EWCA Civ 454.

60 *Higham v IC & Cornwall Council*, EA/2015/0078, 27 September 2016.

61 ICO, *Information on Emissions (Regulation 12 (9))*, Information Commissioner's Office, 2013, ico.org.uk/media/for-organisations/documents/1616/information-on-emissions-eir-guidance.pdf.

62 *G. M. Freeze v Information Commissioner and DEFRA*, EA/2010/0112, 8 March 2011.

63 *R (Evans) & Anor v Attorney General* [2015] UKSC 21.

64 Directive 2003/4/EC, 14 February 2003, op. cit., Recital 19.

Chapter 6

1 Cabinet Office, *FOI Statistics October to December 2017 and Annual Tables*, 26 April 2018, Table 10, www.gov.uk/government/statistics/freedom-of-information-statistics-annual-2017.

2 GDPR, Regulation (EU) 2016/679, Art. 4.

3 ICO, *Personal Information (Section 40 and Regulation 13)*, Information Commissioner's Office, 25 May 2018, 12, ico.org.uk/media/for-organisations/documents/1213/personal-information-section-40-and-regulation-13-foia-and-eir-guidance.pdf.

4 Ibid., 14.

5 *Egan v IC & West Midlands Police*, EA/2014/0297, 16 June 2015.

6 GDPR Recital 43.

7 Data Protection Act 2018, sch. 19.

8 Based on *Goldsmith International Business School v the Information Commissioner and The Home Office* [2014] UKUT 563 (AAC), 16 December 2014.

9 *Corporate Officer of the House of Commons v IC & Leapman, Brooke & Thomas*, EA/2007/0060-63, 122, 123 and 131, 26 February 2008.

10 *Information Commissioner v (1) CF and (2) Nursing and Midwifery Council*, [2015] UKUT 449 (AAC), 10 August 2015.

11 ICO, *Requests for Personal Data About Public Authority Employees*, Information Commissioner's Office, 24 May 2018, para. 35, ico.org.uk/media/for-organisations/documents/1187/section_40_requests_for_personal_data_about_employees.pdf.

12 *Corporate Officer of the House of Commons v IC & Leapman, Brooke & Thomas*,

EA/2007/0060-63, 122, 123 and 131, 26 February 2008, para. 49.

13 *Surrey Heath Borough Council v The Information Commissioner and John Morley* [2014] UKUT 339 (AAC), 21 July 2014.

14 ICO, *Requests for Personal Data About Public Authority Employees*, 2018, op. cit., 7-10.

15 *David Perrin v IC*, EA/2014/0303, 27 November 2015.

16 *McFerran v IC*, EA/2012/0030, 7 September 2012.

17 *Joe McGonagle v Information Commissioner and Ministry of Defence*, EA/2011/0104, 4 November 2011.

18 Department for Communities and Local Government (DCLG), *Local Government Transparency Code 2015*, February 2015, 20, https://assets.publishing.service.gov.uk/government/uploads/system/uploads/attachment_data/file/408386/150227_PUBLICATION_Final_LGTC_2015.pdf.

19 ICO, *Requests for Personal Data About Public Authority Employees*, Information Commissioner's Office, 24 May 2018, op. cit., 16.

20 Accounts and Audit (Amendment no 2) (England) Regulations 2009

21 *Trago Mills v IC and Teignbridge DC*, EA/2012/0028, 22 August 2012.

22 *Corporate Officer of the House of Commons v IC & Leapman, Brooke & Thomas*, EA/2007/0060-63, 122, 123 and 131, 26 February 2008.

23 *Haslam v (1) Information Commissioner (2) Bolton Council*, [2016] UKUT 0139 (AAC), 10 March 2016.

24 *Martyres v ICO and NHS Cambridgeshire*, EA/2011/0209, 11 January 2012.

25 Act Now Training, FOI Requests From Heir Hunters, *Act Now Training Blog*, 4 March 2014, actnowtraining.wordpress.com/2014/03/04/foi-requests-from-heir-hunters/.

26 *Bluck v ICO & Epsom and St Helier University Hospital NHS Trust*, EA/2006/0090, 17 September 2007.

27 Decision Notice FS50618324, Information Commissioner's Office.

28 *Theresa Schleicher on behalf of Medical Justice v Information Commissioner*, EA/2015/0188, 9 June 2016.

29 Decision Notice FS50454267, Information Commissioner's Office.

30 Decision Notice FS50153179, Information Commissioner's Office.

31 BBC News, 'Jihadi John' death at centre of dispute, BBC News, 10 June 2016, www.bbc.co.uk/news/uk-politics-36484376.

Chapter 7

1 TNA, *The Lord Chancellor's Code of Practice on the management of records issued under section 46 of the Freedom of Information Act 2000*, The National Archives and Ministry of Justice, 2009, 4.

2   FOIA, s. 62(1).

3   ISO 15489 *Records Management*, International Standards Organization, 2016, https://committee.iso.org/sites/tc46sc11/home/projects/published/iso-15489-records-management.html.

4   TNA, *Memorandum of Understanding between the Information Commissioner and the Chief Executive of The National Archives/Keeper of Public Records*, The National Archives, August 2015, www.nationalarchives.gov.uk/documents/information-management/mou-as-signed-aug-2015.pdf.

5   Gibbons, P., Denham's Duty to Document, *Freedom of Information Journal*, **13** (3), 2017, 4–7.

6   Ibid.

7   Monetary Penalty Notice ENF0367593, Information Commissioner's Office, 28 May 2012.

8   *Metropolis v Information Commissioner and Donnie Mackenzie* [2014] UKUT 0479 (AAC), 22 October 2014.

9   Shepherd, E., Flinn, A. and Stevenson, A., Information Governance, Records Management and Freedom of Information: a study of local government authorities in England, *Government Information Quarterly*, **27** (4), 2010, 337–45.

10 Ibid.

11 HL Debate, 17 January 2012, vol. 734.

12 Scottish Government, *Scottish Ministers' Code of Practice on Records Management by Scottish Public Authorities Under the Freedom of Information (Scotland) Act 2002*, 16 December 2011.

13 Constitutional Reform and Governance Act 2010, s. 52, Sch. 7 para. 4(2).

14 The Freedom of Information (Definition of Historical Records) (Transitional and Saving Provisions) Order 2012 [2012 No. 3029].

15 Wadham, J. and Griffiths, J., *Blackstone's Guide to the Freedom of Information Act 2000*, Oxford University Press, 2nd edn, 2005, 159.

16 ICO, *Information Intended for Future Publication and Research Information (sections 22 and 22A)*, 18 August 2017, op. cit., 6-7.

17 Decision Notice FS50662278, Information Commissioner's Office.

18 TNA, *Code of Practice for Archivists and Records Managers under section 51(4) of the Data Protection Act 1998*, The National Archives, 2007.

19 Ibid., 28.

20 Decision Notice FS50101391, Information Commissioner's Office, para. 39.

Chapter 8

1   Barrett, P., Publication Schemes. In Carey, P. and Turle, M. (eds), *Freedom of Information Handbook*, The Law Society, 2006, 50.

2   Denham, E., *Trust, Transparency and Just-in-Time FOI: sustainable governance and openness in the digital age*, speech, 22 March 2018, ico.org.uk/about-the-ico/ news-and-events/news-and-blogs/2018/03/trust-transparency-and-just-in-time-foi-sustainable-governance-and-openness-in-the-digital-age/.

3   Independent Commission on Freedom of Information, *Independent Commission on Freedom of Information Report*, 2016, op. cit.

4   Cabinet Office, *Freedom of Information Code of Practice*, 2018, 27.

5   ICO, *Model Publication Scheme: Freedom of Information Act*, Information Commissioner's Office, 2015, ico.org.uk/media/for-organizations/documents/1153/model-publication-scheme.pdf.

6   ICO, *How Should We Comply with the Model Publication Scheme?, Guide to Freedom of Information*, Information Commissioner's Office, n.d., ico.org.uk/for-organizations/guide-to-freedom-of-information/publication-scheme/.

7   Cabinet Office, *Freedom of Information Code of Practice*, 2018, 27.

8   Scottish Information Commissioner, *Model Publication Scheme: guide for Scottish public authorities*, 2017, www.itspublicknowledge.info/ScottishPublicAuthorities/PublicationSchemes/TheModelPublicationScheme.aspx.

9   ICO, *Means of Communicating Information (section 11)*, Information Commissioner's Office, 2015, para. 55, ico.org.uk/media/for-organisations/documents/1163/means-of-communicating-information-foia-guidance.pdf; EIR reg. 6(1)(b).

10   The Transfer of Functions (Digital Government) Order 2018 [2018 No. 526]

11   Cabinet Office and Government Digital Service, *How to Publish Central Government Transparency Data*, 14 December 2017, https://www.gov.uk/government/collections/how-to-publish-central-government-transparency-data.

12   Topping, A., Barr, C. and Duncan, P., Gender Pay Gap Figures Reveal Eight in 10 UK Firms Pay Men More, *The Guardian*, 4 April 2018, https://www.theguardian.com/money/2018/apr/04/gender-pay-gap-figures-reveal-eight-in-10-uk-firms-pay-men-more.

13   ICO, *The Guide to INSPIRE Regulations*, Information Commissioner's Office, 2015, ico.org.uk/for-organisations/inspire-regulations/.

14   *Veolia ES Nottinghamshire Ltd v Nottinghamshire County Council & Others* [2010]

EWCA Civ 1214, paras. 88–103.

15   Local Audit and Accountability Act 2014, s. 26.

16   DCLG, *Local Government Transparency Code 2015*, 2015, op. cit.

17   ICO, *Freedom of Information Act: definition document for principal local authorities
(county councils, unitary authorities, metropolitan district councils, borough councils,
city councils and district councils, the council of the Isles of Scilly and local authorities
in Wales)*, Information Commissioner's Office, 2013, 10,
ico.org.uk/media/1262/definition_document_local_authorities.pdf.

18   Independent Commission on Freedom of Information, *Independent Commission
on Freedom of Information Report*, 2016, op. cit.

19   Cabinet Office, *Freedom of Information Code of Practice*, 2018, op. cit.

20   House of Commons FOI Request & Disclosure Log, n.d.,
www.parliament.uk/site-information/foi/foi-and-eir/commons-request-
disclosure-logs/.

21   Greater London Authority, FOI Disclosure Log, n.d., www.london.gov.uk/
about-us/governance-and-spending/sharing-our-information/
freedom-information/foi-disclosure-log?order=DESC.

Chapter 9

1   Cornish, P., *Copyright: Interpreting the Law for Libraries, Archives and Information
Services*, 6th ed, Facet Publishing, 2015, 7.

2   Open Knowledge International, *Open Data Handbook*, n.d.,
http://opendatahandbook.org/guide/en/what-is-open-data/.

3   World Bank, *Open Data for Economic Growth*, 2014, 6,
www.worldbank.org/content/dam/Worldbank/document/Open-Data-for-
Economic-Growth.pdf.

4   TNA, *Open Government Licence*, v. 3, The National Archives, n.d.,
www.nationalarchives.gov.uk/information-management/re-using-public-sector-
information/uk-government-licensing-framework/open-government-licence/.

5   *Mr V Jordan v Scottish Environment Protection Agency*, SIC 049/2016, 3 March
2016.

6   Decision Notice FS50564815, Information Commissioner's Office.

7   Both examples taken from TNA, *Links Between Access and Re-use*, The National
Archives, v. 1, July 2015 (reproduced here under the Open Government Licence v.
3.0).

8   Ibid.

Chapter 10

1   Department for Constitutional Affairs, *Secretary of State for Constitutional Affairs' Code of Practice on the discharge of public authorities' functions under Part 1 of the Freedom of Information Act 2000, Issued under section 45 of the Act*, 2004, para. 15.

2   Justice Committee, *Post-legislative Scrutiny of the Freedom of Information Act 2000*, 2012, op. cit., chapter 3.

3   Independent Commission on Freedom of Information, *Independent Commission on Freedom of Information Report*, 2016, op. cit.

4   Justice Committee, *Post-legislative Scrutiny of the Freedom of Information Act 2000*, 2012, op. cit., conclusions and recommendations.

5   Worthy, B., *Politics of Freedom of Information*, 2017, op. cit., 168.

6   Burt, E. and Taylor, J., *The Freedom of Information (Scotland) Act 2002: new modes of information management in Scottish public bodies?,* Scottish Information Commissioner, 2007.

7   JISC, *Information Legislation and Management Survey 2016*, Joint Information Systems Committee, 2017, www.jisc.ac.uk/reports/information-legislation-and-management-survey-2016.

8   Hazell, R., Worthy, B. and Glover, M., *Impact of the Freedom of Information Act on Central Government in the UK*, 2010, op. cit., 108

9   Bourke, G. et al., *FOIA 2000 and local government in 2010: the experience of local authorities in England*, UCL Constitution Unit, 2011.

10   Worthy, B., John, P. and Vannoni, M., *Transparency at the Parish Pump: a field experiment to measure the effectiveness of freedom of information requests*, 2015, https://ssrn.com/abstract=2699198.

11   Decision notice FS50652566, Information Commissioner's Office, paras 50–2.

12   UCL Constitution Unit, *Evaluating the Impact of FOI on Local Government: August 2009 – November 2011: surveys*, 2012, www.ucl.ac.uk/constitution-unit/research/foi/foi-and-local-government.

13   JISC, *Information Legislation and Management Survey 2016*, 2017, op. cit.

14   Department of Public Expenditure and Reform (Ireland), *Code of Practice for Freedom of Information for Public Bodies*, 2015, op. cit.

15   Scottish Information Commissioner, *Setting up Your FOI Function*, 2017, 5, www.itspublicknowledge.info/nmsruntime/saveasdialog.aspx?lID=9372&sID=7999.

16   Freedom of Information Act 2009 (Malta), s. 17(1)(d).

17   Freedom of Information Co-ordinating Unit home page, foi.gov.mt.

18   Freedom of Information Act 1982 (Australia), s. 8(2)(i).

19 Right to Information Act 2005 (India), s. 5.

20 Transparency and Access to Government Information Act 2002 (Mexico), Arts. 28–29 (from a translation by C. McAllister provided by K. Doyle, 'Mexico's new Freedom of Information Law', National Security Archive, 2002, www.gwu.edu/~nsarchiv/NSAEBB/NSAEBB68/.

21 Freedom of Information Act, 5 U.S.C., § 552, (j), www.justice.gov/oip/freedom-information-act-5-usc-552.

22 Dept of Public Expenditure and Reform (Ireland), *Code of Practice for Freedom of Information for Public Bodies*, 2015, op. cit., para. 2.4.

23 Ibid., para. 2.9.

24 Ibid., paras. 2.10–2.12.

25 Ibid., paras. 2.13–2.14.

26 Ibid., para. 2.15.

27 Ibid., paras. 2.18–2.19.

28 Ibid., paras. 2.20–2.24.

29 GDPR, Arts. 37–9.

30 Data Protection Act 2018, s. 7.

31 ICO, *The Guide to the General Data Protection Regulation: Data Protection Officers*, Information Commissioner's Office, n.d. (last accessed 6 August 2018), ico.org.uk/for-organisations/guide-to-the-general-data-protection-regulation-gdpr/accountability-and-governance/data-protection-officers/.

32 Email from respondent, 13 February 2018.

33 Reported in Burgess M, *FOI - a practical guide for U.K. journalists*, Routledge, 2015, 102.

34 Pratchett, T. et al., *Practical Tips for Developing Your Staff*, Facet Publishing, 2016, 28.

35 Ibid.

36 Monetary Penalty Notice: Royal Borough of Kensington and Chelsea, Information Commissioner's Office, 10 April 2018, 6.

37 Gibbons, P., You be the Judge, *FOIMan blog*, 10 March 2015, www.foiman.com/archives/1463.

38 HC Debate, vol. 542, col. 133WH, 14 March 2012.

39 Justice Committee, *Post-legislative scrutiny of the Freedom of Information Act 2000*, 2012, vol. III, written evidence from the Association of Chief Police Officers, para. 2.5, https://publications.parliament.uk/pa/cm201213/cmselect/cmjust/96/96vw12.htm.

40 Justice Committee, *Post-legislative Scrutiny of the Freedom of Information Act 2000*, 2012, vol. I, op. cit., para. 50.

41 Stewart, S., Exclusive: Glasgow City Council junkets pruned, *Daily Record*, 2008, www.dailyrecord.co.uk/news/scottish-news/exclusive-glasgow-city-council-junkets-987550 (accessed 12 February 2018).

42 Ibid., 134.

43 Burgess, M., *FOI - a practical guide for U.K. journalists*, 2015, op. cit., 161.

44 Ibid., 103.

Chapter 11

1 Dept of Public Expenditure and Reform (Ireland), *Code of Practice for Freedom of Information for Public Bodies*, 2015, op. cit., para. 2.1.

2 Scottish Information Commissioner, *Setting up Your FOI Function: guidance for Scottish public authorities new to FOI*, 2017, op. cit., 5.

3 Dept of Public Expenditure and Reform (Ireland), *Code of Practice for Freedom of Information for Public Bodies*, 2015, op. cit., para. 2.7.

4 Worthy, B., Amos, J., Hazell, R. and Bourke, G., *Town Hall Transparency? The impact of freedom of information on local government in England*, UCL Constitution Unit, 2011.

5 Dept of Public Expenditure and Reform (Ireland), *Code of Practice for Freedom of Information for Public Bodies*, 2015, op. cit., para. 2.8.

6 Scottish Information Commissioner, *Setting up Your FOI Function*, 2017, op. cit., 14.

7 Response to follow-up email to response 14, 16 March 2018.

8 Cabinet Office and Ministry of Justice, Freedom of Information Statistics, n.d., www.gov.uk/government/collections/government-foi-statistics.

9 Scottish Information Commissioner, FOI and EIR statistics database, n.d., www.itspublicknowledge.info/ScottishPublicAuthorities/StatisticsCollection.aspx.

10 See for example, University of York, *Freedom of Information Policy*, n.d., www.york.ac.uk/records-management/foi/foi-policy/.

11 See for example ICO, *Definition document for principal local Authorities (county councils, unitary authorities, metropolitan district councils, borough councils, city councils and district councils, the council of the Isles of Scilly and local authorities in Wales)*, 2013, Information Commissioner's Office, 8, ico.org.uk/media/for-organisations/documents/1262/definition_document_local_authorities.pdf.

12 Department for Constitutional Affairs, *Secretary of State for Constitutional Affairs' Code of Practice on the discharge of public authorities' functions under Part 1 of the Freedom of Information Act 2000*, 2004, op. cit., para. 26.

13 Cabinet Office, *Freedom of Information Code of Practice*, 2018, 16.

14 *Derry City Council v Information Commissioner*, EA/2006/0014, 11 December 2006.

15 Cabinet Office, *Freedom of Information Code of Practice*, 2018, 31.

16 Ibid., 31–2.

17 Hazell, R., Worthy, B. and Glover, M., *Impact of the Freedom of Information Act on Central Government in the UK*, 2010, op. cit., 114.

18 Response to FOI request, 10 October 2017.

19 Denham, Trust, *Transparency and Just-in-Time FOI*, 2018, op. cit.

20 © Greater London Authority, 2018.

21 Harrow to Make All Data Public in FOI Revolution, *The Lawyer*, 7 February 2011, www.thelawyer.com/issues/7-february-2011/harrow-to-make-all-data-public-in-foi-revolution/.

22 Hazell, Worthy and Glover, *Impact of the Freedom of Information Act on Central Government in the UK*, 2010, op. cit., 108.

23 Ibid.

24 Manchester City Council, *Code of Practice – handling requests for information*, June 2011, https://secure.manchester.gov.uk/info/200031/data_protection_and_freedom_of_information/1322/freedom_of_information/6.

25 Department of Justice (USA), *FAQs: Who Handles FOIA Requests?*, n.d., www.foia.gov/faq.html.

26 Roberts, A. S., Spin Control and Freedom of Information: lessons for the United Kingdom from Canada, *Public Administration*, **83** (1), spring 2005, 7–8, ssrn.com/abstract=1308145.

27 New Zealand Treasury, *OIA Guidance Document*, New Zealand Treasury, v.4.0, September 2016, p.6 (disclosed by New Zealand Treasury, OIA disclosure TOIA 20170165).

28 Scottish Information Commissioner, *Get It Right First Time*, poster, n.d., www.itspublicknowledge.info/Law/FOISA-EIRsGuidance/Briefings.aspx.

29 Anonymous, FOI: a civil servant writes, *FOIMan blog*, 21 March 2012, www.foiman.com/archives/550.

30 Swallow, D. and Bourke, G., *The Freedom of Information Act and Higher Education: the experience of FOI officers in the UK*, UCL Constitution Unit, 2012.

31 Based on Hasson, G., *How to Deal With Difficult People: smart tactics for overcoming the problem people in your life*, Capstone Publishing, 2015.

Chapter 12

1 Cabinet Office, *Freedom of Information Code of Practice*, 2018, 14.

2 Response to follow-up email to response 13, 13 February 2018.

3 Making Better FOI Requests in Hackney, *My Society blog*, 9 February 2018,

www.mysociety.org/2018/02/09/making-better-foi-requests-in-hackney/.

4   Ibid.

5   Hazell, R., Worthy, B. and Glover, M., *Impact of the Freedom of Information Act on Central Government in the UK*, 2010, op. cit., 102.

6   Ministry of Defence, *Freedom of Information & Environmental Information Regulations: hints for practitioners handling FOI/EIR requests*, 2008, ico.org.uk/media/for-organizations/documents/1643/foi_hints_for_practitioners_handing_foi_and_eir_requests_2008.pdf.

7   Ministry of Justice, *Freedom of Information Act 2000 – statistics on implementation in central government: 2010 Annual and Q4: October to December 2010*, 2011, 50, www.gov.uk/government/uploads/system/uploads/attachment_data/file/217848/2010-Annual-and-Q4-FOI-bulletin-vfinal.pdf.

8   Hazell, R., Worthy, B. and Glover, M., *Impact of the Freedom of Information Act on Central Government in the UK*, 2010, op. cit., 105.

9   Quoted in Burgess, M., *FOI - a practical guide for U.K. journalists*, 2015, op. cit., 154.

10 Shepherd, E., Flinn, A. and Stevenson, A., Information Governance, Records Management and Freedom of Information: a study of local government authorities in England, *Government Information Quarterly*, **27** (4), 2010, 337–45.

11 Cabinet Office, *Freedom of Information Code of Practice*, 2018, 11.

12 ICO, *Determining Whether Information Is Held*, 2015, op. cit.

13 ICO, *Official Information Held in Private Email Accounts*, Information Commissioner's Office, 2017, 4, ico.org.uk/media/for-organizations/documents/1147/official_information_held_in_private_email_accounts.pdf.

14 Ibid., 4.

15 ICO, *Information Held by a Public Authority for the Purposes of the Freedom of Information Act*, Information Commissioner's Office, 2012, 7, ico.org.uk/media/for-organizations/documents/1148/information_held_by_a_public_authority_for_purposes_of_foia.pdf.

16 Ibid.

17 The Freedom of Information and Data Protection (Appropriate Limit and Fees) Regulations 2004 [2004 No 3244], reg. 4.

18 *Cardiff Council v IC & Christopher Hastings*, EA/2011/0215, 23 February 2012.

19 Burgess, M., Government's FOI 'round robin list' doesn't comply with data protection rules, *FOI Directory*, 30 June 2016, http://foi.directory/governments-foi-round-robin-list-doesnt-comply-with-data-protection-rules/.

20 Response to follow-up e-mail to response 2, 20 March 2018.

21 Response to follow-up e-mail to response 14, 16 March 2018.

22 Response to follow-up e-mail to response 13, 13 February 2018.

23 Response to follow-up e-mail to response 2, 20 March 2018.

24 Scottish Information Commissioner, *Responding to Information Requests: Guidance and Procedures*, 2017, 14,
www.itspublicknowledge.info/nmsruntime/saveasdialog.aspx?lID=7940&sID=105.

25 TNA, *Redaction Toolkit: editing exempt information from paper and electronic documents prior to release*, The National Archives, 2016,
www.nationalarchives.gov.uk/documents/information-management/redaction_toolkit.pdf.

26 ICO, *How To Disclose Information Safely: removing personal data from information requests and datasets*, Information Commissioner's Office, 2015,
ico.org.uk/media/for-organizations/documents/how-to-disclose-information-safely-removing-personal-data-from-information-requests-and-datasets/2013958/how-to-disclose-information-safely.pdf.

27 ICO, *Retention Schedule*, Information Commissioner's Office, May 2018,
ico.org.uk/media/about-the-ico/policies-and-procedures/2259025/retention-and-disposal-schedule-for-website.pdf.

28 *Home Office and Ministry of Justice v IC*, EWHC 1611 (Admin), 2009.

29 *Davies v IC & Cabinet Office*, EA/2017/0050, 19 July 2017, para. 1.

Chapter 13

1 TNA, http://www.nationalarchives.gov.uk.

2 © TNA, 2018. Contains public sector information licensed under the Open Government Licence, v. 3.0.

3 Cabinet Office, *Freedom of Information Code of Practice*, 2018, 14.

4 *Department for Constitutional Affairs, Secretary of State for Constitutional Affairs' Code of Practice on the discharge of public authorities' functions under Part 1 of the Freedom of Information Act 2000*, 2004, op. cit.

5 *Brown v Information Commissioner*, EA/2006/0088, 2 October 2007.

6 mySociety, www.mysociety.org/about/.

7 ICO, *Recognising a Request made under the Freedom of Information Act (Section 8)*, op. cit., 22.

8 WhatDoTheyKnow, *Powered by Alavateli*, n.d.,
www.whatdotheyknow.com/help/alaveteli.

9 Do Authorities Respond Faster by Email or Through an FOI Website? Our latest research, *MySociety blog*, 10 May 2016, www.mysociety.org/2016/05/10/do-authorities-respond-faster-by-post-or-through-an-foi-website-our-latest-research/.

10 UCL Constitution Unit, *International Focus: Mexico*, n.d.,

www.ucl.ac.uk/constitution-unit/research/foi/countries/mexico.

11 Cabinet Office, *Freedom of Information Code of Practice*, 2018, op. cit., 11.

12 Goddard, L., FoI Costs? University 'spies' only add to them, *Times Higher Education*, 12 May 2016, www.timeshighereducation.com/comment/freedom-of-information-costs-university-spies-only-add-to-them.

13 Based on Roberts, *Spin Control and Freedom of Information*, 2005, op. cit.

14 Burgess, M., *FOI - a practical guide for U.K. journalists*, 2015, op. cit., 14–15.

15 Ibid., 16.

16 Ibid., 155.

17 *DH v (1) IC, (2) Bolton Council* [2016] UKUT 0139 (AAC), 10 March 2016, para. 61.

18 FOIA s. 1(1).

19 FOIA s. 11.

20 Cabinet Office, *Freedom of Information Code of Practice*, 2018, op. cit., 33.

21 ICO, *Refusing a Request: writing a refusal notice (Section 17)*, Information Commissioner's Office, 2012, 5, ico.org.uk/media/for-organisations/documents/1211/refusing_a_request_writing_a_refusal_notice_foi.pdf.

22 Cabinet Office, *Freedom of Information Code of Practice*, 2018, op. cit., 20.

23 Cabinet Office, *Freedom of Information Code of Practice*, 2018, op. cit., 15.

24 ICO, *Dealing with Vexatious Requests (section 14),* Information Commissioner's Office, 2015, https://ico.org.uk/media/for-organisations/documents/1198/dealing-with-vexatious-requests.pdf.

25 ICO, *Refusing a Request*, 2012, op. cit., 4.

26 Smithers, R., Faulty Appliances Cause 60 UK House Fires a Week, Which? Says, *Guardian*, 15 February 2018.

27 Wilkinson, E., GPs Offered up to 50% Cut of Savings Generated by Slashing Their Own Referrals, *The Pulse*, 28 February 2018, www.pulsetoday.co.uk/news/commissioning/commissioning-topics/referrals/gps-offered-up-to-50-cut-of-savings-generated-by-slashing-their-own-referrals/20036235.article.

28 ICO, *Refusing a Request*, 2012, op. cit., 6.

29 Ibid., 12.

Chapter 14

1 FOIA s. 50(2)(a).

2 Hazell, R., Worthy, B. and Glover, M., *Impact of the Freedom of Information Act on Central Government in the UK*, 2010, op. cit., 123.

3   Cabinet Office, *Freedom of Information Statistics in Central Government for 2017*,
    26 April 2018, www.gov.uk/government/statistics/freedom-of-information-
    statistics-annual-2017.

4   Cabinet Office, *Freedom of Information Code of Practice*, 2018, op. cit., 19.

5   Department for Constitutional Affairs, *Secretary of State for Constitutional Affairs'
    Code of Practice on the discharge of public authorities' functions under Part 1 of the
    Freedom of Information Act 2000*, 2004, op. cit.

6   Cabinet Office, *Freedom of Information Code of Practice*, 2018, op. cit., 20.

7   Ibid., 19

8   ICO, *When Can We Refuse a Request for Information?: What if the requester is
    unhappy with the outcome?*, Information Commissioner's Office, n.d.,
    ico.org.uk/for-organisations/guide-to-freedom-of-information/refusing-a-request/.

9   Cabinet Office, *Freedom of Information Code of Practice*, 2018, op. cit., 20.

10 Department for Constitutional Affairs, *Secretary of State for Constitutional Affairs'
    Code of Practice on the discharge of public authorities' functions under Part 1 of the
    Freedom of Information Act 2000*, 2004, op. cit., para. 46.

11 Cabinet Office, *Freedom of Information Code of Practice*, 2018, op. cit., 20.

12 Dept of Public Expenditure and Reform (Ireland), *Code of Practice for Freedom of
    Information for Public Bodies*, 2015, op. cit., 13.

13 Cabinet Office, *Freedom of Information Statistics in Central Government for 2017*,
    op. cit.

14 Hazell, R., Worthy, B. and Glover, M., *Impact of the Freedom of Information Act on
    Central Government in the UK*, 2010, op. cit., pp.126–7.

15 ICO, *Information Commissioner's Annual Report and Financial Statements 2016/17*,
    HC 137, Information Commissioner's Office, 2017, 20, ico.org.uk/media/about-the-
    ico/documents/2014449/ico053-annual-report-201617-s12-aw-web-version.pdf.

16 ICO, *How We Deal With Complaints*, 2011, Information Commissioner's Office,
    2–3 .

17 ICO, *Key Questions for Public Authorities – Freedom of Information Act 2000*,
    Information Commissioner's Office, 2011, ico.org.uk/media/for-organisations/
    documents/1247/key_questions_for_public_authorities_foi_v2.pdf.

18 ICO, *How We Deal With Complaints*, 2011, op. cit., 3.

19 Ibid.

20 Ibid., 4–5.

21 ICO, *Information Commissioner's Annual Report and Financial Statements 2015/16*,
    HC 212, Information Commissioner's Office, 2016, 25, ico.org.uk/media/about-
    the-ico/documents/1624517/annual-report-2015-16.pdf.

22 ICO, *How the Information Commissioner's Office Selects Authorities for Monitoring*,

Information Commissioner's Office, 2017, ico.org.uk/media/action-weve-taken/monitoring/2791/how-the-ico-selects-authorities-for-monitoring.pdf.

23 Contempt of Court Act 1981.

24 Councillor Facing Trial for Destroying Dog Poo Records, *Daily Telegraph*, 25 April 2018, www.telegraph.co.uk/news/2018/04/25/councillor-facing-trial-destroying-records-dog-dna-scheme/.

25 Maltese Government, *FOIA FAQs*, foi.gov.mt/FOI/faqs.

26 UCL Constitution Unit, *International Focus: India*, n.d., www.ucl.ac.uk/constitution-unit/research/foi/countries/india.

27 Office of the Australian Information Commissioner, *Freedom of Information: how to apply*, factsheet, n.d., www.oaic.gov.au/freedom-of-information/foi-resources/foi-fact-sheets/foi-fact-sheet-6-how-to-apply.

28 US Department of Justice, *How Do I File an Administrative Appeal?*, FOIA FAQs, n.d., www.foia.gov/faq.html.

29 ICO, *How We Deal With Complaints*, 2011, op. cit., 6.

30 ICO, *Information Commissioner's Annual Report and Financial Statements 2016/17*, 2017, op. cit., 21.

31 Burgess, M., *FOI - a practical guide for U.K. journalists*, 2015, op. cit., 172.

32 Wadham, J., Harris, K. and Peretz, G., *Blackstone's Guide to the Freedom of Information Act 2000*, 4th edn, Oxford University Press, 2011, 166.

33 *Secretary of State for the Home Department v IC and P. Miller*, EA/2015/0143, 12 January 2016, para. 93.

34 *G. Muttitt v IC and Cabinet Office*, EA/2011/0036, 31 January 2012, para. 34.

Index